IFIP Advances in Information and Communication Technology

525

Editor-in-Chief

Kai Rannenberg, Goethe University Frankfurt, Germany

Editorial Board

TC 1 – Foundations of Computer Science
  Jacques Sakarovitch, Télécom ParisTech, France

TC 2 – Software: Theory and Practice
  Michael Goedicke, University of Duisburg-Essen, Germany

TC 3 – Education
  Arthur Tatnall, Victoria University, Melbourne, Australia

TC 5 – Information Technology Applications
  Erich J. Neuhold, University of Vienna, Austria

TC 6 – Communication Systems
  Aiko Pras, University of Twente, Enschede, The Netherlands

TC 7 – System Modeling and Optimization
  Fredi Tröltzsch, TU Berlin, Germany

TC 8 – Information Systems
  Jan Pries-Heje, Roskilde University, Denmark

TC 9 – ICT and Society
  Diane Whitehouse, The Castlegate Consultancy, Malton, UK

TC 10 – Computer Systems Technology
  Ricardo Reis, Federal University of Rio Grande do Sul, Porto Alegre, Brazil

TC 11 – Security and Privacy Protection in Information Processing Systems
  Steven Furnell, Plymouth University, UK

TC 12 – Artificial Intelligence
  Ulrich Furbach, University of Koblenz-Landau, Germany

TC 13 – Human-Computer Interaction
  Marco Winckler, University Paul Sabatier, Toulouse, France

TC 14 – Entertainment Computing
  Matthias Rauterberg, Eindhoven University of Technology, The Netherlands

IFIP – The International Federation for Information Processing

IFIP was founded in 1960 under the auspices of UNESCO, following the first World Computer Congress held in Paris the previous year. A federation for societies working in information processing, IFIP's aim is two-fold: to support information processing in the countries of its members and to encourage technology transfer to developing nations. As its mission statement clearly states:

IFIP is the global non-profit federation of societies of ICT professionals that aims at achieving a worldwide professional and socially responsible development and application of information and communication technologies.

IFIP is a non-profit-making organization, run almost solely by 2500 volunteers. It operates through a number of technical committees and working groups, which organize events and publications. IFIP's events range from large international open conferences to working conferences and local seminars.

The flagship event is the IFIP World Computer Congress, at which both invited and contributed papers are presented. Contributed papers are rigorously refereed and the rejection rate is high.

As with the Congress, participation in the open conferences is open to all and papers may be invited or submitted. Again, submitted papers are stringently refereed.

The working conferences are structured differently. They are usually run by a working group and attendance is generally smaller and occasionally by invitation only. Their purpose is to create an atmosphere conducive to innovation and development. Refereeing is also rigorous and papers are subjected to extensive group discussion.

Publications arising from IFIP events vary. The papers presented at the IFIP World Computer Congress and at open conferences are published as conference proceedings, while the results of the working conferences are often published as collections of selected and edited papers.

IFIP distinguishes three types of institutional membership: Country Representative Members, Members at Large, and Associate Members. The type of organization that can apply for membership is a wide variety and includes national or international societies of individual computer scientists/ICT professionals, associations or federations of such societies, government institutions/government related organizations, national or international research institutes or consortia, universities, academies of sciences, companies, national or international associations or federations of companies.

More information about this series at http://www.springer.com/series/6102

Ioannis Stamelos · Jesus M. Gonzalez-Barahoña
Iraklis Varlamis · Dimosthenis Anagnostopoulos (Eds.)

Open Source Systems: Enterprise Software and Solutions

14th IFIP WG 2.13 International Conference, OSS 2018
Athens, Greece, June 8–10, 2018
Proceedings

 Springer

Editors
Ioannis Stamelos
Aristotle University of Thessaloniki
Thessaloniki
Greece

Jesus M. Gonzalez-Barahoña ⓘ
King Juan Carlos University
Fuenlabrada
Spain

Iraklis Varlamis ⓘ
Harokopio University of Athens
Tavros, Athens
Greece

Dimosthenis Anagnostopoulos ⓘ
Harokopio University of Athens
Tavros, Athens
Greece

ISSN 1868-4238   ISSN 1868-422X (electronic)
IFIP Advances in Information and Communication Technology
ISBN 978-3-030-06420-4   ISBN 978-3-319-92375-8   (eBook)
https://doi.org/10.1007/978-3-319-92375-8

Printed on acid-free paper

This Springer imprint is published by the registered company Springer International Publishing AG part of Springer Nature
The registered company address is: Gewerbestrasse 11, 6330 Cham, Switzerland

General Chair's Message

I would like to welcome you to the proceedings of the 14th International Conference on Open Source Systems (OSS 2018) held in Athens during June 8–10, 2018. OSS 2018 was an emblematic international conference in the area of open source systems and I was much honored to serve this year as the general chair of this conference.

Apart from being an international forum where professionals from academia and industry gather to share research and discuss all aspects of FLOSS and new FLOSS initiatives, this year's OSS conference also focused on practical experiences, as open source enterprise software has reached a high level of popularity. An increasing number of organizations recognize the benefits that FLOSS offers, bringing open source software into their business.

I am also very proud of this year's program, which included an exceptional line-up of keynote speeches, by Tony Wasserman and Jörn Altman, and a collection of technical papers.

This conference would not have been possible without the contributions and efforts of many, not the least of whom are the program chairs (Iraklis Varlamis, Ioannis Stamelos, and Jesus Gonzalez-Barahoña), the Program Committee members, our local organizers (Konstantinos Tserpes, Dimitrios Michail, and George Dimitrakopoulos), the Greek Open Technologies Alliance (GFOSS) for supporting OSS 2018 and Mara Nikolaidi, the rector of Harokopio University of Athens. I would also like to thank Tony Wasserman for his valuable support throughout all conference organizing activities and most importantly, you, the members of the OSS community.

June 2018   Dimosthenis Anagnostopoulos

Program Chairs' Message

It is a great pleasure to welcome you to the proceedings of the 14th International Conference on Open Source Systems (OSS 2018). The range of papers published in *Open Source Systems: Open Source Enterprise Software and Solutions* cover a range of topics related to free, libre, and open source software (FLOSS), including: licensing, organizational and management issues; best practices and case studies; quality and reusability of projects, tools, and systems.

The OSS series of conferences aims to provide an international forum where a diverse community of professionals from academia, industry, and the public sector, as well as diverse FLOSS initiatives can come together to share research findings and practical experiences. The conference is also a forum to provide information and education to practitioners, identify directions for further research, and to be an ongoing platform for technology transfer, no matter which form of FLOSS is being pursued.

We are very pleased to have received 38 contributions (34 full and four short paper submissions) for the technical program, from which we included 14 full papers and one short paper (representing an acceptance rate of 41% for full papers). Every paper received on average three reviews by members of the Program Committee, and was carefully discussed by Program Committee members until a consensus was reached. Based on the reviews for each paper, one of the two program chairs initiated an online discussion among the reviewers in order to reach consensus. The two program chairs facilitated this process for the different papers. All decisions were based on the quality of the papers, which considered the reviews and the outcome of the discussions.

The program also included two keynotes (by Anthony Wasserman and Jörn Altmann), two tutorials and one "Working Session on Developing a FLOSS Body of Knowledge." We would like to give special thanks to all the people who allowed us to present such an outstanding program, and we would especially like to mention: the Program Committee members and additional reviewers; the community and publicity chairs; the session chairs; all the authors who submitted their papers to OSS 2018; the General Chair (Dimosthenis Anagnostopoulos), and the local organizers (Konstantinos Tserpes, Dimitrios Michail, and George Dimitrakopoulos). We are also grateful to the Greek Open Technologies Alliance (GFOSS) for supporting OSS 2018, the rector of Harokopio University of Athens, Maria Nikolaidi, for her valuable assistance and a number of other people without whom this conference would not have happened.

June 2018

Ioannis Stamelos
Jesus M. Gonzalez-Barahoña
Iraklis Varlamis

Preface

The 14 full and one short papers that were selected for presentation are organized thematically as follows:

Organizational Aspects of OSS Projects

The work of Eckert [1] draws parallels between OSS projects and organizations and explains with paradigms how the components of an organizational framework— people, organization, and assets— map to the respective elements of an OSS community.

Wen et al. [2] investigate a 30-month government–academia partnership in order to depict the differences in project management methods employed by the government and by academia and provide best practices that favor team management in collaborative works.

Ilin et al. [3] perform a study on founders, developers, and managers of 13 crowdfunding initiatives involving open source products to determine how communities, crowdfunding campaigns, and open source are associated. Their findings indicate common characteristics among the three, a family-like relationship between the community and the organizers, who perceive community as a success factor for their crowdfunding campaigns.

OSS Project Validity

Kritikos and Stamelos [4] propose an evaluation approach based on the adaptation of the City Resilience Framework to OSS with the aim of providing a strong theoretical basis for evaluating OSS projects.

Pinto et al. [5] study the subject of opening the software history and investigate the reasons behind removing the software history when open-sourcing and the challenges that developers face with the lack of availability of software history.

Chalal and Saini [6] propose and validate a commit message quality model, and use it to analyze seven OSS projects. Their analysis shows that when a small group of contributors is active at the same time in a project, this leads to high syntactic quality contributions.

Mining OSS Data

Kouzari et al. [7] perform an empirical process-mining research on the Koha open source integrated library system and find that the bug closure process followed in the project is very similar to the declared one but that variations do occur under specific circumstances. In this way, they highlight the importance of process mining in OSS projects in order to investigate the processes followed and identify outliers helping to standardize and improve the processes and to enhance the collaboration among members of the community.

Ribeiro et al. [8] present Kiskadee, a system to support the usage of static analysis during software development by providing carefully ranked static analysis reports. The software runs multiple static analyzers on the source code and then classifies and ranks all the potential bugs by importance.

Caetano et al. [9] introduce an approach based on software issues to support decision-making regarding open source software development activities such as release planning and retrospectives. They form an issue dependency topology and apply a PageRank algorithm to suggest an importance ranking of the software issues, which can then be used by project leaders as an input to planning activities.

OSS in Public Administration

The work of Williams [10] presents how a FLOSS software, Open Source Internet Research Tool, OSIRT, has the opportunity to flourish in the sector of law enforcement, especially because of the cuts to budgets being made to law enforcement services.

Koloniaris et al. [11] record the current penetration and usage of free and open source software in the municipalities of Greece and compare its potential with the current state of computerization and the hardware level. They examine the possibility of improving the services provided to the citizens as well as the cost aspects from the use of OSS.

Vafopoulos et al. [12] propose a model conceptualization (Linked Open Economy, LOE) capable of exploiting the massive amount and variety of open economic data that are gradually becoming available by governments and open source communities. LOE will create a common ground to serve as a catalyst in providing more efficient answers in important economic activities.

OSS Governance

Harutyunyan et al. [13] present a study of ten companies with advanced FLOSS governance practices and conclude with a partial theory of FLOSS governance tool requirements by industry. By providing a detailed hierarchical list of these industry-relevant requirements, they offer a unique insight into industry understanding of FLOSS governance tools and their expectations, alongside existing tools and their features.

OSS Reusability

Routis et al. [14] present the ReWeee Platform, a collaborative community platform, developed exclusively with open source software. Using only OSS components, they manage to develop the platform writing less than 10% code and reusing more than 20 software components.

Kyriakou et al. [15] examine how Rust and Node.js and their respective tooling and package repositories can be used for discovering existing OSS implemented in C/C++. With an incremental methodology applied in a proof-of-concept situation, they show the potential increase in discoverability, code quality, and portability, along with viable performance degradation of portable binaries.

June 2018

Ioannis Stamelos
Jesus M. Gonzalez-Barahoña
Iraklis Varlamis
Dimosthenis Anagnostopoulos

Organization

Organizing Committee

General Chair

Dimosthenis Anagnostopoulos   Harokopio University of Athens, Greece

Program Chairs

Ioannis Stamelos   Aristotle University of Thessaloniki, Greece
Jesus M. Gonzalez-Barahoña   Universidad Rey Juan Carlos, Spain
Iraklis Varlamis   Harokopio University of Athens, Greece

Local Organizing Chairs

Konstantinos Tserpes   Harokopio University of Athens, Greece
Dimitrios Michail   Harokopio University of Athens, Greece

Proceedings Chair

George Dimitrakopoulos   Harokopio University of Athens, Greece

Community Chair

Nikos Roussos   Greenpeace and Greek FOSS, Greece

Publicity Chairs

Europe

Stefano Zacchiroli   Paris Diderot University and Inria, France

Asia

Akinori Ihara   Nara Institute of Science and Technology, Japan

North America

Mei Nagappan   Rochester Institute of Technology, USA

South America

Igor Steinmacher	UTFPR, Brazil

Advisory Committee

Tony Wasserman	Carnegie Mellon University, USA
Diomidis Spinellis	Athens University of Economics and Business, Greece
Gregorio Robles	Universidad Rey Juan Carlos, Spain
Imed Hammouda	Chalmers and University of Gothenburg, Sweden

Program Committee

Ampatzoglou Apostolos	Aristotle University of Thessaloniki, Greece
Anagnostopoulos Ioannis	University of Thessaly, Greece
Andreatos Antonios	Hellenic Air Force Academy, Greece
Angelis Lefteris	Aristotle University of Thessaloniki, Greece
Assaf Anwar	KADDB, Jordan
Bibi Stamatia	University of Western Macedonia, Greece
Boldyreff Cornelia	University of East London, UK
Cánovas Izquierdo Javier Luis	Open University of Catalonia, Spain
Capiluppi Andrea	Brunel University, UK
Chatzigewrgiiou Alexandros	University of Macedonia, Greece
Crowston Kevin	Syracuse University, USA
Dasygenis Minas	University of Western Macedonia, Greece
El Baamrani Khalid	Université Cadi Ayyad, Morocco
Fermigier Stéfane	Nuxeo, France
Ihara Akinori	Nara Institute of Science and Technology, Japan
Kakarontzas George	TEI of Thessaly, Greece
Karam Walid	University of Balamand, Lebanon
Koch Stefan	Johannes Kepler University, Austria
Kon Fabio	University of São Paulo, Brazil
Labastida i Juan Ignasi	University of Barcelona, Spain
Lanubile Filippo	University of Bari, Italy
Lavazza Luigi	Università degli Studi dell'Insubria, Italy
Lenarduzzi Valentina	Tampere University of Technology, Finland
Louridas Panagiotis	Athens University of Economics and Business, Greece
Michail Dimitrios	Harokopio University of Athens, Greece
Mikkonen Tommi	Tampere University of Technology, Finland
Morasca Sandro	Università degli Studi dell'Insubria, Italy
Nagappan Mei	Rochester Institute of Technology, USA
Nikolaidi Maria	Harokopio University of Athens, Greece
Ottom Mohammad Ashraf	Yarmouk University, Jordan
Papaspyrou Nikolaos	National Technical University of Athens, Greece

Riehle Dirk	Friedrich Alexander University Erlangen-Nürnberg, Germany
Rizomiliotis Panagiotis	University of the Aegean, Greece
Russo Barbara	Free University of Bozen-Bolzano, Italy
Steinmacher Igor	Universidade Tecnológica Federal do Paraná, Brazil
Taibi Davide	University of Bozen-Bolzano, Italy
Theodoros Karounos	Open Technologies Alliance (GFOSS), Greece
Travassos Guilherme	COPPE/UFRJ, Brazil
Tserpes Konstantinos	Harokopio University of Athens, Greece
Tzotsos Angelos	National Technical University of Athens, Greece
Vassilakis Costas	University of the Peloponnese, Greece
Vavalis Manolis	University of Thessaly, Greece
Vlachos Vasileios	TEI of Larissa, Greece
Voyiatzis Ioannis	Athens University of Applied Sciences, Greece
Weber Jens	University of Victoria, Canada
Zacchiroli Stefano	Paris Diderot University, France
Zavras Alexis	Intel Corporation, Germany

Sponsors

With the Support of

Contents

OSS in Public Administration

OSS Governance

OSS Reusability

Organizational Aspects of OSS Projects

How Can Open Source Software Projects Be Compared with Organizations?

Remo Eckert[(✉)]

University of Bern, Bern, Switzerland
remo.eckert@iwi.unibe.ch

Abstract. The existence of a community plays a central role in the development of Open Source Software (OSS). Communities are commonly defined as a group of people sharing common norms or values. The common interest of an OSS project is obvious: to develop software under an OSS license. When we look at the rather general definition of a community, we see that there is a similarity to the term 'organization'. This paper draws parallels between OSS projects and the general elements of an organization and shows the different elements comprised in an OSS community: people, organization and assets. Each of those elements is enriched with examples from different research in the corresponding OSS research stream and provides a broad overview of the elements of OSS projects. With the help of this comparison, research on OSS can be made more focused and aligned with organizational research.

Keywords: Open Source Software · OSS governance · OSS framework

1 Introduction

The phenomenon of OSS has attained much attention over the years. In the academic literature, different aspects of OSS and its development have been examined and discussed. Quite often, however, the terms used to describe the different phenomena around OSS are not exactly defined and even more the relationship between different concepts is not clarified. For example, OSS research often uses various different concepts of a collective that works together to reach a common goal, such like community, project, organization, or foundation. This results in a situation where it is not always clear what is exactly meant with the concepts, what do they comprise and how they relate to each other.

The development of OSS takes place in an OSS project. By creating a three-phase model, de Laat [1] describes the structural evolution of an OSS project. In phase one, governance is spontaneous and explicit coordination and control are non-existent. Phase two introduces internal governance with formal tools, e.g. division of roles, training, modularization or decision-making. This enables an OSS project to be governed internally in order to increase efficiency and effectiveness as the community grows. Eventually, in phase three, if the OSS project is successful and both companies and other organizations wish to participate, there is a need for institutionalization (a legal entity such as a foundation) to involve outside parties such as organizations [1].

I. Stamelos et al. (Eds.): OSS 2018, IFIP AICT 525, pp. 3–14, 2018.
https://doi.org/10.1007/978-3-319-92375-8_1

Governance within OSS projects has been widely discussed for many years [2–4]. One frequently used definition of OSS governance is "the means of achieving the direction, control, and coordination of wholly or partially autonomous individuals and organizations on behalf of an OSS development project to which they jointly contribute" [5]. In order to better understand what governance of an OSS project is, one needs first to understand the different elements of what is to be governed. However, there is no research that attempts to explain those different elements of an OSS project. Thus, there is a need for studies that contribute to a better understanding of the different elements comprised within an OSS project. Therefore, this paper attempts to answer the following question: *What are the different elements comprised within an OSS project?* To answer our research question, we have developed a framework in which OSS projects are compared to the elements of an organization.

The remainder of this paper is structured as follows: Sect. 2 shows the elements of an organization because we perceive an OSS project as an organization in the most generic sense. Section 3 adapts these elements to OSS projects and explains the different elements of an OSS project. Section 4 discusses the results and the implications thereof for both theory and practice.

2   The Elements of an Organization

An organization is defined as an entity comprising multiple actors with a collective goal [6]. According to organizational research, governance combines various mechanisms to encourage people to do things that align with the organization's goals [7].

According to Luhmann [6], there are three characteristics that highlight the organization: first, an organization can decide which people are part of it and which are not. The organization can define restrictions and rules; failure to observe these rules can result in exclusion. Second, organizations have goals and the decisions an organization takes are oriented around these goals. Generally, organizations have several processes, which can be structured either in management processes, in core processes or in supporting processes. Core processes are central for an organization to earn money, whereas management processes structure an organization to achieve those core processes. Supporting processes are necessary to run the core processes, but are not central to an organization [8]. Third, organizations have hierarchies, which regulate the position of members within the organization. Processes and hierarchies enable an organization to coordinate its people. Processes and hierarchies, both formal and informal, therefore represent mechanisms of governance to align the behavior of people according to organizational goals [7].

Besides people, common goals, roles, rules and structures, most - if not all - organizations are in need of assets. Assets are tangible or intangible goods and can be owned or controlled to produce and have a positive economic value. Moreover, they can be converted into cash [9]. From an accounting viewpoint, an asset is a resource controlled by an entity as a result of past events and from which future economic benefits are expected to flow to the entity. An asset can be tangible or intangible [10].

The establishment of a legal entity helps to protect an organization from various threats such as liability. Figure 1 combines Luhmann [6] and the accounting viewpoint

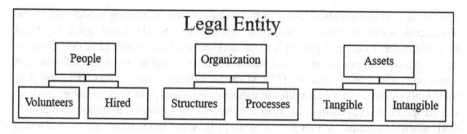

Fig. 1. Organizational framework.

and shows the different elements of an organization. Although Fig. 1 implies a well-defined structure, each element is closely interlinked with the other elements.

3 Organizational Framework of OSS Projects

In the following subsections, we explain how each of the corresponding elements of people, organization and assets can be understood in regards to OSS projects. The following subsections show that the similarities between an organization and OSS can be structured according to our organizational framework.

3.1 People

OSS projects are associations consisting of people who come together virtually in pursuit of a common goal [11]. The motivation to contribute to an OSS project differs: contributors to an OSS project can either be paid by an employer, or are volunteers. In general, their reasons for contributing to OSS projects can be categorized as either intrinsic or extrinsic motivation [12]. An action is extrinsically motivated when it is performed in order to obtain some separable outcome, whereas an intrinsically motivated action is carried out for the mere interest in or joy of performing it [13]. However, the motivations behind employees and volunteers contributing to an OSS projects differ [14]. A developer's "itch worth scratching", as stated by Raymond, might be not as strong for a paid developer as for a volunteer [15]. Tasks such as project design, coordination, testing, documentation and bug-fixing are usually less attractive for volunteers and could therefore be carried out by hired people to ensure that these tasks will be done properly [16]. We therefore distinguish between hired people and volunteers.

Volunteers. The involvement of a community in an OSS project is a vital factor for the success of the project because the community promotes the project and its development [17, 18]. Therefore, attracting and gaining volunteers for a new OSS-project is one of the main focus of community building. The community can ease the way in which new volunteers can join the community by defining guidelines, compiling mailing lists and wikis and answering project-related questions [19]. Moreover, the software quality itself may increase the success rate of attracting new members, whereas several methods of enhancing the quality of the code exist, ranging from code refactoring to documentation [20]. On the technical side, increasing modularity of the source code is one incentive for attracting new developers [21]. Another way to attract more volunteers to an OSS project is to use an issue tracking system [22]. OSS projects typically have an open issue tracker where developers and users of the software can report bugs and feature requests [23]. With the help of issue trackers, potential new contributors can get in touch with the existing community. In their literature review, von Krogh et al. [12] distinguish between intrinsic, internalized extrinsic or extrinsic motivations. As stated by von Krogh et al. [12], some motivations are by definition extrinsic, but could be internalized by developers so that they are perceived as self-regulating behavior rather than external impositions.

Hired Contributors. A high number of developers are paid by an employer for their OSS efforts [24]. In a study by O'Mahony and Bechky [25], 63% of respondents were paid by a corporate sponsor. In the GNOME project, tasks which are usually less attractive to volunteers, such as project design and coordination, testing, documentation and bug-fixing are carried out by employees [16]. People who are paid to contribute to an OSS project may be paid directly by an organization which benefits from the developed software. For example, Red Hat will make more money on support if Linux is used more. Another example is Intel. It will sell more semiconductors if an operating system is free, and a computer therefore costs less. As a result, such companies hope to benefit from allocating their own employees to an OSS project [26, 27]. Berdou [28] distinguishes between free sponsorship, clear mandate, OSS-friendly jobs and sub-contracting. In free sponsorship, developers receive no clear instruction from their employer about what they should work on. For the most part, they are former volunteers, who are expected to work on more or less the same things they used to. In contrast to free sponsorship, those who have a clear mandate from their employer, are told what they ought to work on, such as integrating different aspects of the project into company products, or building on their projects' platform to create commercial applications. OSS-friendly jobs are jobs where people are expected to develop proprietary software, but are also allowed to spend part of their time working on OSS projects. Their terms of work can be formal or informal and resemble part-time free sponsorship. In sub-contracting, meanwhile, people are paid to solve a problem or develop a specific application. This form could also include bounty programs (cash reward offered for development) and self-employed developers. However, people can also be paid by an OSS foundation, as it is in the GNOME Foundation, where the executive director and an administrator, as well as other contractors, are paid via membership fees to accelerate community growth and sustainability [29].

3.2 Organization

Some OSS projects, especially bigger ones, have formal membership rules and agreements, such as the membership fee and bylaws with different roles and functions [19]. Bylaws are rules established by the community to regulate itself in a structural and in a procedural way. As an example, the bylaws of the Eclipse Foundation regulate the overall purpose of the community, the powers and duties of the various roles within the community, how and when members are elected and how meetings are organized.

Moreover, the Eclipse Foundation bylaws explain how decisions are made, explain the tasks of the different committees, councils, boards and the different forms of membership [30]. Contributions not only help the software to evolve, but also redefine the role of the contributors, thereby changing the social dynamics of the community. Consequently, project leaders and core members should focus not only on the evolution of the software itself, but also on the creation of an environment and culture that fosters and encourage new members to move toward the center of the OSS community. This can happen by means of both formal and informal mechanisms. Such mechanisms allow developers to work independently, by encouraging or helping other developers to work in ways that are expected by the community [31].

Structures. Relationships with external groups, leadership and control are common sources of conflict in an OSS project. In the worst case, these can even lead to a breakdown or a software fork where a subgroup of contributors develop their own version of the code [32, 33]. A structure regulates the coordination efforts between different actors. Although there is no strict hierarchy in some OSS communities, their structure is not completely flat. According to [34], roles and their associated influence can be earned through contributions to the community. The resulting informal community structure, called the "onion-model" can be depicted as layers, where the roles closer to the center (e.g. the project leader and core members) have a greater influence than the roles in the outer layers (e.g. readers and passive users). The roles are not fixed and can change over time, depending on the contributions of the community members involved. The processes are in many cases more informal than formal, anyone can join and the relations and roles change over time [35]. Roles do not imply authority, but instead responsibility. Authority, as an example in the NetBeans community, is based on reputation and respect [31].

O'Mahony and Ferraro [36] show how a community uses a formal bureaucratic basis of authority to reinforce its meritocratic norms. They show how an OSS project designed a governance system that combines a constitutional basis of authority with democratic mechanisms to ensure control by the majority. A governance system shapes the way in which project-wide decisions are made. Moreover, governance structures ensure that a project could survive a change in leadership or crucial positions within the project. The need to coordinate member activities and integrate their contributions necessitates a structure. Analyzing the Debian project, O'Mahony and Ferraro [36] distinguish between four different forms of governance, where the community develops from an informal to a formal structure. In the Debian project, the de facto governance worked well for the first five years. There were no formal means of governance. In the designing governance phase, a formal definition of roles, rights and responsibilities was established. The resulting governance system embraced two elements - the formal positional authority and the limitation of that authority through democratic means. In phase three, implementing governance, the new formal governance structure accepted by the community, was implemented. Candidates nominated themselves and the community could give them their vote. In phase four, stabilizing governance, the leadership forms began to reach settlement.

Processes. Like an organization, an OSS project also has various processes, which can be structured in core processes, management processes and support processes.

Core Processes. While many OSS projects are built by a small number of individuals, in large projects, a significant number of individuals and firms contribute to the project [5, 27, 37]. Formal rules about the development process ensure that operational tasks, such as requirements elicitation, assignment of people to tasks, release control, etc. are organized [5]. The Eclipse development process, for example, describes the principles upon which the process should rely: openness, transparency and meritocracy. Moreover, each project is supposed to make a project plan available to the community at the beginning of each development cycle (for each major and minor release) [38]. Another core process is requirements engineering. German [16] illustrates how several leaders in the GNOME project provide a list of requirements that the system should satisfy and reference applications the project should replace. However, not all requirements are an output of the leaders. Requirements for a new module or components are born from discussions in mailing lists or on an issue tracker [22]. Requirements can be formulated in a vision developed by community leaders; by imitating the features from reference applications; by discussions in a mailing list; by providing a prototype with the implemented requirements to work on; or by a post-hoc requirement where the requirements are unknown to the rest of the community and are fulfilled by the developer seeking those requirements. What those methods have in common is that they are usually informal and prioritized by the leaders of the project, maintainers of the module or by a foundation [37].

Management Processes. OSS projects, especially larger ones, exhibit formal structures that can be described in bylaws. German [16] describes how the board of directors in the GNOME community is elected. The board of directors is democratically elected by the rest of the foundation members. In addition, the community has a rule that restricts the power of a single organization by imposing a maximum number of board seats. Moreover, board members must represent the interests of the GNOME community, not the interests of their own organization. This rule, as stated, has already been enforced several times in the past.

Supporting Processes. The developed software asset needs to be protected from lawsuits from the legal entity that owns it [39]. Therefore, the OSS community needs to ensure that contributions do not infringe third-party IP-rights. For example, a contributor agreement ensures that the OSS community cannot be subject to a firm's ownership claim and is therefore seen in some OSS projects as a precondition to any code contribution [25]. Another example of a supporting process is the funding process. Since there are different forms of memberships and fees, the Eclipse Bylaws define which people have to pay for becoming a member and how much [30]. The secretary is responsible for invoicing membership fees and collecting fees, if necessary with a dues notice. The annual report, which is publicly available, provides an overview of the financial situation of the Eclipse community in terms of revenues and expenses. This report, which encompasses far more than just the financial situation, also constitutes a supporting process.

3.3 Assets

We distinguish between tangible and intangible assets, which are described in detail in the following.

Tangible Assets. With respect to the development of software, the availability of an IT Infrastructure is an important aspect. Gutwin et al. [40] found that distributed developers do need to maintain awareness of one another, more specifically, both a general awareness of the entire team and more detailed knowledge of the individuals they plan to work with. The main mechanisms for maintaining this awareness of who is involved in the project and what their activities are, are text-based communication tools that are commonly used in OSS project, e.g. mailing lists, wikis or text chats. For specific awareness, such as people's expertise and activities, an operating IT Infrastructure with a decentralized version control system such as GIT [41], bug trackers for submitting bugs and feature requests, e.g. Bugzilla [22] and mailing lists [5, 36] are needed. Collaboration among the participating members takes place with the help of these tools and simplifies the effort required for distributed software development [16]. As recommended by German [16], communication should be carried out via a variety of tools. All such tools, including the servers they run on, represent IT Infrastructure [16, 42].

If an OSS project wants to obtain contributions, it needs to market itself. This includes hosting a website with the published source code of the OSS project. Therefore, a webserver is required. As an example, a committer must have access to the latest code base in order to insert changes into that base [43]. Normally, this is done using a decentralized version control system (DVCS) such as GIT, which facilitates collaboration among various developers [41]. However, a DVCS and a website need to run on a server with guaranteed Internet access. As described by German [16], at the level of community IT Infrastructure, servers as well as bandwidth are required to communicate and share collaborators' progress. As an example, the GNOME community relies upon donations from the Autonomous University of Mexico and other organizations that provide its IT Infrastructure [16].

Because the majority of work in an OSS project is performed by globally distributed individuals, face-to-face meetings are rather rare. However, they help to better communicate and resolve potential conflicts [40]. Consequently, infrastructure in the form of rooms for meetings and an internet connection can help to reduce potential communication problems. Moreover, if the OSS project has a legal entity, its address can be used for corresponding purposes.

Intangible Assets. Although OSS does not fully meet the conditions to be included as an asset in financial reports [44], it can be protected in different ways, such as intellectual property rights (IPR), trademarks and brands. As stated by Fitzgerald [45], trademarks or brands are alternative mechanisms to protect IPR in addition to the license itself. A trademark can protect the OSS project's reputation by preventing other projects using their name or brand (e.g. a software fork with other goals than the main project). The goal of a trademark is to prevent customers from confusion as to the origins of the product or service [46]. A common practice among OSS foundations is to own the copyright of the source code and related texts, as stated by Riehle [47].

However, a legal basis for a growing community, especially when firms are involved, is necessary. Firms are reluctant to donate code to a project without transferring responsibility for it. Without a legal owner, firms hesitate to donate code and transfer responsibility for future maintenance. The establishment of a foundation offers firms a legal entity to which ownership can be transferred [16, 25]. IPR are better defined and more defensible when owned by a single legal entity as opposed to various individuals. Having a single and central copyright holder means that it holds the asset and therefore can protect it more easily compared to the situation when hundreds of contributors hold the individual rights to their parts. Furthermore, a legal entity ensures that volunteer contributors are protected against individual liability, and can enter into agreements collectively and protect their code, trademarks, licenses and brands on their behalf [39].

4 Discussion

Our organizational framework compares OSS projects with the typical elements of an organization by showing the different elements exhibited by an OSS project and comparing these with the elements of an organization. According to our framework, the three main elements of an OSS project are people, organization and assets. Each of those elements is enriched with examples from different research in the corresponding OSS research stream and provides a broad overview of the elements of OSS projects.

The people dimension refers to the concept of a community. Contributors to an OSS project therefore can either be hired or volunteers. OSS projects are associations consisting of people who come together virtually in pursuit of a common goal [11]. Tasks such as the project design, coordination, testing, documentation and bug-fixing are less attractive for volunteers and could therefore be carried out hired staff to ensure that these tasks are done [16]. Due to the fact that, in some OSS projects, more than half of the contributors are paid by a corporate sponsor [25], we see that OSS governance is becoming increasingly important. A key aspect of OSS governance is therefore managing the community [5].

What we call the organizational dimension as well as the asset dimension, can be compared to the concept of governance. Similar to Markus [5], we see formal and informal structures and norms as one of the main elements of OSS governance. Different projects have a varying degree of formalism, with some lacking any formal descriptions at all on how decisions are made. However, there are a number of OSS projects with formal rules and agreements, such the bylaws, with different roles and functions [19]. When firms participate in an OSS project, the degree of formalism may increase [25]. Similar to Markus [5], we see ownership of assets as one of the main areas of OSS governance. Although OSS does not fully meet the conditions to be included in financial reports as an asset [44], OSS projects often possess other assets, such as IPR, trademarks, brands or IT Infrastructure [16, 45]. However, there are plenty of opportunities for OSS projects to use IT Infrastructure from other organizations without possessing them (e.g. GitHub as a DVCS).

What de Laat [1] describes as institutionalization in order to involve outside parties, is what the legal entity is in our framework.

In their paper, Lindman and Hammouda [48] illustrate the role of OSS foundations and the relationships between OSS communities and other OSS foundations. Although their unit of analysis was OSS foundations, the taxonomy can be compared to the organizational framework in our study; each of their elements can also be found in our organizational framework.

Our framework describes the different elements comprised within a single OSS project and shows the broad variety and complex constellation surrounding such a project. However, as an example, an OSS community may have different projects (e.g. different software products with different goals) and therefore a project does not correspond to the organization (the three dimensions of our framework). Moreover, an umbrella organization such as the Linux Foundation may offer their legal entity in order to protect the project and to offer services relating those three dimensions of our framework. Therefore, the legal aspect of the organizations does not need to correspond to the project. We see our framework as a first step to better understand and differentiate the concepts and different elements in order to ask more specific questions relating OSS research.

Our organizational framework broadens the view of Riehle and Berschneider [49] that shows 3 different ways in which a mature OSS project can govern itself in the future: (1) continue as is, (2) create its own legal entity or (3) affiliate with an existing OSS foundation. In our view, in addition to these 3 forms, an "in-between" solution involving collaboration with different OSS foundations is also possible. Such collaboration can be in all areas of our organizational framework or in specific areas only. This is the case in the LibreOffice community which has its own legal entity (The Document Foundation), but buys some services in the funding process from another foundation [50].

For practitioners, our framework will help to provide a better understanding of the structure an OSS project can have and how the different elements can be organized, similar to an organization. Moreover, our framework can provide practitioners valuable insights on several managerial aspects relating to OSS governance.

References

1. De Laat, P.B.: Governance of open source software: state of the art. J. Manag. Gov. **11**, 165–177 (2007)
2. De Noni, I., Ganzaroli, A., Orsi, L.: The evolution of OSS governance: a dimensional comparative analysis. Scand. J. Manag. **29**, 247–263 (2013)
3. Franck, E., Jungwirth, C.: Reconciling rent-seekers and donators–the governance structure of open source. J. Manag. Gov. **7**, 401–421 (2003)
4. Schaarschmidt, M., Walsh, G., von Kortzfleisch, H.F.O.: How do firms influence open source software communities? A framework and empirical analysis of different governance modes. Inf. Organ. **25**, 99–114 (2015)
5. Markus, M.L.: The governance of free/open source software projects: monolithic, multidimensional, or configurational? J. Manag. Gov. **11**, 151–163 (2007)
6. Luhmann, N.: Funktionen und Folgen formaler Organisation. Duncker & Humblot, Berlin (1964)

7. Choudhury, V., Sabherwal, R.: Portfolios of control in outsourced software development projects. Inf. Syst. Res. **14**, 291–314 (2003)
8. Becker, J., Kahn, D.: The process in focus. In: Becker, J., Kugeler, M., Rosemann, M. (eds.) Process Management: A Guide for the Design of Business Processes, pp. 1–12. Springer, Heidelberg (2003)
9. O'Sullivan, A., Sheffrin, S.M.: Economics: Principles in Action. Pearson Prentice Hall, Upper Saddle River (2003)
10. IFRS Foundation: International Financial Reporting Standards. http://www.ifrs.org/issued-standards/list-of-standards/. Accessed 19 Jan 2018
11. Rheingold, H.: The Virtual Community: Homesteading on the Electronic Frontier. MIT Press, Cambridge (2000)
12. von Krogh, G., Haefliger, S., Spaeth, S., Wallin, M.W.: Carrots and rainbows: motivation and social practice in open source software development. MIS Q. **36**, 649–676 (2012)
13. Deci, E.L., Ryan, R.M.: The general causality orientations scale: self-determination in personality. J. Res. Pers. **19**, 109–134 (1985)
14. Roberson, Q.M., Stewart, M.M.: Understanding the motivational effects of procedural and informational justice in feedback processes. Br. J. Psychol. **97**, 281–298 (2006)
15. Raymond, E.S.: The Cathedral & The Bazaar: Musings on Linux and Open Source by an Accidental Revolutionary. O'Reilly Media Inc., Sebastopol (2001)
16. German, D.M.: The GNOME project: a case study of open source, global software development. Softw. Process Improv. Pract. **8**, 201–215 (2003)
17. Bagozzi, R.P., Dholakia, U.M.: Open source software user communities: a study of participation in Linux user groups. Manag. Sci. **52**, 1099–1115 (2006)
18. Iivari, N.: Empowering the users? A critical textual analysis of the role of users in open source software development. AI Soc. **23**, 511–528 (2009)
19. von Krogh, G., Spaeth, S., Lakhani, K.R.: Community, joining, and specialization in open source software innovation: a case study. Res. Policy **32**, 1217–1241 (2003)
20. Kilamo, T., Hammouda, I., Mikkonen, T., Aaltonen, T.: From proprietary to open source-growing an open source ecosystem. J. Syst. Softw. **85**, 1467–1478 (2012)
21. MacCormack, A., Rusnak, J., Baldwin, C.Y.: Exploring the structure of complex software designs: an empirical study of open source and proprietary code. Manag. Sci. **52**, 1015–1030 (2006)
22. Heppler, L., Eckert, R., Stuermer, M.: Who cares about my feature request? In: Crowston, K., Hammouda, I., Lundell, B., Robles, G., Gamalielsson, J., Lindman, J. (eds.) OSS 2016. IAICT, vol. 472, pp. 85–96. Springer, Cham (2016). https://doi.org/10.1007/978-3-319-39225-7_7
23. Anvik, J., Hiew, L., Murphy, G.C.: Who should fix this bug? In: Proceedings of the 28th International Conference on Software Engineering, pp. 361–370. ACM, New York (2006)
24. Hars, A., Ou, S.: Working for free? Motivations of participating in open source projects. In: Proceedings of the 34th Annual Hawaii International Conference on System Sciences, pp. 25–39. IEEE (2001)
25. O'Mahony, S., Bechky, B.A.: Boundary organizations: enabling collaboration among unexpected allies. Adm. Sci. Q. **53**, 422–459 (2008)
26. Bonaccorsi, A., Rossi, C.: Comparing motivations of individual programmers and firms to take part in the open source movement: from community to business. Knowl. Technol. Policy **18**, 40–64 (2006)
27. Lerner, J., Tirole, J.: Some simple economics of open source. J. Ind. Econ. **50**, 197–234 (2002)

28. Berdou, E.: Insiders and outsiders: paid contributors and the dynamics of cooperation in community led F/OS projects. In: Damiani, E., Fitzgerald, B., Scacchi, W., Scotto, M., Succi, G. (eds.) OSS 2006. IIFIP, vol. 203, pp. 201–208. Springer, Boston, MA (2006). https://doi.org/10.1007/0-387-34226-5_20

29. GNOME Foundation: GNOME Foundation - Fiscal Year 2016 Annual Report. https://www.gnome.org/wp-content/uploads/2017/07/GAR2016-web.pdf. Accessed 19 Jan 2018

30. The Eclipse Foundation: Bylaws of Eclipse Foundation, Inc. https://www.eclipse.org/org/documents/Eclipse%20BYLAWS%202011_08_15%20Final.pdf. Accessed 19 Jan 2018

31. Jensen, C., Scacchi, W.: Collaboration, leadership, control, and conflict negotiation and the netbeans.org open source software development community. In: System Sciences, p. 196b. IEEE (2005)

32. Gamalielsson, J., Lundell, B.: Sustainability of open source software communities beyond a fork: how and why has the LibreOffice project evolved? J. Syst. Softw. **89**, 128–145 (2014)

33. West, J., O'Mahony, S.: Contrasting community building in sponsored and community founded open source projects. In: Proceedings of the 38th Annual Hawaii International Conference on System Sciences, HICSS 2005 (2005)

34. Nakakoji, K., Yamamoto, Y., Nishinaka, Y., Kishida, K., Ye, Y.: Evolution patterns of open-source software systems and communities. In: Proceedings of the International Workshop on Principles of Software Evolution, pp. 76–85. ACM (2002)

35. Dahlander, L., Magnusson, M.G.: Relationships between open source software companies and communities: observations from Nordic firms. Res. Policy **34**, 481–493 (2005)

36. O'Mahony, S., Ferraro, F.: The emergence of governance in an open source community. Acad. Manag. J. **50**, 1079–1106 (2007)

37. Scacchi, W.: Understanding the requirements for developing open source software systems. IEE Softw. Proc. **149**, 24–39 (2002)

38. The eclipse foundation: eclipse development process. https://www.eclipse.org/projects/dev_process/development_process.php. Accessed 19 Jan 2018

39. O'Mahony, S.: Guarding the commons: how community managed software projects protect their work. Res. Policy **32**, 1179–1198 (2003)

40. Gutwin, C., Penner, R., Schneider, K.: Group awareness in distributed software development. In: Proceedings of the 2004 ACM Conference on Computer Supported Cooperative Work, pp. 72–81 (2004)

41. Kalliamvakou, E., Damian, D., Blincoe, K., Singer, L., German, D.M.: Open source-style collaborative development practices in commercial projects using Github. In: Proceedings of the 37th International Conference on Software Engineering, pp. 574–585. IEEE Press (2015)

42. Ducheneaut, N.: Socialization in an open source software community: a socio-technical analysis. Comput. Support. Coop. Work (CSCW) **14**, 323–368 (2005)

43. Jørgensen, N.: Putting it all in the trunk: incremental software development in the FreeBSD open source project. Inf. Syst. J. **11**, 321–336 (2001)

44. García-García, J., Alonso de Magdaleno, M.I.: Valuation of open source software: how do you put a value on free? Revista de Gestão, Finanças e Contabilidade **3** (2013)

45. Fitzgerald, B.: The transformation of open source software. MIS Q. **30**, 587–598 (2006)

46. Anderson, H., Dare, T.: Passport without a Visa: open source software licensing and trademarks. Int. Free Open Source Softw. Law Rev. **1**, 99–110 (2010)

47. Riehle, D.: The economic case for open source foundations. Computer **43**, 86–90 (2010)

48. Jung, Y., Kim, J., Shin, J., Yi, K.: Taming false alarms from a domain-unaware C analyzer by a Bayesian statistical post analysis. In: Hankin, C., Siveroni, I. (eds.) SAS 2005. LNCS, vol. 3672, pp. 203–217. Springer, Heidelberg (2005). https://doi.org/10.1007/11547662_15

49. Riehle, D., Berschneider, S.: A model of open source developer foundations. In: Hammouda, I., Lundell, B., Mikkonen, T., Scacchi, W. (eds.) OSS 2012. IAICT, vol. 378, pp. 15–28. Springer, Heidelberg (2012). https://doi.org/10.1007/978-3-642-33442-9_2
50. Software in the Public Interest, Inc. http://www.spi-inc.org/projects/libreoffice. Accessed 19 Jan 2019

FLOSS Project Management
in Government-Academia Collaboration

Melissa Wen, Paulo Meirelles, Rodrigo Siqueira$^{(\boxtimes)}$, and Fabio Kon

FLOSS Competence Center, University of São Paulo, São Paulo, Brazil
{wen,paulormm,siqueira,fabio.kon}@ime.usp.br

Abstract. Government and academia can collaborate on bringing innovation and filling design-reality gaps in e-government projects. However, differences in project management methods employed by the organizations is often a challenge for collaborative works. Bearing that in mind, we investigated a 30-month government-academia partnership to find appropriate ways to get around this obstacle. From the analysis of *post-mortem* data, we present a set of best practices based on FLOSS and agile software development approaches that favors team management in government-academia collaborations in e-government development projects.

Keywords: Open source software · Free software
Project management

1 Introduction

E-government projects differ from others due to their complexity and extension [2]. They are complex because they combine development, innovation, information & communications technologies, politics, and social impact. They are extensive, however, regarding their scope, target audience, organizational size, time, and the corresponding resistance to change. Developing an innovative e-government project that meets the needs of society is a issue that may be addressed alternatively through collaborative projects between government and academia. This collaborative work has challenges such as organizing the collaboration project, aligning goals, synchronizing the pace of between government and academia, and overcoming the failure trend of e-government projects [7].

One of the leading causes of e-government project failure is poor project management [2]. In this sense, the proper management of the collaboration project should be a relevant concern when government and academia combine efforts to develop an e-government solution. Academia commonly works on cutting-edge development methodologies while the government still relies on traditional techniques. Changing the development process of one of this large-size institutions represents an organizational disturbance with impacts on structure, culture, and

I. Stamelos et al. (Eds.): OSS 2018, IFIP AICT 525, pp. 15–25, 2018.
https://doi.org/10.1007/978-3-319-92375-8_2

management practices [10]. As a result, government and academia have to harmonize their view to increasing the chances of success in projects with tight deadlines and short budgets.

We have investigated the adoption of recommended community standards from Free/Libre and Open Source Software (FLOSS) and agile values as a strategy to harmonize different management approaches, due to the plurality of FLOSS ecosystems and the diversity favored by agile methodologies. Open communication, project modularity, the community of users, and fast response to problems are just a few of the FLOSS ecosystem practices [5,15]. Individuals and interactions, working software, customer collaboration, responding to change are the values agile development [3]. With this in mind, FLOSS and agile practices may improve the cooperation of distinct teams.

In this work, we examine the empirical method developed during 30 months of a government-academia project that helped to harmonize the differences between both organization management cultures. We discuss both quantitative and qualitative analyses of the benefits of FLOSS and agile practices in an e-government project. We identify and trace the best practices based on FLOSS ecosystems and agile methodology. We collect and analyze data from the project repository. Finally, we conduct a survey target at projects participants to find their perception around the set of best practices, and which of them are useful to government-academia collaboration. In doing so, we aim to help academia better understand critical issues they will be confronted with when engaging in a government-academia software project.

2   Related Work

Discussions on how to introduce new management methods into an organization are present in several works. Nerur et al. recognized critical issues concerning the migration from traditional to agile software development by comparing practices of both methodologies [10]. The authors point out managerial, organizational, people, process, and technological issues to be rethought and reconfigured in an organization for a successful migration. Strode et al. investigated the relationship between the adoption of agile methodologies and organizational culture [14] by evaluating nine projects. They identified a set of six factors directly linked to agile methods and concluded that the presence of these aspects in an organization is proportional to the value of agile methodologies usage for their projects. As Nerur et al., Strode et al. also said that the adoption of agile development techniques does indeed produce changes in an organization's culture.

Some works also discuss how academia can collaborate with the industry in the management of software projects. Chookittikul et al. evaluated the increasing use of the agile techniques in software development companies in Thailand. The authors suggested that universities should create curricula that develop in their undergraduate students practical skills required by industry (mainly agile practices) to promote growth in local software businesses [6]. Sandberg et al. report the use of Scrum in an industry-academia research consortium (involving ten industry partners and five universities in Sweden) [12]. Through a case study, they demonstrate that being able to bring together the meaningful activities of the stakeholders is essential to the success of collaborative research between industry and academia.

Complex and large-scale organizations, such as the public administration, have to deal with multiple project variables. Alleman et al. describe a production deployment for the US government, focusing on the methodology applied to address long-term planning and value estimation [1]. In the Brazilian context, Melo et al. [9] investigates the growing adoption of agile methodologies in this country's IT industry. The results of their survey highlight some mismatch that companies faces when developing software for public administration.

Several works tried to highlight the FLOSS practices, while others attempted to determine the relationship between FLOSS practices and agile methods. Capiluppi et al. examined about 400 projects to find FLOSS project properties [5]. In their work, they extracted generic characterization (project size, age, license, and programming language), analyzed the average number of people involved in the project, the community of users, and documentation characteristics. Warsta et al. found differences and similarities between agile development and FLOSS practices [15]. The authors argued that FLOSS development may differ from agile in their philosophical and economic perspectives, on the other hand, both share the definition of work. Finally, Eric Raymond describes many of his experiences and decisions in his work with FLOSS communities [11], and his report in 1999 has many intersections with the agile manifesto in 2001.

This paper differs itself from others by studying the government-academia collaboration for developing a production-level solution. From questionnaires, interviews, and development activities data, we extracted best practices that helped to harmonize the interactions between two different development process and satisfied the management process of both sides. We analyzed the decisions made from the FLOSS and agile perspectives.

3 Research Design

We studied practical alternatives to harmonize the software project lifecycle when confronting different development processes from crucial stakeholders. We are interested in the relationship between government and academia from the project management perspective, without the enforcement of changing their internal processes. We present two research questions that guided this work:

RQ1. *How to introduce FLOSS and agile best practices into government-academia collaboration projects?*

RQ2. *What practices favor effective team management in government-academia collaborative projects?*

To answer these questions, we used the case study as research method. We selected as a case the evolution of the Brazilian Public Software (SPB) portal [8], a government-academia collaborative project based on FLOSS systems. To validate our answers, we covered three different points of view: developers, government agent, and data collected from the project repository.

3.1 The Case Study

The project to evolve the SPB portal was a partnership between government and academia held between 2014 and 2016 [8]. The old version of SPB suffered from maintenance problems and design-reality gaps. In this sense, the Ministry of Planning (MPOG) decided to join the University of Brasília (UnB) and the University of São Paulo (USP) to develop a new platform. This platform had the primary requirement to be based on existing FLOSS projects and integrate multiple systems into one, providing the end user with a unified experience.

In short, the SPB portal evolved into a Collaborative Development Environment (CDE) [4]. It was a novelty in the context of the Brazilian government, due to the technologies employed and its diverse features, which includes social networking, mailing lists, version control system, and source code quality monitoring. All software is integrated using a system-of-systems framework [8]. These characteristics led the project to interact with different FLOSS projects and communities.

The platform development took place at the Advanced Laboratory of Production, Research, and Innovation in Software Engineering (LAPPIS/UnB) and the FLOSS Competence Center at USP (CCSL/USP), both with experience in FLOSS development. Undergraduate interns, IT professionals, and professors formed a partially distributed development team. Their activities followed the workflow of biweekly sprints and 4-month releases.

On the managerial aspect, at the project beginning, the collaboration management and strategic discussions happened only once a month, when project leaders and MPOG directors met in person at the ministry's headquarters. Table 1 summarizes the organizational differences in both involved sides.

Table 1. Differences between academia and government sides.

Characteristics	Academia	Goverment
Responsibilities	Platform development activites	Contracts and collaboration management
	42 undergraduate interns	
	2 professors	1 director
Team size	6 senior developers with significant	1 coordinator
	experience in FLOSS projects	2 requirement analysts
	2 Designers (UX specialists)	
Workplace	LAPPIS at UnB and CCSL at USP	MPOG headquarters
Management approaches	FLOSS practices and Agile values	Mindset from RUP, CMMI, and PMBOK

During the course of the project, we were unable to fully extract all the possible benefits from this workflow. Conflicts between the internal management processes and differences in pace and goals of each institution were compromising the platform development. To improve the project management process and reducing the mismatch between government and academia, professors, with the senior developers' collaboration, incrementally employed a set of best practices based on FLOSS and agile values.

Although the government initiative to work with the university, they had a natural barrier to accept the non-traditional development approaches. The development leaders made decisions in a non-systematic way to promote the usage of

FLOSS and agile techniques in such way that the government understood the value of the collaboration. In this scenario, the SPB project became a proper case to comprehend the processes harmonization between government and university. In this paper, we analyzed and codified the set of project decisions and how they favored the collaboration progress.

3.2 Survey, Interview and Data Collection

We separated the project team into three groups: undergraduate interns, IT professionals (senior developers and designers), and MPOG analysts. For the first two, we sent online questionnaires, and for the last ones, we conducted 2-h interviews. Table 2 presents the details of these processes.

Table 2. Surveying the project participants

	Undergraduate Interns	Senior Developers	MPOG Analysts
Research technique	Online questionnaire	Online questionnaire	Interview
Discussed topics	(1) project organization (2) the development process (3) communication and relationship with members (4) knowledge sharing (5) experience with FLOSS projects		(1) professional profile (2) organization, communication and development methodologies (3) satisfaction with the developed platform (4) lessons learned
Number of interviewed	42	8	2
Rate of responses	88% (37)	100%	100%
Average age at the end of the project	22 years old	30 years old	30 years old
Gender	8% women 92% man	13% women 87% man	100% women
Experience background	43% of the interns had the SPB project as their first contact with FLOSS	11 years of experience; worked in at least 5 companies; participated in 4 to 80 distinct projects; 86% of them had some background with FLOSS before the SPB project	more than 7 years working in the government; SPB project represented their first experience of government-academia collaboration

Finally, we analyzed the data from the central project repository considering all the issues and commits. From April 2015 to June 2016, 59 distinct authors opened 879 issues, 64 different users made the total of 4,658 comments. The development team made 3,256 commits in this above-mentioned repository.

4   Results

The SPB portal project had two phases according to the traceability of project management activities. The first one, between January 2014 and March 2015, is non-traceable since only the universities managed the development activities. The communication between government and academia was, generally, in private channels, such as professional e-mails, personal meetings, and telephone calls. Therefore, the quantitative data found for this period are not conclusive or have little expressiveness, and we do not examine them.

The second phase, from April 2015 to the end of the project (June 2016), has meaningful data. Much of the management and communication activities were recorded and published on online channels and tools. During this period, the development leaders consolidated several FLOSS practices and agile values employed in the development process. At the end, the academic team had an empirical management approach for meeting the government bureaucracies.

Decision 1: Use of the system under development to develop the system itself. Due to the platform features for software development and social network, the development coordinators decided to use the platform under construction to develop the system itself. Gradually, in addition to development activities, government and academia migrated the project management and the communication between teams to the portal environment.

In short, the wiki feature was used for logging meetings, defining goals, planning sprints, documenting deployment procedures and user guides. The issue tracker was used for discussing requirements, monitoring features under development, requesting and recording changes, and validating the delivered functionalities. Finally, the mailing list was used for collaborative construction of requirements, defining schedules, and scheduling meetings between institutions.

Our surveys report Mailing list (100%) and Issue Tracker (62.5%) as the main means of interaction between senior developers and interns. The development team and MPOG staff also interacted mostly via Mailing List (87.5%) and Issue tracker (50%). According to one of the interviewees, this movement made the communication more transparent and efficient. An MPOG analyst said that *"Communicating well goes far beyond the speed. It means enabling someone to tell everyone about everything that is happening in the project. We did not use emails, we use more mailing list and avoid emails. This usage helped us considerably. Everything was public and did not pollute our email box. So, when you wanted to know something, you could access the SPB list and see everything".*

Migrating to the SPB platform also easied monitoring of activities and increased interactions between developers and public servants. The data collected from the repository highlight the frequent use of the platform by both sides teams. In the last 15 months of the project, 59 different authors opened the central repository issues, 8 of them were MPOG agents. These issues received comments from 64 distinct users, 9 of them from MPOG. When we consider the issues with more interactions, those which had ten comments or more, we notice that the government team also felt comfortable in using the tool to interact directly with the development team. In a set of 102 active issues, MPOG staff created 43 of them (this represents 42% of the most active issues).

For the MPOG analysts, interaction via repository improved communication. *"There was a big evolution, we increased our communication via Gitlab".* Migrating to the platform also led MPOG staff to trust the developed code: *"Everything was validated. We tested the functionalities and developed the project on the SPB platform itself. Hence, the use of the system homologated most of its features. From the moment we began to use it for developing, this validation was constant. We felt confident in the code produced".*

The above-mentioned decision also collaborated to meet the government's demand for meticulous documentation of the software design and stages of development without bureaucratizing or modifying the development process. The usage of the platform for project team management conducted the organic production of documentation and records, as mentioned in one of the MPOG responses: *"It was a great learning experience. There are many things documented in emails as well as in the portal itself. We can access the tools at any time and find out how we develop a solution. We can remember the positive points"*.

Decision 2: Brings together government staff and development team. In the first phase of the project, the interviewed MPOG analysts did not participate in any direct interaction with any university representative, even though they were the ones in charge of the government in ensuring the collaboration agreement and the delivery of the products. Because of this, they relied on feedback from their superiors on inter-institutional meetings. They reported that there was significant communication noise in the internal dialogues with their superiors, as well as between their superiors and the development team.

In the second phase of the project, these analysts became direct representatives of the government and started to visit the university's laboratory bi-weekly. One of the analysts believed that *"at this point, the communication started to change"*. The new dynamics reduced communication misunderstandings and unified both sides, as reported by another interviewee: *"It was very positive. We liked to go there and to interact with the team. I think it brought more unity, more integration into the project"*. 73% of the interns considered positive the direct participation of the MPOG staff, and 81% of them believed the presence of government staff in sprint ceremonies was relevant for the project development. For 76% of the interns, writing the requirements together with the MPOG staff was very important to better meet expectations of both sides. According to one of them, *"Joint planning and timely meetings were very important for understanding the needs of MPOG"*.

The closest dialogue between government and academia generated empathy, as reported by one of the interviewees: *"Knowing people in person makes a big difference in the relationship because it causes empathy. You know who that person is. He's not merly a name"*. Consequently, this empathy helped to synchronize the execution pace of activities: *"Visiting the lab and meeting the developers encouraged us to validate resources faster and give faster feedback to the team. In return, they also quickly answered us any question"*.

The implementation of a Continuous Delivery pipeline also reinforced the teams' synchronization [13]. For 81% of the interns and 75% of the IT professionals, deploying new versions of the SPB portal in production was a motivator during the project. On the government side, this approach helped to overcome the government bias toward low productivity of collaborative projects with academia, as mentioned by themselves: *"Government staff has a bias that universities do not deliver products. However, in this project, we made many deliveries with high quality. Nowadays, I think if we had paid the same amount for a company, it would not have done the amount of features we did with the technical quality we have"*. Additionally, the deployment of each new version also share a common understanding of the process from one side to the other, as mentioned by a MPOG analyst: *"We had only the strategic vision of the project. When we needed to deal with technical issues, we had some difficulty planning the four-month releases. However, in the last stages of the project I realized that this was not a problem. The team was delivering and the results were available in production. The team was qualified, the code had quality, and the project was well executed. So in practice, our difficulty in interpreting the technical details did not impact the release planning"*.

Decision 3: Organized development team into priority fronts, and for each one, hire at least one specialist from the IT market. The development team had four work areas divided by the main demands of the project: User Experience, DevOps, Integration of Systems, and Social Networking. For each segment, at least one professional in the IT market was hired to raise the quality of the product. Senior developers have been selected based on their vast experience in FLOSS systems and their knowledge on tools used in the project.

The presence of senior developers in the project contributed to conciliate the development processes of each institution and make better technical decisions, as quoted in one of the answers to the senior developer's questionnaire: *"I think my main contribution was to balance the relations between the MPOG staff and the university team"*. 63% of the IT professionals believed they have collaborated to conciliate the management and development process between the two institutions and also 63% of them helped MPOG staff express their requests more clearly. Government analysts were also more open to suggestions from these developers: *"They are upstream developers of the systems that integrate the platform. They conveyed trust, and then we trust in the developed code"*. According to questionnaire responses, IT professionals largely agreed with the project development process. For 63%, this process has close similarity to their previous experiences. In contrast, 62.5% of them did not understand the MPOG's project management process and 50% believed this process could affect their project productivity.

The senior developers were also responsible for improving the management and technical knowledge of the interns about practices from industry and open source projects. 91% of the interns believed that working with professionals was essential for learning, and, for all of them, working with IT professionals was important during the project. 75% of the IT professionals believed that "Working in pairs with a senior" and 63% that "Participate in joint review tasks" were the tasks with the involvement of them that most contributed to the evolution of the interns in the project. 75% believed that the knowledge shared by them to one intern was widespread among the others in the team. Government analysts also pointed this knowledge sharing: *"On the university side, we noticed a significant improvement in the platform with the hiring of the systems original developers. They had a guide on how to best develop each feature and were able to solve non-trivial problems quickly"*.

Organizing the development team and hiring of the IT professionals allowed each team to self-organize and gain more autonomy in the management of their tasks. There was a development coach to lead each team, and a "meta-coach" supported all of them in their internal management activities. The coaches (most advanced interns) were points of reference in the development process. 89% of the interns said that the presence of the coach was essential to the sprint's running, and for 88% of the of the IT professionals the coaches was essential for their interaction with the development team. MPOG analysts saw the coaches as facilitators their activities and communication with the development team. They said *"I interacted more with the project coordinator (professor) and team coaches"*, *"Usually, we contact a coach to clarify some requirements or to understand some feature. The coaches were more available than senior developers and, sometimes, they would take our question to a senior developer"*.

5 Discussion

Our results reveal a set of nine management practices successfully employed in above-mentioned case. We analyzed unsystematic decisions made during a 30-month collaborative project and identified three macro-decisions that harmonized the differences of the management processes of each organization. We collected evidence from the gathered data that demonstrates the benefits obtained with the adoption of a collection of practices. Table 3 summarizes macro-decisions, practices, and benefits.

Table 3. Empirical SPB management decisions and its benefits.

Decision	Practice Explanation	Benefits
Use of the system under development to develop the system itself	– The features and tools of the platform under development supported the project management and communication activities.	– Communicating with transparency and efficiency. – Easy monitoring of activities. – More interactions between developers and public servants. – Confidence in the developed code. – Organic documentation.
Bring together government staff and development team	– Government staff, academic coordinators, senior developers and team coaches biweekly meet at the university lab, academia headquarters, for sprint planning and review. – Conduct on the platform technical discussions between government staff and the development team. – Involve government board directors only in strategic planning of the project. – Build a continuous delivery pipeline with stages involving both sides.	– Reducing communication misunderstanding. – Better meeting expectations of both sides. – Improvement of the decision-making process. – Overcoming the government bias regarding low productivity of collaborative projects with academia. – Synchronizing the execution pace of activities. – Sharing a common understanding of the process from one side to the other.
Organize the development team into priority fronts, and for each one, hire at least one specialist from the IT market	– The coordinators separated the development team into priority work areas considering the main demands of the project. – IT market professionals with recognized experience on each front were hired to work in person or remotely. – Define among the interns the leadership roles: a coach for each front, and a meta-coach of the entire development team. – Each team has certain self-organization, being guided by one intern-coach and at least one senior developer.	– Conciliating the development processes of each institution, taking better technical decisions. – Improving the management and technical knowledge. – Self-organizing and gaining autonomy in the management of their tasks.

The results presented here corroborate the lessons learned in our previous work on studying the SPB project case [8]. Evidence from the data collected, responses to questionnaires, and interviews reinforce what has been reported by the academic coordination of the project, adding the point of views of government and other roles involved on the academic side. In short, the government staff took time to understand how collaboration works and to realize that the project should not assume a client-executor relationship, but rather that both organizations were at the same hierarchical level in the work plan.

The decisions, practices, and benefits presented presented in Table 3 should be evaluated and used in contexts with more substantial plurality and diversity of government stakeholders. This study has a few obvious limitations. First, we point out the lack of communication records and low traceability of the management data referring to the first phase of the project. Second, we consider a drawback the hiatus between the completion of the project and the conduction of interviews and questionnaires, since we rely on the memory of the interviewees to rescue the events. Finally, the current situation of the respondents, such as their current working mindset, may also alter their perception on the topics addressed in the questionnaire and consequently their responses.

6   Conclusion

Organizational culture is built and reinforced every life year of a large organization. These cultural values reflect on the internal management processes and the norms of communication among its members. In the context of software development projects, each institution adopts development methods that best meet its managerial procedures and organizational routines. When two large organizations decide to develop a solution collaboratively, the development methods and workflow of one may conflict with the interests of the other. In a case of government-academia collaboration, conciliating their different management processes is crucial, since the poor and unadaptable management could lead the project to fail, resulting in the waste of tax-payer resources.

In this study, we investigated the management method employed at the SPB portal project, a partnership between the Brazilian government and universities. As a result, we identified a set of FLOSS and agile best practices, empirically employed by the development leaders, which improved the workflow and relationship between the organizations involved.

Regarding our first research question *"How to introduce FLOSS and agile best practices into government-academia collaboration projects?"*, we examined the SPB project and identified three macro-decisions taken by the academic coordinators that drove them to intuitively and unsystematically adopt nine FLOSS and agile best practices in the development process.

The interviews responses allowed us to understand how FLOSS and agile practices have benefited the project management. Based on that, we answered our second research question *"What practices favor effective team management in government-academia collaborative projects?"*, making explicit 14 benefits obtained from the use of the nine best practices, presented in Table 3.

Finally, we collected a significant amount of data and testimonials related to the teaching of software engineering. We consider the studied project an educational case, an example of teaching FLOSS and agile techniques applied to real-world software development. As future work, we intend to analyze this collected information to propose improvements in educational methods for teaching software engineering to undergraduate students as well.

References

1. Alleman, G.B., Henderson, M., Seggelke, R.: Making agile development work in a government contracting environment-measuring velocity with earned value. In: Proceedings of the Agile Development Conference, ADC 2003, pp. 114–119. IEEE (2003)
2. Anthopoulos, L., Reddick, C.G., Giannakidou, I., Mavridis, N.: Why e-government projects fail? An analysis of the healthcare.gov website. Gov. Inf. Q. **33**, 161–173 (2016)
3. Beck, K., Beedle, M., Bennekum, A., et al.: Manifesto for agile software development. Agile alliance (2001). Accessed 14 June 2010
4. Booch, G., Brown, A.W.: Collaborative Development Environments. Advances in Computers, vol. 59, pp. 1–27. Elsevier (2003)
5. Capiluppi, A., Lago, P., Morisio, M.: Characteristics of open source projects. In: Proceedings of the Seventh European Conference on Software Maintenance and Reengineering, pp. 317–327. IEEE (2003)
6. Chookittikul, W., Kourik, J., Maher, P.E.: Reducing the gap between academia and industry: the case for agile methods in Thailand, pp. 239–244 (2011)
7. Goldfinch, S.: Pessimism, computer failure, and information systems development in the public sector. Public Adm. Rev. **67**, 917–929 (2007)
8. Meirelles, P., Wen, M., Terceiro, A., Siqueira, R., Kanashiro, L., Neri, H.: Brazilian public software portal: an integrated platform for collaborative development. In: Proceedings of the 13th International Symposium on Open Collaboration, OpenSym 2017, pp. 16:1–16:10. ACM (2017)
9. Melo, C., Santos, V., Katayama, E., Corbucci, H., Prikladnicki, R., Goldman, A., Kon, F.: The evolution of agile software development in Brazil. J. Braz. Comput. Soc. **19**, 523–552 (2013)
10. Nerur, S., Mahapatra, R., Mangalaraj, G.: Challenges of migrating to agile methodologies. Commun. ACM **48**(5), 72–78 (2005)
11. Raymond, E.: The cathedral and the bazaar. Philos. Technol. **12**(3), 23 (1999)
12. Sandberg, A.B., Crnkovic, I.: Meeting industry: academia research collaboration challenges with agile methodologies. In: Proceedings of the 39th International Conference on Software Engineering: Software Engineering in Practice Track, ICSE-SEIP 2017, pp. 73–82. IEEE Press (2017)
13. Siqueira, R., Camarinha, D., Wen, M., Meirelles, P., Kon, F.: Continuous delivery: building trust in a large-scale, complex government organization. IEEE Softw. **35**(2), 38–43 (2018)
14. Strode, D.E., Huff, S.L., Tretiakov, A.: The impact of organizational culture on agile method use. In: 42nd Hawaii International Conference on System Sciences, HICSS 2009, pp. 1–9. IEEE (2009)
15. Warsta, J., Abrahamsson, P.: Is open source software development essentially an agile method. In: Proceedings of the 3rd Workshop on Open Source Software Engineering, pp. 143–147 (2003)

Insights into the Trilateral Relationship of Crowdfunding Campaigns, Open Source and Communities

Patricija Ilin[1], Dimitrios Platis[2(✉)], and Imed Hammouda[3,4]

[1] Univerity of Gothenburg, Gothenburg, Sweden
ilinpatricia@outlook.com
[2] Aptiv PLC, Gothenburg, Sweden
dimitrios.platis@aptiv.com
[3] Mediterranean Institute of Technology, South Mediterranean University,
Tunis, Tunisia
imed.hammouda@medtech.tn
[4] Chalmers and University of Gothenburg, Gothenburg, Sweden

Abstract. Crowdfunding campaigns enable individuals to bring their ideas to production by appealing directly to the end-market and the global community. A number of these projects are open source, seemingly, counteracting the funding process. We interviewed founders, developers and managers of 13 crowdfunding initiatives involving open source products to determine how communities, crowdfunding campaigns and open source are associated. Our findings verified the existence of common characteristics among the cases, the emergence of a family-like relationship between the organizers and the community, as well as the community perceived as a success factor. We suggest that the development of certain niche products inherently leads to the adoption of open source as a licensing model and crowdfunding as the capital gathering process.

1 Introduction

During the recent years, we have seen the rise of start-up companies as well as their contribution to the economy by creating job positions, enabling the youths to innovate and taking their ideas to the market. One way these ideas get investment to reach the market and influence market trends is via crowdfunding platforms with crowd raised contributions, such as Kickstarter, Indiegogo and Crowd Supply. According to Massolution's crowdfunding report, summed up in [2], the total global crowdfunding revenue was over \$16.2 billion worldwide in 2014. The report further shows that the leading regions were N. America, Asia and Europe, and the crowdfunding models that had grown the most in percentage were the donation and the equity-based models.

Lately, we have witnessed the merge of these two trends, open source and crowdfunding, often ending up in successful projects. What ties the open source

I. Stamelos et al. (Eds.): OSS 2018, IFIP AICT 525, pp. 26–36, 2018.
https://doi.org/10.1007/978-3-319-92375-8_3

and crowdfunding together is the idea of social influence from a devoted crowd movement that supports the organizers and steers the outcome of a project. Social networking is, in this case, a fundamental component for both of the cases. Because of the networking attribute, the crowdfunding backers who support a project, typically help invest in it and market it through word of mouth among their friends and families on websites such as Facebook and Twitter. Likewise in open source, communities can be formed that lead to companionship and inspire the individuals to not only contribute to a project but also engage into activities to popularize it, as in the case of Linux User Groups [1].

Previous research in this area is mainly focused on what motivations people have for investing in a crowdfunding project (e.g. [3,4]) or what motivations they have for participating in an open source community (e.g. [5–7]). Other research also sheds a light on what impact social media has on crowdfunding projects (e.g. [8]) or what role communities in general play in crowdfunding projects (e.g. [9,10]).

Despite many open source products being crowdfunded during the latest years, there has not been enough research to shed light on the characteristics of those campaigns and how they are associated with the corresponding communities. This study will aim to fill this gap, by attempting to determine the characteristics the specific crowdfunding campaigns, the communication process between the campaign organizers and the communities as well as the possible impact of the communities when crowdfunding an open source project.

2   Background

2.1   Crowdfunding

Obtaining resources for a start-up or a product is often considered challenging. Typically, it can require a loan, finding investors, applying for a grant etc. When these tactics are not fruitful or sufficient, online crowdfunding can come in handy. Crowdfunding is an alternative way to raise money with the help of a large number of individuals from all over the world, who see potential in a product, project, social cause or service. The project can be anything from a physical product such as a smartphone case to a trip, book publishing, the start-up of a business, a concert or an expense (e.g. medical). The crowdfunding methods are typically based on donations, peer-to-peer or peer-to-business loans, rewards or equity, meaning that people who fund products can become co-owners.

In our research, we investigate initiatives launched on reward-based platforms, focused on physical products. They have adopted an *all-or-nothing model*, i.e. contributions will be returned unless the project reaches its funding goal.

2.2   Communities

Throughout the years, communities have been examined from different perspectives by researchers. Shared values and interests are what pervades the communities and results in mutual relationships and unselfish acts of kindness to one another. Findings by Li et al. (2006) [12] as well as Wu et al. (2010) [13] show that the more values the members of a community share such as goals, appropriate behavior and policies, the stronger the competence, commitment and altruism is among the members. Additionally, the members' bond results in a higher level of satisfaction and enhances *belongingness*.

This view is further elaborated in [14] where it is claimed that apart from homogeneous behaviors, interpersonal relationships and bonds need be the foundation of the community for it to thrive. This leads to a knowledge community or network of practice, traditionally called a *community of practice*. These communities describe big groups or networks of people online, that may or may not know each other or meet face to face. They share common goals and purposes and use communication to fulfill these goals [15, 16].

2.3 Doing Business with Open Source

One of the most crucial decisions when doing business with open source software is the license under which the derived works can be distributed. That being said, not all open source products have the same profit potential. Krishnamurthy (2003) divides OSS products into categories based on their importance and customer applicability [17]. In this study, we investigated cases with products of lower customer applicability which, depending on their importance, can be regarded as high or low profile nichers.

Based on the nature of typical open source crowdfunding campaigns, we determined three business models as most applicable, taken from [18,19]. The *Support seller* model, which involves releasing the source while charging for services such as packaging, branding, distribution, customizing and supporting it. *Brand licensing* aims to sell the trademark. Finally, in *Loss leader* model, an open source product is used for marketing purposes to attract attention towards another, more profitable, product.

2.4 Previous Studies

Gerber et al. (2012) have been looking at the motivations for posting and funding crowdfunding projects online. Their study shows that the participation-motivations among crowdfunding project creators depend on the idea of strengthening commitment to community members and their feedback [3]. Similarly, Brabham (2010:1139–1140) reveals that members are driven by opportunities in the form of money, skills and creating a portfolio. Additionally, he characterizes members "vibrant and obsessed" and deems these traits essential for a thriving crowdsourcing community.

Moreover, Hars and Ou (2001) have divided the motivation of members in an open source community in *intrinsic* e.g. altruism and identification with a community and *extrinsic*, direct compensation and personal needs [7]. On the other hand, Lakhani and Wolf (2003), propose creativity as the main motive [6].

Regarding the impact of social media on crowdfunding projects, Lu et al. (2014) mapped principles that have a positive effect on crowdfunding. They have observed that early promotional activities are strongly connected to the outcome and stress the benefit of using multiple platforms for promotion [8]. As to the impact of communities, Bard et al. (2014) highlight the importance of recognizing them as more than just financers. They are a devoted group sharing ideas and information [10]. Finally, Matheus (2016) suggests the success rate of a crowdfunding platform depends on creators backing other projects, lessons learned and connection with the backers [9].

3   Research Questions and Methodology

In the current work we investigate the *socio-technical* attributes present in crowdfunding campaigns of open source products, from the perspective of the campaign organizers. Utilizing the research questions as the protocol to help us explore the topic, we begin by identifying the advantages and disadvantages hereditary in such campaigns as well as the business aspects are relevant. Next, we track the communication tools and how they are used as well as investigate the relationship between the organizers and the community. Finally, we attempt to determine the impact of the communities by combining the results of the previous questions with empirical data.

– RQ1: What are the characteristics of a crowdfunding campaign of open source products?
– RQ2: How can the relationship and communication between the campaign organizers and the community be described?
– RQ3: What is the impact of the community on an open source crowdfunding campaign according to the organizers perspective?

Due to the scarcity of previous literature on the specific topic, we opted for a qualitative research method which enables handling of ambiguous data and paves the way for the subjects' viewpoints. Moreover, it leads to a more in-depth description of characteristics, settings and practices which would otherwise not emerge with quantitative methods. Stemming from the open-ended goal of our research, we conducted semi-structured interviews to collect the necessary empirical data. This technique allows the suggestion of further follow-up questions, formulating a dialogue through the question-answer approach.

The initial goal was to conduct face to face interviews with campaign organizers from Sweden. However, when this was proven neither possible nor sufficient we shifted our attention to the global scene. The interviewees were sought after in major online crowdfunding platforms, i.e. Kickstarter, Indiegogo and Crowd Supply. The primary criteria for selecting campaigns included open source elements to have been developed for the respective products as well as contact information to be available. Altogether, we approached 53 campaign organizers via their email and social media accounts. 20 of them responded. Eventually, 12 interviews were conducted via Skype and 1 via email. The majority (8) of the projects published both software and hardware, 2 of them only software and 1 just the hardware. The rest planned an open source release in the near future.

Based on the research questions, we compiled an interview guide consisting of 20 interviews, which were slightly modified on the course of time to suit each case better. This was deemed necessary as some questions were not always applicable. For example, some worked alone or had a well-established business prior to the campaign while others worked in teams or did not create a company at all. To ensure participants did not feel distant or estranged, they were introduced to the topic via emails prior to the interview and whenever the connection quality permitted, video calls were made.

4   Results and Analysis

During the interviews, we collected a plethora of data, documenting the experiences, perspectives and actions of 13 campaign organizers. This section shall present some interesting excerpts, present and discuss the collected information as well as correlate them, where applicable, with existing literature.

4.1   Characteristics

"I want to be someone who contributes back because I'm rather taking huge advantage of other people's work." - Study participant

The motivation behind organizing a campaign of an open source product can be split into four categories. The first concerns creating inspiration and facilitating innovation through the released source, in exchange for feedback and help. This was also seen in the elements of open communication and shared improvements that constitute the pillars of the hacker culture and techno-meritocracy [11]. Moreover, organizers perceived the crowdfunding campaigns as the means to popularize their product, by broadening the awareness around it and its domain. The third perspective that was encountered during this research was that hobbyists (e.g. Makers) often desire or expect products to be open source. Finally, some viewed open source as a gesture of gratitude for the help they had received. This sense of altruism and identification is also encountered in [7].

Next, using a bottom-up approach, such as crowdfunding, makes the campaign perceived as less profit-oriented. Due to the open source nature of the products, the organizers feel like they get more publicity among hobbyists and enthusiasts. Releasing the code makes it easier to reach the crowd and inspires generosity, goodwill and altruistic feelings which translate into financial support for the campaign. Interestingly, keeping supporters in suspense was an explanation for not releasing the source before the campaign. Therefore open source is not just the catalyst that increases engagement and loyalty but also a marketing tool, which is in alignment with the findings of Krishnamurthy [17].

Furthermore, crowdfunding campaigns often appeared to be the sole viable option for commercializing a niche open source product. One of the reasons is that customers who can provide most revenue, such as businesses and public institutions, will not normally take the risk to purchase an unfinished product.

Secondly, many investors either do not take open source seriously, seeing the product as "less professional" or worse, view open source as a threat. From their perspective, a competitor can utilize the existing source to beat the original developers to the market. Lastly, if a community has already been formulated around a project, crowdfunding is a relatively secure way to gather resources, as it is likely for the community to support it financially. This can be linked to the research of Gerber et al. (2012), who argue about the extrinsic motivation of campaign organizers in the pursue to secure funding [3].

> "You're using Kickstarter, not only to get the money but also to raise awareness and to start building a community. With open source, the only way it can survive is people using and contributing to it every day, so, it's really gotta be a thriving community." - Study participant

Open source, being a factor that facilitates the formulation of communities, appears to integrate well with crowdfunding campaigns. During the interviews, an organizer mentioned the importance of early community members who, with their ideas and discussions, helped to boost the crowdfunding campaign, especially in the beginning. This importance is in pair with the observations by Lu, Xie, Kong and Lu (2014) on the relation between the outcome of a campaign and early promotional activities [8]. Moreover, the positive effects of the open source nature are also prevalent after the campaign when the supporters get their hands on the product and start to engage or contribute to it in diverse ways. These factors deem open source highly compatible with crowdfunding.

> "We encourage copying. We spread the word and we give all the things you need to create your own project. [..] The only thing we try to work against is the use of our brand name." - Study participant

Having a product open exposes it to the risk of getting cloned and beaten to the market. This can increase competition and damage the profitability. To tackle this, some of the interviewees did not release the source until the end of the campaign. What is more, a proposal for mitigating this risk involved keeping parts of the product closed, such as the hardware. On the other hand, others were not as negative when it comes to cloning. They either embraced it as inevitable and a sign of success or viewed it as a non-threat since the existence of a dedicated community around the product would allow it to be financially viable. Protection against clones can explain the organizer efforts to present themselves as equals among the community and not as a party that simply intends to financially exploit them.

Additionally, it is usually expected for a crowdfunding campaign of an open source product not to offer just software. Particularly, software is expected to come at no cost. More importantly, it became evident that the target audience prefers to pay for hardware or services around the software, rather than just the software itself. This can be interpreted by the fact that the source of the software, once acquired, can be easily transformed into a functional artifact. This is not the case with hardware which needs to be fabricated, the necessary components to be acquired at a retail price and assembled. Equivalently, additional software services (e.g. cloud storage or servers) are also hard or costly to set up by individual users, therefore they would be more inclined to purchase them. We documented tendency to support products, someone would have to pay for regardless of whether they were open source or not.

Most organizers initially had no other goal than to test the product's marketability. A formal business perspective surfaced along the way. Their crowdfunding goal became to eventually establish a line of products, reach out to a big market and grow a business. Surprisingly or not, the participants showed no awareness of open source business models. That being said, the model they mainly identified themselves with was that of the support seller [19]. The interviewees aligned themselves with the specific model on the grounds of the support that they and their communities offer to each other. In this instance, support is given for free. However, we can perceive the hardware, that typically accompanies the software, as packaging that is shipped to the campaign backers. Therefore, the combination of packaging, distribution and branding feasibly places these cases under the support seller business model.

4.2   Relationship

"A community is much like a garden. Fertile soil, plenty of water, plenty of attention and you know, sometimes, as well, it's a bit of luck. It's good weather. But you get out of a community as much as you put in. And only by being incredibly active and giving a community the tools and the resources they need to become engaged, is the only way you can not only build a bigger community but build a more powerful community. One that can really empower themselves." - Study participant

Looking at the relationship between the communities and the organizers, we should first note that we did not discover any norm as to *when* a dedicated community, around the product, is created. Moreover, previous involvement in open source communities and projects did not play a significant role. This might come as a surprise, as one could assume prior engagement with the community would help the audience identify themselves easier with the organizers.

With Makers being the primary target group, both online and offline communication channels were utilized. The most popular online channels were Twitter, Facebook and mailing lists. Interestingly, some of the organizers maintained separate channels, based on technical skills. The most common offline means were talks on conferences and participation in Maker Faires. Despite many engaging face-to-face with their target group, some participants stressed how these types of activities are time-consuming and ultimately not effective *during* a campaign.

Furthermore, we saw that involvement with the communities came with mutual communication and a close connection. This involved shared attitudes, reciprocity, selflessness and a sense of goodwill. Many organizers became emotionally tangled with the communities, concerning them as family members rather than merely customers and sensing a bond to them regardless of geographical location. Moreover, four elements surfaced, outlining the organizers' role: listening, asking, answering and supporting the communities. Important elements that characterized the communication was selflessness and a positive, proactive attitude. The latter was worded as "being nice" while the campaign organizers mentioned they witnessed a similar stance as a response.

This show of goodwill can be traced in Brabham (2010) who explains how members are enthusiastic and committed to the same cause as the organizers, recognizing themselves as more than just customers [4]. Community members not identifying as mere customers but as organic parts of the project is an attribute also prevalent in the hacker culture ethics. They have the power to influence its direction, help it evolve and are defined by reciprocity and altruism [20].

4.3   Impact

"Maker community doesn't like closed sourced products. From a marketing perspective, they are more into open source." - Study participant

To evaluate the impact of the community on a crowdfunding campaign, we examine its effect on the following activities: (a) the promotion, (b) the received contributions and feedback and (c) the business aspects.

As discussed previously, communities can catalyze the reach of a campaign and boost the marketing efforts. A noteworthy factor regarding the promotion of the products was that the majority did not have open source as their primary marketing point. They preferred to focus more on facts, need and usage. Therefore, it is not surprising that some of the interviewees claimed open source had no major effect on their publicity. Furthermore, two of them pointed out mainstream media proved to be unfamiliar with the field or regarded it as unprofessional. On the contrary, the hobbyist community valued open source. Thus, despite open source not being the primary statement of the promotion, it did eventually become relevant since organizers had to be careful not to depict themselves as "too business oriented". A company's intentions to generate revenue can conflict with the open source communitie' norms and value, therefore great attention should be paid to keep everyone aligned.

Next, in most occasions software was released after the campaign, therefore limiting the interaction with the community to inquiries regarding the functionality and feature requests. The most significant reasons behind this were to ensure a final bug-free product and avoid being beaten to the market. In the case of products that had released the source before the beginning of the campaign, all but two received a large amount of contribution. It typically consisted of features, usability remarks, code issues and bug reports. Furthermore, a point that was often stressed out, was the importance of listening to feedback. Feedback would come in forms of suggestions, constructive criticism and in some cases negative and questionable comments about the work done on the product. Sorting through it could be time-consuming, but still proved to be vital for a

Fig. 1. Dependencies around a niche product

healthy relationship with the community members as well as for the progress of the product.

Nearly half of the campaign organizers aimed to create a line of products utilizing the crowdfunding campaign as the basis for this initiative. The existence of a vibrant and active community that offers feedback, develops and raises awareness can be viewed as fundamental for a long-lasting and successful product ecosystem. Additionally, most of the products involved in this research should be considered as high and low profile nichers targeting a crowd that values open source. This target group expects parts of the product to be open and therefore this translates into going down the open source path, business-wise.

Moreover, crowdfunding is often regarded as the only viable option to finance an open source product. Combining these two points, we come to realize that the impact of the community is not only the deciding factor behind the product being open source but also behind selecting crowdfunding as the means to commercialize it. By taking a step back we can generalize the above observation. Figure 1 visualizes the interdependent relationships between crowdfunding, communities and open source around niche products. We discover the coupling between these three concepts compels the creators to open source and crowdfund their product, once they attempt to gain the support of a relevant community.

5   Validity Threats

Threats to validity is a typical concern related to open-ended, qualitative studies with semi-structured interviews. This can be, up to a point, attributed to authors having to use creativity, critical thinking, improvisation and therefore exhibit a certain degree of subjectivity in order to maintain vivid and interesting discussions [21]. We utilized the scheme by Runeson and Höst (2009) [22] to classify the different threats so to employ mitigation tactics against them.

Internal validity is related to risks around the research process which increase the bias. We made an effort to approach a diverse crowd in terms of technology, geographical location and sex. However, the responses we received were primarily by males who were involved in campaigns of products that had both software and hardware elements. Additionally, one interview was conducted via email, instead of a call, which could have inadvertently influenced the collected data.

Furthermore, most of the cases appealed to a rather specific market segment, i.e. Makers and Hackers. This constitutes a serious external validity constraint, thus we do not deem it feasible to generalize our results beyond this class of products. Moreover, participants were selected on a rather ad-hoc basis, having to manually determine whether they *developed* open source elements as well as the availability of contact details. This leaves room for selection bias. To minimize it we tried to involve a large and diverse sample which also offers us a degree of reproducibility. Lastly, interviews were conducted in English, i.e. not the native tongue of all participants, which could threaten construct validity.

6   Conclusion

Open source and crowdfunding share a common pillar, communities, which enables their union to be compatible and often fruitful. The first question when contemplating upon open source being crowdfunded is why would someone assume the risk of investing in a product not yet in the market, considering that at some point in time its source will be released. It appears what backers are usually willing to pay for is, difficult to reproduce, hardware that incorporates open source software. Open source and the potential of a developer community around the product safeguard its evolution and user support.

Communities are perceived to play an important role in crowdfunding campaigns. Metaphorically speaking, if sales to high-profile customers allow a product to walk then communities, supporting it through its early stages, allow it to stand up. This importance becomes even more prevailing when open source is involved, as communities are one of the determining factors behind the success or demise of an open source project. Campaign organizers repeatedly emphasized the need to engage as often as possible with the community and place themselves among their customers to increase the sense of belongingness. Moreover, they avoided appearing as business-oriented outsiders who just want to sell a product.

Furthermore, launching a product with low customer applicability targeting communities accustomed to open source, paves the way for the product itself becoming open source and eventually acquiring resources via a crowdfunding campaign. This signifies the magnitude of influence communities have on such products. As future research, we suggest the verification our results through the prism of backers as well as examining the platform characteristics that facilitate crowdfunding of open source projects.

References

1. Bagozzi, R., Dholakia, U.: Open source software user communities: a study of participation in Linux user groups. Manage. Sci. **52**(7), 1099–1115 (2006)
2. Marketwired: Crowdfunding Market Grows 167% in 2014: Crowdfunding Platforms Raise $16.2 Billion, 31 March 2015. https://goo.gl/v5QyrG. Accessed 10 Mar 2017
3. Gerber, E., Hui, J., Kou, P.: Crowdfunding: Why People Are Motivated to Post and Fund Projects on Crowdfunding Platforms. Northwestern University Creative Action Lab., USA (2012)
4. Brabham, D.C.: Moving the crowd at threadless: motivations for participation in a crowdsourcing application. Inf. Commun. Soc. **13**(8), 1122–1145 (2010)
5. Budhathoki, N.R., Haythornthwaite, C.: Motivation for open collaboration: crowd and community models and the case of OpenStreetMap. Am. Behav. Sci. **57**(5), 548–575 (2013)
6. Lakhani, K.R., Wolf, R.G.: Why hackers do what they do: understanding motivation and effort in free/open source software projects. Perspect. Free Open Sour. Softw. **1**, 3–22 (2005)
7. Hars, A., Ou, S.: Working for free? Motivations of participating in open source projects. In: Proceedings of the 34th Annual Hawaii International Conference on System Sciences, pp. 25–39. IEEE (2001)
8. Lu, C.T., Xie, S., Kong, X., Yu, P.S.: Inferring the impacts of social media on crowdfunding. In: Proceedings of the 7th ACM International Conference on Web Search and Data Mining, pp. 573–582. ACM, February 2014
9. Matheus, A.A.R.: The Role of Online Crowdfunding Communities in Funding Cycle Success: Evidence from Kickstarter. Universidade do Porto (2016)
10. Bard, A., Brännström, E., Fahlberg, D.: Crowdfunding – En ständig kommunikation. En studie på en communitys relevans runt ett crowdfundat projekt. Institutionen för informatik. Umeå Universitet (2014)
11. Castells, M.: The Internet Galaxy: Reflections on the Internet, Business, and Society. Oxford University Press on Demand, Oxford (2002)
12. Li, D., Browne, G.J., Wetherbe, J.C.: Why do internet users stick with a specific web site? a relationship perspective. Int. J. Electron. Commer. **10**(4), 105–141 (2006)
13. Wu, J.J., Chen, Y.H., Chung, Y.S.: Trust factors influencing virtual community members: a study of transaction communities. J. Bus. Res. **63**(9), 1025–1032 (2010)
14. Parks, M.R.: Social network sites as virtual communities. In: Papacharissi, Z. (ed.) A Networked Self: Identity, Community, and Culture on Social Network Sites, pp. 108–109. Taylor & Francis, USA (2011)
15. Borg, E.: Discourse Community. ELT J. **57**(4), 398–400 (2003)
16. Wasko, M.M., Faraj, S.: Why should i share? Examining social capital and knowledge contribution in electronic networks of practice. MIS Q. **29**, 35–57 (2005)
17. Krishnamurthy, S.: An Analysis of Open Source Business Models. MIT Press, Cambridge (2003)
18. Raymond, E.S.: The magic cauldron (1999)
19. Raymond, E.S.: The Cathedral and the Bazaar: Musings on Linux and Open Source by An Accidental Revolutionary. O'Reilly Media Inc., Sebastopol (2001)
20. Raymond, E.S.: How to become a hacker. Database Netw. J. **33**(2), 8–9 (2003)
21. Maxwell, J.A.: Understanding and validity in qualitative research. Harv. Educ. Rev. **62**(3), 279 (1992)
22. Runeson, P., Höst, M.: Guidelines for conducting and reporting case study research in software engineering. Empir. Softw. Eng. **14**(2), 131 (2009)

OSS Projects Validity

Open Source Software Resilience Framework

Apostolos Kritikos[✉] and Ioannis Stamelos

Aristotle University of Thessaloniki, University Campus,
54124 Thessaloniki, Greece
{akritiko,stamelos}@csd.auth.gr
http://www.csd.auth.gr

Abstract. An Open Source Software (OSS) project can be utilized either as is, to serve specific needs on an application level, or on the source code level, as a part of another software system serving as a component, a library, or even an autonomous third party dependency. There are several OSS quality models that provide metrics to measure specific aspects of the project, like its structural quality. Although other dimensions, like community health and activity, software governance principles or license permissiveness, are taken into account, there is no universally accepted OSS assessment model. In this work we are proposing an evaluation approach based on the adaptation of the City Resilience Framework to OSS with the aim of providing a strong theoretical basis for evaluating OSS projects.

Keywords: Open source software · Software resilience
Software engineering · Software quality · Software metrics

1 Background

Open Source Software (OSS) has been continuously growing and evolving for over two decades now. It started as a revolutionary software engineering approach, producing software that was freely and openly available to be used, edited, copied, even commercially utilized. Since then, it has been fueling the development process of companies with source code, testing and bug fixing. Moreover it has been one of the main drivers for the birth of healthy, successful companies [1,2].

In the beginning, the focus about OSS revolved mainly around its development style. Eric Raymond in [3] compares closed source development to a Cathedral because of its structured and concrete definition of work and roles. In contrast, open source development resembles to a bazaar, a place with no strict rules, where people can openly and freely contribute. As Raymond specifically states *"No quiet, reverent cathedral-building here rather, the Linux community*

© IFIP International Federation for Information Processing 2018
Published by Springer International Publishing AG 2018. All Rights Reserved
I. Stamelos et al. (Eds.): OSS 2018, IFIP AICT 525, pp. 39–49, 2018.
https://doi.org/10.1007/978-3-319-92375-8_4

seemed to resemble a great babbling bazaar of differing agendas and approaches (aptly symbolized by the Linux archive sites, who'd take submissions from anyone) out of which a coherent and stable system could seemingly emerge only by a succession of miracles" meaning that in a time where closed (or proprietary) software development was the norm, an open approach of collectively developed software seemed odd and likely to fail.

The fact that OSS succeeded is a result of several factors. A primary and extensively studied factor is structural quality which led to the proposal of several quality models like ISO25010 [4] for evaluating software in general or Open Source specific ones like OpenBRR [5]. In [6] Midha and Palvia identify several other factors outside the scope of source code and software structure. The level of permissiveness of the license under which the OSS is published, community aspects such as number of active developers and end users, language translations are some indicative examples. In [7] the authors study Open Source Governance models, another important factor for OSS success.

In [8] Miguel presents the evolution of quality models between 1977 and 2013. The models are further categorized to Basic Models (1977–2001) with the aim of evaluating the software product as a whole and Tailored Quality Models (2001–2013) which extend to component evaluation. The latter category includes the OSS specific quality models as well. The study compares and contrasts the models based on their characteristics and concludes that generic quality evaluation models cannot easily be applied in specific cases. On the other hand tailored quality models usually cover the needs of very specific domains limiting their applicability.

In [9] Wasserman describes the evolution of Business Readiness Rating (BRR) model to OSSpal. As Wasserman very aptly states, software quality, maturity, stability, documentation, community and so forth vary in different OSS projects and continuously change as those projects evolve. Therefore it is important for OSS evaluation models to include, apart from numerical scores and metrics, qualitative criteria as well.

In [10] the authors are combining quality assurance methodologies with social network analysis techniques to study competition and collaboration in large OSS ecosystems. Community wise, in [11] the authors are proposing a reference model for evaluating the maturity of an OSS project's community. They focus on the socio-technical practices of OSS software development and try to combine characteristics of existing software quality models to this end.

The aforementioned diverse set of factors which are responsible for the success of an OSS dictates the need to approach it as an evolving system in order to be able to study it in a holistic way. Moreover, in order for an OSS to be able to succeed and achieve longevity, it is crucial to be resilient to survive potential stresses and crises that might occur. Such stresses or crises could be related with forks of the project that might drive the attention of the original project's community away, migration of lead developers or even part of the development community to other forks or projects, an unsuccessful major release that might hurt the reputation of the project, changes to the license, migration to another forge and so forth. In [12] Gamalielsson and Lundell study the case of Libre Office, an OSS project that started as a fork of Open Office, but managed to retain the development community and evolve, as of the time of writing, to a successful OSS project.

In this publication we are trying to adapt the concept of City Resilience, a term found in the scientific field of Urban Planning and Architecture, to OSS evolution. The term resilience is defined in [13] as the ability [of a system] to cope with change. In [14] the author defines a resilient system as one that can take a hit to a critical component and recover and come back for more in a known, bounded and generally acceptable period of times. In [15] the authors of the City Resilience Framework, which inspired this paper, define city resilience as follows: *"city resilience describes the capacity of cities to function, so that the people living and working in cities particularly the poor and vulnerable survive and thrive no matter what stresses or shocks they encounter"*.

From the aforementioned literature it becomes clear that an OSS project can be approached from several perspectives. The structure of its source code, the community that was built around it (developers, end users, testers), business related aspects (license, business models). In order to be able to holistically evaluate an OSS project we need to study it as a continuously evolving system. In this work we are proposing a framework with the aim of studying the resilience of an OSS project trying to combine several of the aforementioned perspectives.

The rest of the paper is organized as follows. In Sect. 2 we analyze the City Resilience Framework, a framework designed to measure Urban Resilience, which inspired our work. In Sect. 3 we present the adaptation of the City Resilience Framework to OSS. In Sect. 4 we demonstrate the application of the Open Source Resilience Framework to two (2) Open Source projects. In Sect. 5 we discuss possible threats to validity and, finally, in Sect. 6 we summarize our conclusions and we discuss ideas for future work.

2   City Resilience Framework

The City Resilience Framework (CRF), as presented in [15], is the result of research undertaken with the aim of establishing an accessible, evidence-based definition of Urban Resilience by Arup and the Rockefeller Foundation. The CRF is, as of the time of writing, used by the 100 Resilient Cities [16] a non profit organization to primarily evaluate the Urban Resilience of more than 90 cities around the world and, additionally, to assist the cities on crises with tailored made resilience strategies.

Trying to tackle the fact that every city is unique the City Resilient Index (CRI) was proposed. It is a set of indicators, variables and metrics that allow cities to understand, baseline and subsequently measure local resilience over time. As the authors of [17] state *"The CRI will measure relative performance over time rather than comparison between cities. It will not deliver an overall single score for comparing performance between cities, neither will it provide a world ranking of the most resilient cities."*

2.1   City Resilience Index

City Resilience Index (CRI) suggests that resilience of a city is related to four (4) key dimensions that are further decomposed to twelve (12) goals that can help a city achieve resilience. These dimensions and goals are the following:

1. **Health & well-being:** Related to **people**, working and living in the city. <u>Goals:</u> (1) Minimal human vulnerability, (2) Diverse livelihoods & employment (3) Effective safeguards to human health & life.
2. **Economy & society:** Related to the **organization** of cities on a social and economical level. <u>Goals:</u> (1) Sustainable economy, (2) Comprehensive security & rule of law, (3) Collective identity & community support.
3. **Infrastructure & environment:** Related to **place**, the quality of infrastructure and ecosystems. <u>Goals:</u> (1) Reliable mobility & communications, (2) Effective provision of critical services, Reduced exposure & fragility.
4. **Leadership & strategy:** Related to **knowledge** of the past and adapting appropriately for the future. <u>Goals:</u> (1) Effective leadership & management, (2) Empowered stakeholders, (3) Integrated development planning.

Finally, the aforementioned goals are, on a third level, analyzed in indicators in order to identify the critical factors that contribute towards the resilience of urban systems.

3   Adaptation of City Resilience Index to Open Source Software

We argue that Open Source Software projects share a conceptual similarity with cities. They are dynamic and continuously evolving systems with their own structural properties, they attract people that form communities around them which, on a second level, may utilize a governance model. Some OSS projects have commercial activity. As it is happening with cities, OSS projects can face stresses and crises (i.e. developers abandoning the project to work on a fork or users massively migrate to a competitive project).

In this section we are presenting our attempt to adapt the City Resilience Index to Open Source Software projects. We aim in utilizing the models and metrics of the extensive literature on OSS quality, metrics and evaluation and provide a framework that will measure the relative performance of an OSS project over time rather than a comparison between projects.

3.1   Open Source Software Resilience Framework (OSSRF)

Following the City Resilience Framework paradigm, Open Source Software Resiliency Framework (OSSRF) is also being primarily structured to four (4) dimensions that are then analyzed in twelve (12) goals and, on a third level, on a set of indicators for each goal.

3.1.1   Dimensions

As in the CRF we propose four key dimensions related to Open Source Software as follows:

1. **Source Code:** The first dimension of CRF is Health & Well-being and it is related with people. In Open Source Software we consider source code (i.e. classes) to be the structural unit of the project. In this dimension we will take under consideration aspects like the activity and growth rate of an OSS project along with some other related aspects.
2. **Business & Legal:** The second dimension of CRF is Economy & Society and is related with organization. In Open Source Software the norm is voluntary work but, more mature projects are utilizing Open Source Business Models to offer commercial services (be it pro features or support). For those types of projects licensing plays a key role when it comes to commercialization.
3. **Integration & Reuse:** The third dimension of CRF is related to place. Open Source Software projects usually reuse components of other OSS projects or are being reused themselves. In this spirit, in the third dimension of the Open Source Software Resilience Framework we will be dealing with the aspects of integration and reuse.
4. **Social (Community):** Finally the last dimension of CRF is about Leadership & Strategy and is related with utilizing knowledge from the past to become better and more resilient in the future. In Open Source Software both leadership and strategy related processes are usually connected with the community. Moreover most of the knowledge related to an Open Source Software usually comes from its community activity (i.e. feature proposal, bug reports, translations, documentation, testing and so forth).

3.1.2   Goals

The aforementioned dimensions are further decomposed to the following twelve (12) goals:

Source Code

1. Continuous Growth
2. Holistic Documentation
3. Systematic Testing & Violation Minimization

Business & Legal

1. Economic Sustainability
2. Flexible Licensing
3. External Organization Support

Integration & Reuse

1. Low Dependability
2. Low Complexity
3. Ease of Integration

Social (Community)

1. Well defined Project Standards
2. Well Defined Governance
3. Developer Base Activity

3.1.3   Indicators

Finally, the twelve (12) goals are further analyzed to indicators in order to provide a more specific description of the goals. For the purposes of this paper we will analyze the indicators related to the goals of the Business & Legal dimension. Due to space limitations, we provide the full analysis of the indicators to the following url: http://users.auth.gr/akritiko/ossrf_indicators.html for the intended audience.

1. **Economic Sustainability**
   1.1. Donations: 0 (no) or 1 (yes) based on whether the OSS project accepts donations. 0 is considered a non resilient value.
   1.2. Commercial features: 0 (no) or 1 (yes) based on whether the OSS project offers commercial features or a pro (paid) version. The indicator was based to the work of [18]. 0 is considered a non resilient value.
   1.3. Paid support: 0 (no) or 1 (yes) based on whether the OSS project offers a paid plan for support [18]. 0 is considered a non resilient value.
2. **Flexible Licensing**
   2.1. Level or permissiveness: 0 (all restrictive - i.e. commercial), 1 (persistent i.e. GPL), 2 (all permissive - i.e. BSD). We base the indicator to the of [19]. The indicator is considered non resilient when it is less than 1.
   2.2. Level of persistence: 0 (no) or 1 (yes) based on whether there are parts of the project's code or dependencies published under persistent licenses (i.e. GPL). We base the indicator to the of [19]. 1 is considered a non resilient value.
3. **External Organization Support:** 0 (no) or 1 (yes) based on whether the OSS project is supported by an external organization (non profit, governmental or corporate). 0 is considered a non resilient value.

3.1.4   Resilience Determination Mechanism

Since the evaluation of a project regarding its resilience is based on indicators we need a mechanism to determine whether the OSS project under review is resilient and, on a second level, how its resiliency changes as it evolves. Starting to the indicators level we will consider an OSS project successful towards a resilience goal when it is considered resilient at least to 50% of the goals ingredients.

Moving to the dimensions level, an OSS project will be considered successful towards a resilience dimension when it is considered resilient at least to 50% of the goals of the specific dimension. Likewise, on a project level, the OSS project is considered resilient when at least two (2) out of four (4) dimension (50%) are considered resilient.

4   Open Source Software Resilience Framework Application

In this section we will be demonstrating the application of the OSSRF to two OSS projects, the OKapi and WooCommerce, using the indicators analyzed in the previous sections. Due to space limitations, for our demonstration purposes will be using only the fully analyzed dimension "Business & Legal".

Since the OSSRF takes under consideration the evolution of OSS projects we would normally have to apply the framework to all the major releases of the two projects. Due to limitation spaces we chose to use the last major release of each year from the beginning of each project until either the year the project became inactive (i.e. for the case of OKapi) or the last full year (i.e. 2017) for the case of WooCommerce. We do not consider alpha, beta releases or release candidates so if some early years of the project have been excluded is because there were no major release back then.

4.1   OKapi - A Non Resilient Project

The first project, OKapi is a small framework for building web applications. It's built on PHP and is hosted in Github [20]. It started during 2008 and hasn't been updated since July 2011. We selected this case in order to test our framework to a project that intuitively seems non resilient.

The versions of the releases of OKapi to which we will be applying the OSSRF, with their corresponding dating (year/month) are shown to the following table: By applying the Business & Legal dimension's indicators to OKapi we are getting the results as shown in Table 1. In order to make the demonstration of the Resilience Determination Mechanism we proposed at Sect. 3.1.4 easier, we have marked the values of the indicators to Table 2 with (F), if an indicator is considered non resilient, and (S) if it is considered resilient.

Table 1. OKapi releases

Version	1.1.5	1.2.1	1.2.3
Date	2008/12	2009/12	2010/12

OKapi is officially not maintained but even when it was there is no indication that supported donations, commercial features or support. There is no official website or reference in any related document, to our best knowledge, about revenue streams for the project. Therefore we consider the project non resilient regarding the indicators of the first goal. As far as the licensing part is concerned, there is no license defined to the project and OKapi does not seem to reuse other open source projects. Therefore the project is considered non resilient as far as the "Level of permissiveness" is concerned but it is considered resilient towards the "Level of persistence". Therefore regarding the goal "Flexible Licensing"

Table 2. OKapi - Business & Legal dimension. Goals & indicators

Indicator	v1.1.5	v1.2.1	v1.2.3
Economic Sustainability			
Donations	0 (F)	0 (F)	0 (F)
Commercial features	0 (F)	0 (F)	0 (F)
Paid support	0 (F)	0 (F)	0 (F)
Flexible Licensing			
Level or permissiveness	0 (F)	0 (F)	0 (F)
Level of persistence	0 (S)	0 (S)	0 (S)
External Organization Support			
External Organization Support	0 (F)	0 (F)	0 (F)

OKapi is considered resilient. Finally, there is no indication that OKapi was ever supported by an external organization therefore we consider the project non resilient towards this goal. The aforementioned results apply to all the versions of the project.

Based on the results two out of three goals are considered non resilient for the OKapi project. Therefore based on OSSRF, the project is considered <u>non resilient</u>.

4.2 WooCommerce - A Resilient Project

The second project is WooCommerce, an open source eCommerce plug-in for WordPress content management system, written also in PHP and hosted in Github [21]. It started as an OSS project in 2011 and, as of the time of writing, is still active. We selected this case in order to test our framework to a project that intuitively seems resilient.

The versions of the releases of WooCommerce to which we will be applying the OSSRF, with their corresponding dating (year/month) are shown to Table 3. By applying the Business & Legal dimension's indicators to WooCommerce we are getting the results as shown in the Table 4.

Table 3. WooCommerce releases

Version	1.3.2	1.6.6	2.0.20	2.0.10	2.0.12	2.6.11	3.2.6
Date	2011/12	2012/12	2013/12	2014/12	2015/12	2016/12	2017/12

WooCommerce is a free and OSS WordPress plug-in but there are commercial plug-ins created for WooCommerce. There is also paid support offered. To our best knowledge it does not support donations. Additionally, WooCommerce is published under GPL license and some of its dependencies are published under

Table 4. WooCommerce - Business & Legal dimension. Goals & indicators

Indicator	v1.3.2	v1.6.6	v2.0.20	v2.0.10	v2.0.12	v2.6.11	v3.2.6
Economic Sustainability							
Donations	0 (F)	0 (F)	0 (F)	0 (F)	0 (F)	0 (F)	0 (F)
Commercial features	1 (S)	1 (S)	1 (S)	1 (S)	1 (S)	1 (S)	1 (S)
Paid support	1 (S)	1 (S)	1 (S)	1 (S)	1 (S)	1 (S)	1 (S)
Flexible Licensing							
Level or permissiveness	1 (S)	1 (S)	1 (S)	1 (S)	1 (S)	1 (S)	1 (S)
Level of persistence	1 (F)	1 (F)	1 (F)	1 (F)	1 (F)	1 (F)	1 (F)
External Organization Support							
External Organization Support	1 (S)	1 (S)	1 (S)	1 (S)	1 (S)	1 (S)	1 (S)

persistent license (i.e. wc-e2e-page-objects). Finally WooCommerce is backed from both the WordPress Foundation and the Automattic Company, both well-known organizations. Towards "Economic Sustainability" goal the project is considered resilient since 2 out of 3 indicators are considered resilient. Regarding "Flexible Licensing" it is also considered resilient since 1 of 2 indicators is considered resilient. Finally, "External Organization Support" is also considered resilient. The aforementioned findings apply to all versions.

Therefore based on OSSRF, the project is considered <u>resilient</u>.

5 Threats to Validity

We should note that OSSRF should be applied to project of a relative maturity in terms of community and age (we would intuitively suggest at least 10 contributors and a maturity of more than a year). Applying it in solo maintained OSS projects, or projects that not yet have reached the proposed maturity may lead to misleading results.

OSSRF is an adaptation of the City Resilience framework to Open Source Software. Although the structure of the original framework was retained, despite the conceptual similarities that we have already mentioned earlier, the mapping of dimensions, goals and indicators is a product of the subjective lens of the authors.

In the application of the OSSRF to the two projects we have applied the indicators of one of the four available dimensions of the OSSRF, "Business & Legal" dimension.

Regarding the goals and indicators, some of them are based on metrics available for object oriented source code. Additionally, as far as control version systems are concerned, for the needs of this publication we selected projects that are hosted in Github.

As far as the scales and their aggregation is concerned, in this preliminary approach we considered each criterion equally important and the threshold for defining a project as resilient or non resilient is 50%.

Finally, both of the projects analyzed in this paper, were developed in PHP and their domains are close (OKapi was a framework for web applications and WooCommerce is a plugin for a WordPress which is also considered by some a kind of web framework).

6   Conclusions and Future Work

This is a preliminary work proposing an evaluation approach with the aim of providing a strong theoretical basis for evaluating OSS projects adapting the concept of Urban Resilience to OSS. By doing so, we are trying to benefit form the advantage of resiliency to follow the evolution of a dynamic system (such as a city or an OSS) while at the same time we are providing a framework that can take under consideration concepts such as crises and or stresses that can theoretically impact the survival of an OSS. We applied a single dimension of the OSSRF to an intuitively non resilient OSS project and an intuitively resilient one and the results seem to concur with the initial intuitions.

For future work we intend to thoroughly fine-tune the rest of the indicators by testing it to a variety of OSS projects. This will also allow us to investigate how the OSSRF responds to projects of different age, community size or source code size and complexity. We also intend to investigate whether the software domain of an OSS project affects the results of the application of the OSSRF.

Regarding the framework itself we will experiment with other approached regarding the "Resilience determination mechanism" (i.e. weighted goals).

In addition we will be extending the OSSRF to be able to work with a variety of control version systems (not only git-like but also Mercurial, SVN, CVS). In a similar spirit will would like to experiment with projects of different programming languages (i.e. Java).

Another challenging idea for future work would be to apply OSSRF to OSS projects that are known to have faced specific stresses or crises in order to identify how those crises relate with the resiliency levels of an OSS project.

Finally we intend to attempt and request feedback, in the form of a survey, from key players of the Open Source Software international community (lead developers, stakeholders, academics and so forth) about OSSRF.

References

1. Weber, S.: The Success of Open Source. Harvard University Press, Cambridge (2004)
2. Thakker, D., Schireson, M.: The Money In Open-Source Software (2016). https://techcrunch.com/2016/02/09/the-money-in-open-source-software/
3. Raymond, E.: The Cathedral and the bazaar. Philos. Technol. **12**(3), 23 (1999)

4. Organización Internacional de Normalización: ISO-IEC 25010: 2011 Systems and Software Engineering-Systems and Software Quality Requirements and Evaluation (SQuaRE)-System and Software Quality Models. ISO (2011)
5. Wasserman, A., Pal, M., Chan, C.: The business readiness rating model: an evaluation framework for open source. In: Proceedings of the EFOSS Workshop, Como, Italy (2006)
6. Midha, V., Palvia, P.: Factors affecting the success of open source software. J. Syst. Softw. **85**(4), 895–905 (2012)
7. Vision Mobile: Open governance index-measuring the true openness of open source projects from android to WebKit (2011)
8. Miguel, J.P., Mauricio, D., Rodríguez, G.: A review of software quality models for the evaluation of software products. arXiv preprint arXiv:1412.2977 (2014)
9. Wasserman, A.I., Guo, X., McMillian, B., Qian, K., Wei, M.-Y., Xu, Q.: OSSpal: finding and evaluating open source software. In: Balaguer, F., Di Cosmo, R., Garrido, A., Kon, F., Robles, G., Zacchiroli, S. (eds.) OSS 2017. IAICT, vol. 496, pp. 193–203. Springer, Cham (2017). https://doi.org/10.1007/978-3-319-57735-7_18
10. Teixeira, J., Robles, G., González-Barahona, J.M.: Lessons learned from applying social network analysis on an industrial free/libre/open source software ecosystem. J. Internet Serv. Appl. **6**(1), 14 (2015)
11. Andrade, S., Saraiva, F.: Principled evaluation of strengths and weaknesses in FLOSS communities: a systematic mixed methods maturity model approach. In: Balaguer, F., Di Cosmo, R., Garrido, A., Kon, F., Robles, G., Zacchiroli, S. (eds.) OSS 2017. IAICT, vol. 496, pp. 34–46. Springer, Cham (2017). https://doi.org/10.1007/978-3-319-57735-7_4
12. Gamalielsson, J., Lundell, B.: Sustainability of open source software communities beyond a fork: how and why has the libreoffice project evolved? J. Syst. Softw. **89**, 128–145 (2014)
13. Wieland, A., Wallenburg, C.M.: The influence of relational competencies on supply chain resilience: a relational view. Int. J. Phys. Distrib. Logist. Manag. **43**(4), 300–320 (2013)
14. Axelrod, C.W.: Investing in software resiliency (2009)
15. Da Silva, J., Morera, B.: City resilience framework. Arup & Rockefeller Foundation (2014). http://publications.arup.com/Publications/C/City_Resilience_Framework.aspx. Accessed 15 Dec 2015
16. Resilient Cities (2013). http://www.100resilientcities.org/
17. City Resilience Index: City resilience framework. The Rockefeller Foundation and ARUP (2014)
18. Munga, N., Fogwill, T., Williams, Q.: The adoption of open source software in business models: a red hat and IBM case study. In: Proceedings of the 2009 Annual Research Conference of the South African Institute of Computer Scientists and Information Technologists, pp. 112–121. ACM (2009)
19. Välimäki, M., Oksanen, V.: Evaluation of open source licensing models for a company developing mass market software. Law and Technology (2002)
20. OKapi Github Repository. https://github.com/liip/Okapi
21. WooCommerce Github Repository. https://github.com/liip/Okapi

Leaving Behind the Software History When Transitioning to Open Source: Reasons and Implications

Gustavo Pinto[1], Igor Steinmacher[2,3](✉), and Marco Gerosa[3]

[1] Federal University of Pará, Belém, PA, Brazil
gpinto@ufpa.br
[2] Federal University of Technology, Campo Mourão, Paraná, Brazil
igorfs@utfpr.edu.br
[3] Northern Arizona University, Flagstaff, USA
Marco.Gerosa@nau.edu

Abstract. Maintenance of software history is regarded to be one of the most relevant features of Version Control Systems (VCS) and is well-known to be indispensable for software developers. However, transitioning from proprietary to open source software poses a challenge: keeping the software history might make available years of historical records and internal matters from the company that built the software. On the other hand, removing the software history may disturb the development and may be harmful to new contributors. We conducted a survey with open source software projects that made this shift to investigate (1) the reasons why they removed the software history and (2) the challenges that developers face with the lack of availability of software history. Among the results, we found that the most common reason for removing the software history is because it is entangled with proprietary code (the fact that the history contains sensitive information appears next). Interestingly, most core developers believed that the lack of software history is, in the worst case, "*a very minor inconvenience.*"

1 Introduction

Maintaining software history, or commit history, is one of the main benefits of Version Controls Systems (VCSs). Developers refer to the software history not only when they need to navigate through changes related to their tasks, but also to learn from previous mistakes or to decide what to do next [23]. Indeed, a recent survey evidenced that software history is indispensable for developers: 61% of the respondents said to examine history up to a few times a day [4]. Practitioners also report acquiring knowledge when examining software history [14]. In particular, the recent introduction of social coding hosting websites made software history of open source software projects more accessible and understandable. As a consequence, even end users are taking advantage of the software

I. Stamelos et al. (Eds.): OSS 2018, IFIP AICT 525, pp. 50–60, 2018.
https://doi.org/10.1007/978-3-319-92375-8_5

history [11]. Researchers also leverage software history to conduct several studies, for instance, regarding the impact of co-changes on software maintenance activities [5], to estimate defects [20], or to fix bugs [3].

However, when open-sourcing their projects, several companies chose not to open the commit history. If decision makers decide to keep the software history with information from the entire development process, they might share sensitive data that is only supposed to be accessed by internal members of the software company (*e.g.,* database passwords). However, if decision makers decide not to keep the software history, they might introduce an additional burden for the software development team (*e.g.,* when dealing with maintenance tasks) or even for new contributors interested in joining the new open source project.

This kind of trade-off is relevant since many software companies, even those that were well-restrictive when it comes to publishing their software artifacts, are now releasing their former proprietary projects under open source licenses. As a notable example, in 2015, Apple released Swift, a programming language designed to be the successor of Objective-C on mobile platforms, under Apache 2, an open source software license. A quick search on HackerNews[1] — a developer-oriented news aggregator — reveals that there are more than 200 news regarding proprietary software projects that became open source[2].

To shed some light on the trade-offs of keeping the software history, we surveyed proprietary software projects that made the shift to open-source and did not open the software history. We selected 50 projects by searching at news aggregators, mailing lists, or README files (details in Sect. 2.2). To understand the reasons and challenges of working with a non-trivial, yet history-free open source project, we posted questions in the project issue trackers or mailing lists. Based on the responses, we characterized a variety of reasons that explain the lack of software history, such as: "[the history] contains sensitive information," "housekeeping needed," and "licensing and legal reasons." Still, regarding the challenges associated with the lack of software history, although some respondents acknowledge the importance of such history, they reported to have very few problems with it, as one maintainer mentioned, *"I'm probably the person most likely to access it, and I'd estimate that I use it only a few times per year".*

In summary, this paper makes the following main contributions:

- The reasons that lead project maintainers to leave behind the software history when transitioning to open source;
- The discovery that some project maintainers do not value software history as predicted by the literature.

2   Method

In this section, we describe our research questions (Sect. 2.1), the projects studied and how we found them (Sect. 2.2), and our survey design and application (Sect. 2.3).

---

[1] https://news.ycombinator.com/.

[2] https://hn.algolia.com/?query=%22is%20now%20open%20source%22

2.1 Research Questions

To guide our research, we investigated the following important but overlooked research questions:

RQ1: Why some projects do not open the software history when going open source?
Why: Although one might believe that the reasons behind the removal of the software history are straightforward (e.g., to protect sensitive data about the company), this research question is intended to bring evidence to confirm or refute this belief, as well as to uncover additional reasons.

RQ2: What are the challenges associated with the lack of software history?
Why: To understand the hidden challenges triggered by the lack of software history. This better understanding can, in turn, motivate researchers and tool makers to improve existing VCS tools in order to mitigate these challenges, or even to avoid the need of leaving behind the software history.

2.2 Studied Projects

We selected a set of active and non-trivial proprietary software projects that recently (*i.e.*, no later than 2014) became open source. To identify these projects, we used a convenience sampling approach: we searched in mailing lists, blog posts, and newsletters for indication of whether a proprietary project became open source. We double checked the first commit(s) for anything indicating whether the source code was imported all at once or not. Such commit usually has an informative message and a high number of additions. For instance, the first commit from project `deepvariant` was named "Initial release of Deep-Variant", and had 49,522 additions (0 deletions) in 270 files.[3] We started this search in June 2016 and proceeded until we found 50 instances of proprietary projects that deleted their software history when transitioning to open source. Among them were `IndexTank` from LinkedIn, `caravel` from Airbnb, `msbuild` from Microsoft, and `Haxl` from Facebook. Throughout this process, we found only eight projects that kept the software history. We sent open questions to the 50 selected projects and received answers from 35 projects, which had been considered for this study; the list of the 35 projects is available at Table 1. Although the list of studied projects is not exhaustive, it contains a variety of projects, with relation to their domains, programming language use, and size in terms of lines of code. Figure 1 depicts some characteristics of the studied projects.

2.3 Survey

To better understand the reasons for the removal and the problems related with the lack of history, we designed a survey aimed at gathering insights about the importance of the lack of software history. We asked four open questions:

---

[3] https://github.com/google/deepvariant/commit/8b84eab.

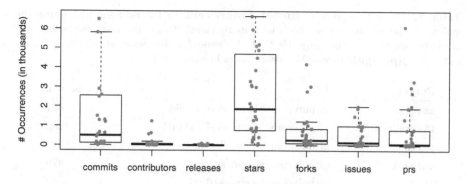

Fig. 1. Characteristics of the analyzed projects

Q1. Why did the software development team decide not to keep the software history?

Q2. Did the *core developers* face any kind of problems when trying to refer to the old history? If so, how did they solve these problems?

Q3. Did the *newcomers* face any kind of problems when trying to refer to the old history? If so, how did they solve these problems?

Q4. How does the lack of software history impact understanding and evolution of software?

We sent the questionnaire by creating issues in the issue trackers of the selected projects. This approach has been successfully employed in recent related work (e.g., [2]). Projects `Tensorflow` and `Scratch` closed the issues, suggesting other means to send research inquiries.[4],[5] We, therefore, approached these projects through their mailing lists (`tensorflow` indeed replied our research inquiries through the mailing list: http://bit.ly/2qR3Mm1). When doing so, one mailing list user contacted us, asking: *"If you'd like another proprietary project that went open source and left behind its history, card.io did that,"* which we promptly accepted. In total, we collect answers from developers of 35 open source projects (totalizing 41 answers; we received up to four answers per project). For the majority of projects (project `ChakraCore` is the only exception), the respondents were within the top-10 most active ones.

To compile the survey results, we qualitatively analyzed the answers following coding procedures [22]. The qualitative analysis was conducted independently by the first two authors, followed by a consensus meeting. To enrich some of the findings, we opted to use some quotes throughout the results section. Among similar opinions, we chose to quote only the one we considered the most representative for each case.

---

[4] https://github.com/LLK/scratch-flash/issues/1112.

[5] https://github.com/tensorflow/tensorflow/issues/2361.

Table 1. The list of projects studied. Project `card.io` has no issue id because the maintainer personally got in touch with us by email. To see the response online, one needs to concatenate the project's URL + /issues/ + the issue id, resulting in, for instance, https://github.com/Microsoft/msbuild/issues/621.

Projects	URL	Issue Id
`msbuild`	github.com/Microsoft/msbuild	621
`ChakraCore`	github.com/Microsoft/ChakraCore	1280
`heron`	github.com/twitter/heron	1018
`caravel`	github.com/airbnb/superset	470
`fbctf`	github.com/facebook/fbctf	49
`Tensorflow`	github.com/tensorflow/tensorflow	2361
`jsaction`	github.com/google/jsaction	11
`card.io`	github.com/card-io/card.io-dmz	– – –
`openwebrtc`	github.com/EricssonResearch/openwebrtc	611
`manta`	github.com/joyent/manta	14
`triton`	github.com/joyent/triton	202
`Dshell`	github.com/USArmyResearchLab/Dshell	87
`buffer-ios`	github.com/bufferapp/buffer-ios-image-viewer	42
`django-knowledge`	github.com/zapier/django-knowledge	70
`warp-ctc`	github.com/baidu-research/warp-ctc	42
`codecombat`	github.com/codecombat/codecombat	3775
`djinni`	github.com/dropbox/djinni	253
`superpowers-core`	github.com/superpowers/superpowers-core	143
`GameMaker`	github.com/gandrewstone/GameMaker	2
`opentoonz`	github.com/opentoonz/opentoonz	640
`magento2`	github.com/magento/magento2	5654
`IndexTank`	github.com/linkedin/indextank-engine	43
`ShareLatex`	github.com/sharelatex/web-sharelatex	282
`Haxl`	github.com/facebook/Haxl	52
`reason`	github.com/facebook/reason	651
`redex`	github.com/facebook/redex	164
`torchnet`	github.com/torchnet/torchnet	28
`torch`	github.com/facebook/fb.resnet.torch	86
`draft-js`	github.com/facebook/draft-js	555
`pinball`	github.com/pinterest/pinball	74
`decoda`	github.com/unknownworlds/decoda	33
`mrjob`	github.com/Yelp/mrjob	1356
`deepvariant`	github.com/google/deepvariant	36
`fsharp-support`	github.com/JetBrains/fsharp-support	6
`escape`	github.com/ankyra/escape	4

3   RQ1: Why Some Projects Do Not Open the Software History?

While analyzing the answers, we observed that the lack of software history occurs for several reasons (some respondents described more than one reason):

Entangled with proprietary code (11 occurrences). We found that some projects became open source by open-sourcing a small part of a bigger project. As one respondent mentioned *"Extracting just the subfolder would have been difficult, and older versions would not have built."* Another respondent summarized this process as: *"first get something working, and then disentangle it from your own proprietary code, configuration, etc."* The same respondent also suggested that this might be a common pattern in OSS projects.

Contains sensitive information (11 occurrences). Some projects had hard-coded sensitive information (*e.g.*, credentials of a remote database) in the source code, e.g., *"DeepVariant was originally developed within Google, using our internal systems. [...] the earliest commits may contain information we cannot share, so upon releasing DeepVariant we squashed the history."* Although one could simply delete the commits that alter this information, one respondent mentioned that they *"have to do an audit of the change descriptions to make sure the descriptions are appropriate for being published publicly,"* which they were unwilling to do. As another respondent said: *"Going through potentially thousands of commits, realistically, means no one will take on the heroic task of even open-sourcing the product."* Thus, the only way to effectively remove this sensitive information is removing the entire software history.

Housekeeping needed (7 occurrences). As Fogel already anticipated [8], prior to releasing a proprietary software as open source, one needs to exert some effort toward improving code quality and documentation, as stated by one respondent: *"We cleaned out embarrassing or inappropriate comments, brought the code up to OSS standards, and generally improved code hygiene, robustness, and security."* However, it was unexpected that the amount of refactoring required would prevent the software history from being useful, as another respondent said: *"the amount of reorganization that happened *just before* open-sourcing meant that it would be harder to track the history than to just understand the current state."*

Of less importance (4 occurrences). Contrary to recent studies (*e.g.*, [4]), some developers believed that the software history does not deserve such importance. One respondent suggested that *"two of the primary motivations for keeping history are egos and understanding bug fixes. [our project] was low on ego, and we were careful to comment non-trivial or subtle bug fixes, so those two historical artifacts weighed less heavily."* Another respondent highlighted another aspect of this lack of importance: *"remember that often something started as one person's random weekend project. Keeping a pristine history might not have been a priority."*

License and legal reasons (4 occurrences). We also found non-technical and legal reasons. As one respondent mentioned: *"[Deleting the software history] also made it much easier to get the lawyers at our parent company to agree to open source it–instead of having to review the entire history for safety, they could review just the current state."* Another reason is that some now open source applications rely on proprietary code. Therefore, to maintain license compliance, the developers have to maintain that code internally. Ultimately, one respondent summarized this reason: *"Legal and policy reasons created incentives to release less source."*

Did not use a VCS before (3 occurrences). Some projects became open source shortly after their bootstrap. Thus, there was no need to use any VCS, as one respondent said, *"there simply was no formal software history kept, and direct cooperation between experienced developers was sufficient to develop it to a releasable state."* For these projects, the first commit at GitHub was their first use of a version control system.

Used another VCS before (3 occurrences). One respondent said that *"Before moving to GitHub, TensorFlow was developed on a system other than Git, and transferring history was not straightforward."* Moreover, the same respondent suggested that the effort needed for migrating the software history from one VCS to another does not outweigh the benefits of keeping it: *"[the] value [of keeping the software history] was at best unclear, so we didn't do it."*

4   RQ2: What Are the Challenges Associated with the Lack of Software History?

Most of the project maintainers reported that they had few problems with the lack of software history; as one respondent mentioned: *"none of the core developers has wanted or needed to go look back through the history."* Another respondent stated that *"based on practical experience, a history [of] more than a year is used very rarely"*, which might explain this behavior. Moreover, another respondent suggested that institutional knowledge, i.e., the combined knowledge of the many contributors to a project, can be an effective substitute for formal software history, for instance: *"communication between developers, documentation in and outside of the source code, and the easily understood idiomatic expressions of the Python language were/are sufficient to maintain project coherency."*

Even though these comments are in sharp contradiction with recent related work [4], it does not suggest that the software history is unimportant. Indeed, some respondents acknowledged its importance (*e.g., "We very much agree that the software history is extremely useful for developers"*). Still, ten respondents suggested that the original software history is internally maintained, as one respondent highlighted: *"we still use the non-git system internally and can refer to history if we need to."* However, the respondents also suggested that the internal software history is not actively used, as one respondent indicated: *"The old history is still available internally. I'm probably the person most likely to access it, and I'd estimate that I use it only a few times per year."* Nevertheless, maintaining two software histories for the same project might require additional effort, which can make it difficult to track down the origins of the code.

Similarly, we found that maintainers do not think that the lack of software history is a significant problem for newcomers; all respondents shared this belief. However, most of the respondents said that they are not *aware* of any problems. Some newcomers may have faced problems, but not reported them, or gave up contributing. Project maintainers often suggested different ways that newcomers can mitigate this problem, as one respondent mentioned: *"they have the code to look at and also code which is non-obvious should anyway have comments, else they could ask people who worked on the code before it was released."*

Finally, regarding software evolution, we found a remarkable uniformity among the respondents; all of them believed that the lack of software history does not greatly impact software evolution and understanding. In the worse case, one respondent characterized the lack of history *"as a very minor inconvenience."* Even more interestingly, one respondent said that software history of an active project loses importance over time: *"For a fast-moving project, history from more than half a year ago is not particularly valuable for development."*

Along with this line of thought, Codoban *et al.* [4] observed that software developers need better tools to visualize software history. We believe that this lack of tools to properly visualize software history might create the perception that it is "not particularly valuable for development." Ultimately, we observed that the burden the lack of history may cause is *"certainly not enough to outweigh the costs of making it public,"* which is particularly relevant to the software projects under study.

5 Implications and Limitations

In this section we discuss some implications of our findings, and state the limitations of this work.

5.1 Implications

Based on our findings, we discuss some implications for stakeholders. We observed that some respondents mentioned a lack of tools to ease the migration between version control systems, for instance: *"I think this one may have been moving between source code repository technologies (SVN to Git) and the tools did not work well enough."* Researchers and tool builders can propose a new set of tools to better support the transition between VCSs. Additionally, we observed that a common way to open-source a software project is by extracting only a small part of an existing project. However, this activity might be extremely difficult to conduct without appropriated tool support. As a result, developers leave behind the software history. Researchers can explore better techniques to extract only parts (or features) of the software while keeping only the relevant software history. Since some respondents mentioned that old software history is not particularly valuable for development, VCS designers can also propose lightweight VCSs, in which only the N most recent changes are kept, where N is based on project's activity or user choice. Programming language designers can also introduce programming language constructs that keep track of the evolution of certain parts of the code.

5.2 Limitations

As any empirical study, this one has limitations and threats to validity. First, we selected our projects by searching blog posts, newsletters, and README files; the first author manually conducted this process. Due to the qualitative nature of this approach (and the timeliness of a proprietary project becoming open source), one could find different projects. Moreover, we used GitHub's issues to send out our questionnaires. Such public participation can also be a threat since anyone could answer our questions. To mitigate this threat, we verified whether the respondents were active project members. We found that the majority of the respondents were among the top-10 most active contributors (only one respondent was not in the top-10). However, nine respondents do not appear as a contributor of the studied project. This might happen because the software history was removed and their contributions might have been removed as well. By comparing the user's affiliation and the project's affiliation on GitHub, we confirmed the affiliation of five of them. The remaining four did not state any affiliation. Also, we observed that some open source projects do not use issues for discussions. We, therefore, got in touch through the mailing list. Still, we certainly did not discover all challenges and reasons behind the lack of software history. Replications are necessary to fully understand the phenomenon. To facilitate replication, we made available the list of studied projects and the responses received in our survey on the companion website: http://bit.ly/dataset-oss2018.

6 Related Work

Some studies focus specifically on GitHub's features, which allow developers to track activities and form detailed impressions of social and technical abilities [12,24]. Community size, interest, and activeness have also being explored [17,21]. Moreover, there is a recent growth of studies targeting proprietary projects under development in social coding websites. Kalliamvakou *et al.* [10] examined how proprietary software projects use GitHub. They found that these projects apply practices such as reduced communication, independent work, and self-organization. Some research has investigated how proprietary projects adopt OSS-related practices to mitigate challenges related to the lack of communication and awareness [18,19]. More recently, we conducted some studies to understand how the contributions from employees (the ones hired by a software company) differs from volunteers (the ones the contribute in their free time) [7,15]. Regarding licensing, some studies investigated licenses inconsistencies and violations [1,9,13], and other focus on license evolution [6,25,26].

The closest work is an in-depth investigation of the contribution characteristics of Company-Owned OSS projects that kept the software history [16]. However, to the best of our knowledge, there is no study targeting the impact of the lack of the software history on proprietary projects that made the shift to open source software.

7   Conclusion

In this paper, we challenge an important belief related to the importance of software history. After the identification of a set of projects that left behind their entire software history after transitioning to open source, we deployed a survey to better understand (1) the reasons that lead to this removal and (2) the hidden challenges that arose due to its lack. We found eight reasons that might justify the decision of removing the software history, such as "entangled with proprietary code," "housekeeping needed," and "license and legal reasons." More interestingly, however, is the fact that when asked whether the lack of software history might impact understanding and evolving of the software, some respondents believed that the lack of history does not place any significant burden on developers.

For future work, we plan to better understand the newcomers' perception of the lack of software history and contrast our results with the analysis of projects that kept the history when migrating to open source.

Acknowledgments. We thank our respondents and the reviewers. This work is supported by CNPq #406308/2016-0; PROPESP/UFPA; and FAPESP #2015/24527-3.

References

1. Almeida, D.A., Murphy, G.C., Wilson, G., Hoye, M.: Do software developers understand open source licenses? In: ICPC 2017, pp. 1–11. IEEE Press (2017)
2. Avelino, G., Passos, L., Hora, A., Valente, M.T.: A novel approach for estimating truck factors. In: ICPC 2016, pp. 1–10 (2016)
3. Bachmann, A., Bird, C., Rahman, F., Devanbu, P., Bernstein, A.: The missing links: bugs and bug-fix commits. In: FSE 2010, pp. 97–106 (2010)
4. Codoban, M., Ragavan, S.S., Dig, D., Bailey, B.: Software history under the lens: a study on why and how developers examine it. In: ICSME 2015, pp. 1–10 (2015)
5. de Oliveira, M.C., Bonifácio, R., Ramos, G.N., Ribeiro, M.: Unveiling and reasoning about co-change dependencies. In: Modularity 2016, pp. 25–36 (2016)
6. Di Penta, M., German, D.M., Guéhéneuc, Y.-G., Antoniol, G.: An exploratory study of the evolution of software licensing. In: ICSE 2010, vol. 1, pp. 145–154. IEEE (2010)
7. Dias, L.F., Steinmacher, I., Pinto, G.: Who drives company-owned OSS projects: Employees or volunteers? In: V Workshop on Software Visualization, Evolution and Maintenance, VEM, p. 10 (2017)
8. Fogel, K.: Producing Open Source Software: How to Run a Successful Free Software Project, 1st edn. O'Reilly Media, Sebastopol (2013)

9. German, D.M., Di Penta, M., Davies, J.: Understanding and auditing the licensing of open source software distributions. In: ICPC 2010, pp. 84–93. IEEE (2010)

10. Kalliamvakou, E., Damian, D., Blincoe, K., Singer, L., German, D.M.: Open source-style collaborative development practices in commercial projects using GitHub. In: ICSE 2015, pp. 574–585 (2015)

11. Kuttal, S.K., Sarma, A., Rothermel, G.: On the benefits of providing versioning support for end users: an empirical study. ACM Trans. Comput.-Hum. Interact. **21**(2), 9:1–9:43 (2014)

12. Marlow, J., Dabbish, L., Herbsleb, J.: Impression formation in online peer production: activity traces and personal profiles in GitHub. In: CSCW (2013)

13. Meloca, R.M., Pinto, G., Baiser, L.P., Mattos, M., Polato, I., Wiese, I.S., German, D.M.: A study of non-approved open-source licenses. In: MSR 2018. IEEE Press (2018)

14. Pham, R., Singer, L., Liskin, O., Filho, F.F., Schneider, K.: Creating a shared understanding of testing culture on a social coding site. In: ICSE 2013, pp. 112–121 (2013)

15. Pinto, G., Dias, L.F., Steinmacher, I.: Who gets a patch accepted first? comparing the contributions of employees and volunteers. In: 2018 11th IEEE/ACM International Workshop on Cooperative and Human Aspects of Software Engineering, CHASE@ICSE 2018, Gothenburg, Sweden, May 2018

16. Pinto, G., Steinmacher, I., Dias, L.F., Gerosa, M.: On the challenges of opensourcing proprietary software projects. Empir. Softw. Eng. 1–27 (2018)

17. Pinto, G., Steinmacher, I., Gerosa, M.A.: More common than you think: an indepth study of casual contributors. In: SANER 2016, pp. 112–123 (2016)

18. Riehle, D., Ellenberger, J., Menahem, T., Mikhailovski, B., Natchetoi, Y., Naveh, B., Odenwald, T.: Open collaboration within corporations using software forges. IEEE Softw. **26**(2), 52–58 (2009)

19. Sharma, S., Sugumaran, V., Rajagopalan, B.: A framework for creating hybrid-open source software communities. Inf. Syst. J. **12**(1), 7–26 (2002)

20. Steff, M., Russo, B.: Co-evolution of logical couplings and commits for defect estimation. In: MSR 2012, pp. 213–216 (2012)

21. Steinmacher, I., Pinto, G., Wiese, I., Gerosa, M.A.: Almost there: a study on quasi-contributors in open-source software projects. In: ICSE 2018 (2018)

22. Strauss, A., Corbin, J.M.: Basics of Qualitative Research: Techniques and Procedures for Developing Grounded Theory, 3rd edn. SAGE, Thousand Oaks (2007)

23. Tao, Y., Dang, Y., Xie, T., Zhang, D., Kim, S.: How do software engineers understand code changes?: An exploratory study in industry. In: FSE 2012, pp. 51:1–51:11 (2012)

24. Tsay, J., Dabbish, L., Herbsleb, J.: Influence of social and technical factors for evaluating contribution in GitHub. In: ICSE 2014, pp. 356–366 (2014)

25. Vendome, C., Bavota, G., Di Penta, M., Linares-Vásquez, M., German, D., Poshyvanyk, D.: License usage and changes: a large-scale study on github. Empir Softw. Eng. **22**(3), 1–41 (2017)

26. Vendome, C., Linares-Vásquez, M., Bavota, G., Di Penta, M., German, D., Poshyvanyk, D.: Machine learning-based detection of open source license exceptions. In: ICSE 2017, pp. 118–129 (2017)

Developer Dynamics and Syntactic Quality of Commit Messages in OSS Projects

Kuljit Kaur Chahal[✉] and Munish Saini

Department of Computer Science, Guru Nanak Dev University, Amritsar, India
kuljitchahal@yahoo.com

Abstract. Community dynamics play an important role in the Open Source Software (OSS) development paradigm. Researchers have extensively studied the human aspects of the OSS paradigm from the point of view of community formation to community evolution. A few studies relate community dynamics with OSS product attributes such as code quality. However, the impact of community dynamics on non-code contributions such as commits has not been explored. In this paper, the aim is to analyze the impact of community dynamics on syntactic quality of commit messages of an OSS project. We first propose and validate a commit message quality model, and then use that model to analyze the OSS projects. Empirical analysis of seven OSS projects available in the Git repository shows that a small group of contributors active at the same time in a project leads to high syntactic quality contributions. These observations may prove useful to developers as well as project managers who need quantifiable techniques for monitoring the OSS projects.

CCS Concepts: CCS → Software and its engineering → Software notations and tools → Software configuration management and version control systems

Keywords: Open Source Software (OSS) · Software evolution
Source code management · Commit activity · Commit message quality

1 Introduction

Open Source Software (OSS) development is presumed to entail collaborative participation of geographically distributed developers for creating a successful project. A source code management system such as Git records and manages contributions of participants in the project repository. Majority of the participants are volunteers. Major motivations for participants include developing and improving skills, getting recognition for the skills, and building a reputation which in turn helps them in furthering their commercial endeavors [8]. Sans any organization control, they can join or leave an OSS project as per their own convenience. Unlike commercial software in which committed employees contribute regularly, an OSS project generally depends upon contributions from self-motivated individuals who belong to different geographical locations, and diverse cultures and backgrounds. More recently, corporate backed OSS projects are also emerging on the landscape. Large corporates such as IBM, HP support OSS development with their own resources (i.e. their paid workforce contributes) in

© IFIP International Federation for Information Processing 2018
Published by Springer International Publishing AG 2018. All Rights Reserved
I. Stamelos et al. (Eds.): OSS 2018, IFIP AICT 525, pp. 61–76, 2018.
https://doi.org/10.1007/978-3-319-92375-8_6

various projects that they use in their own products. Whatever the mode of partici-pation, we can say that OSS community plays an important role in the OSS devel-opment paradigm.

However, this is not static but a very dynamic community. There are no fixed roles. A member can contribute to an OSS project in a number of ways depending upon his skill set (as a developer, tester, or documenter). Not only this, he/she can fluidly shift from being an end user to a developer (for example a tool user can work on improving the tool). Due to the volunteer nature of participation, there could be many lean periods in a project's activity when participants are busy in their regular life activities, for example working on a full-time job on weekdays, enjoying vacations, or not con-tributing due to inexplicable reasons. It will be interesting to investigate community dynamics and its impacts on OSS development processes.

In this paper, we are interested in understanding the impact of community dynamics on the quality of contributions committed to a project's repository.

A commit, a software change that involves a source code or other type of contri-bution such as documentation, is a fundamental component of an OSS development process. In the recent past, commit analysis has been a topic of active research to understand the software development processes of OSS projects [8, 12, 13]. For example commit activity (measured as the number of commits in a unit of time) of an OSS project is correlated with successfulness of the project [13]. A developer with high commit frequency is more productive. A project with high commit frequency is healthy as it gets regular contributions. There is not much research on this topic to define commit quality or to use commit quality information to characterize OSS projects or developers' contribution practices. A few studies have analyzed commits of software projects from quality perspective [1], though there is a lot of work focusing on evaluating the code quality of OSS projects. In this paper, we propose to answer the following question:

What is the impact of community dynamics on commit message (syntactic) quality in the context of OSS projects?

A good quality commit contains a well-crafted message with all the necessary details (meta-data) to effectively convey the change to current or future developers [5]. It not only makes the changes contributed by others easy to understand but also helps in recalling one's own changes contributed in the past. A good commit message should follow a simple and consistent style for specifying commit meta-data and content.

With respect to commit message quality in OSS projects, we propose a commit message syntactic quality model in Sect. 3. Following this model, each commit mes-sage can be assigned a commit score. In this study, we are focusing only on the syntactic view of commit messages. The syntactic analysis shows "writing styles of the contributors" i.e. whether they follow the rules of the syntax while describing their commits. We analyzed 202,561 commit messages of seven OSS projects to understand the way committers commit changes in a Source Code Management (SCM) system specifically Git.

Paper organization: The rest of the paper is organized as follows. Next section presents the related work. Rest of the sections present the commit quality model, the data collection steps, and the results in that order. In the end, a section mentions limitations of the study followed by conclusions and future work.

2   Related Work

The success of an OSS project suggestively depends upon the type of community support available to the project as social aspects significantly determine evolution [6, 16]. However, in the context of the OSS paradigm, the community itself is dynamic in nature. This section discusses the prior work related to community dynamics and its impact on OSS processes. A few of the works related to commit quality and commit analysis are also mentioned.

Some studies in the past focused only on static community structure to understand the demographic diversity of community members [14], gender differences [15], and role of the core members [22]. While [4] studied community dynamics using social network analysis to understand the changes that happen to a community over a period of time. Changes in the community structure are presented with the help of temporal visualization and quantitative analysis.

Bird and Nagappan [7] analyzed two large OSS projects, Firefox and Eclipse, to investigate the impact of distributed locations of the developers on the quality of the code they contributed. They found that quality of components (measured using the number of defects) developed by distributed teams was bad in comparison to the quality of components developed by collocated teams.

Ahmed *et al.* [2] relate poor coding practices with growth in the number of developers. The study concludes that code as well as design quality declines as the number of developers increases. Souza and Silva [21] analyze effect of developer sentiment levels (as expressed in commit messages) on build status of Travis, a Continuous Integration server. The results suggest that negative sentiment reduces the chances of a successful build, though the effect is minor.

Santos and Hindle [18] studied the unusualness of commit messages by training n-gram language models on 120,000 commits of OSS projects and used cross-entropy as an indicator of a commit message's "unusualness". Their work focused mainly on finding the unusualness of a commit message, and further correlating it with code quality. Agrawal *et al.* [1] studied the commit quality of five high-performance computing projects and compared the performance of the projects with three low performance computing projects.

Most of the works in the research literature on commit analysis of OSS projects deal with identifying commit size distribution [3], commit frequency distribution [13], commit characterization [17, 23], and contributor's commit activity distribution [8]. Chełkowski *et al.* [8] analyzed commit contributions of Apache contributors to highlight inequalities among open source contributors' in producing content in the OSS paradigm which is often described as collaborative.

Lack of literature on the subject and the broad nature of practitioner recommendations suggest a need for a research study regarding the quality analysis of the commit messages recorded in a source code management system. We followed a Multi-vocal Literature Review (MLR) approach [8]. In this study, our focus is on measuring commit message quality syntactically by using 11 syntactical metrics by introducing a novel approach to calculate commit quality. Moreover, we focused on finding if there is any relation between community evolution and the commit message quality of the OSS projects. The commit message quality is correlated with the number of contributors to understand the impact of community dynamics on development processes of the OSS projects.

3   The Proposed Model and Its Validation

A set of measures, to calculate the syntactic quality of commit messages recorded in SCM system of the OSS projects, are devised after consulting a bulk of literature (published [1], or available online [9]) to understand "how to write a good commit message". The online search to this topic "how to write a good commit message" or "good commit logs" yielded a large number of results. We followed a double cross-check approach to select the commit quality metrics. Both the authors analyzed the top 33 web links (beyond this the content was repeated) individually, and noted all the rules and identified the possible list of attributes that can act as commit quality measures. At the last, we combined the rules and the lists of attributes that were identified by both the authors. This double cross-check approach avoided any rule or attribute to get skipped from the analysis. After consulting the literature, common rules indicating a good quality commit message are identified as shown in Table 1:

Table 1. Rules for writing a good commit

1.	Title (subject line) of commit message should be short (between 50–72 characters)
2.	Subject line should end with a dot
3.	Capitalize the subject line i.e. first character of the subject line should be capital
4.	Use imperative mood in the subject line for example use words like fix, add, update in place of fixing, adding, and updating etc.
5.	Subject line should be concise and limit the number of "and", "or"
6.	Subject line should not include details such as bug number, file name, ticket number, and any other external references
7.	Subject line and body must be separated by a blank line
8.	Body of a commit message must have multiline description. It should be well explanatory detailing why and what is changed
9.	Body of a commit message should not contain lots of bullets, hyphens, or asterisks
10.	Commit should have one logical change

By considering all these rules, we devised 11 commit quality measures (see Table 2). Out of which, seven are for subject line (title), and the rest four are for the body (multiline description) of a commit message. After evaluating the count and values for the commit messages, the proposed approach assigns scores to each measure on a scale of 1 to 5 (as shown in Table 2).

Next step was to see whether the proposed rules and the corresponding metric definitions sound reasonable from practitioners' point of view. We chose the survey based method to get inputs from practitioners. In response to a survey request, 20 developers volunteered to participate in the survey. Most of the participants were

Table 2. Commit message syntactic quality measures

Commit quality measures	Commit score					Unit
	1	2	3	4	5	
Length of title	=0 or >72	1–10	11–30	31–50	51–72	Number of characters
Title ends with dots	No	Yes				$y \rightarrow 1, n \rightarrow 0$
Title first character capital	No	Yes				$y \rightarrow 1, n \rightarrow 0$
Count number of "and" "or" in title	>6	5–6	3–4	1–2	0	Count
Count number of "file name" in title	>6	5–6	3–4	1–2	0	Count
Count number of external references in title	>6	5–6	3–4	1–2	0	Count
Imperative mode in title	No	Yes				$y \rightarrow 1, n \rightarrow 0$
Commit body existence	No	Yes				$y \rightarrow 1, n \rightarrow 0$
Count number of "file name" in body	0	10>	6–10	3–5	1–2	Count
Count number of external references in body	0	10>	6–10	3–5	1–2	Count
Count number of paragraph in body	0	10>	5–10	3–4	1–2	Count

graduates, with a total of 16 graduate and 4 undergraduate degree holders. Their industrial experience varied from 5 to 7 years in software projects based on Java/C#. In the survey, the participants were provided a sample of commits and were asked to upvote a rule if they agree, downvote a rule if they don't agree, or post a neutral response if it does not matter to them while reading a commit message. They also reported their votes on metric definitions.

As a result of this survey (see Table 3), we concluded that the rules and the metrics to evaluate the commits were useful and reasonable.

Then we calculated the total score for each commit message. We cannot use these scores of individual measures as such to calculate the total score of message quality of a commit as different commit measures have different scales (few commit measures have values on scale 1–5, whereas other have values on the scale 1–2). Therefore, we first normalized the commit scores of individual measures to a common scale [0, 1]. The normalization of commit measures is done by using the following formula [20]:

$$\text{Normalized commit message score} = \text{ActualScore/MaxScore} \qquad (1)$$

$$\text{Total commit score} = \sum_{1}^{11} WCS\_CommitMeasure\_i \qquad (2)$$

In order to further validate the results of the commit message quality score, the results of the proposed model for a sample of 100 commits messages (50 with commit

Table 3. Survey responses

	Rule	Upvotes	Downvotes	Neutral
1.	Title (subject line) of commit message should be short (between 50–72 characters)	15	4	1
2.	Subject line should end with a dot	10	7	3
3.	Capitalize the subject line i.e. first character of the subject line should be capital	8	6	6
4.	Use imperative mood in the subject line for example use words like fix, add, update in place of fixing, adding, and updating etc.	20	–	–
5.	Subject line should be concise and limit the number of "and", "or"	18	–	2
6.	Subject line should not include details such as bug number, file name, ticket number, and any other external references	17	–	3
7.	Subject line and body must be separated by a blank line	12	2	6
8.	Body of a commit message must have multiline description. It should be well explanatory detailing why and what is changed	19	–	1
9.	Body of a commit message should not contain lots of bullets, hyphens, or asterisks	18	–	2
10.	Commit should have one logical change	20	–	–

messages as per the rules and 50 otherwise) were compared with the assessment results made available by the same survey participants. The results show that 84% of the commit messages were correctly judged by the proposed model. Specifically, for commit messages with good quality, about 88% of messages were correctly judged, and about 80% of messages with poor quality were correctly judged by the proposed model. This shows that the proposed model is effective.

4 Data Collection

Seven OSS projects were selected on the basis of their popularity, age, size, number of people involved, and availability of the project repository in Git (an open source distributed version control system).

PostGreSQL is an object-relational data base management system. glibc is a GNU C library used in the GNU/Linux systems. Eclipse-CDT is an industrial strength IDE for developing C/C++ programs and plug-in tools. GnuCash is a double entry accounting software for personal and small enterprises. WordPress is web publishing software. Firebug is a web browser extension for Mozilla Firefox for debugging and performance analysis of web pages rendered in the browser. Rhino is a JavaScript engine. It is an open source application of JavaScript. It is regularly implanted into Java applications to give scripting to end users.

Development repositories of the OSS projects are obtained from the Github (www.github.com). A repository is downloaded by making a clone of the original repository onto the local machine by using Gitbash (www.git-scm.com). A script is written in Java to fetch the commit messages and number of contributors for the observation period for all the OSS projects. Table 4 summarizes the statistics of the datasets collected for all the seven projects.

Table 4. Descriptive statistics of the OSS projects

OSS projects	Origin date	Number of months	Number of contributors	Commit messages
PostgreSQL	Jul, 1996	239	43	54355
glibc	Feb, 1989	321	410	43313
Eclipse-CDT	Jun, 2002	168	203	28817
GnuCash	Nov, 1997	222	105	21969
WordPress	Apr, 2003	158	73	37333
Firebug	Aug, 2007	181	45	13043
Rhino	Apr, 1999	105	56	3721

5 Result and Analysis

This study explores the commit messages of seven OSS projects to calculate and analyze the commit quality of these commit messages. Further, the commit message quality measures are used to answer the research question specified in Sect. 1.

In this section, we first analyze the commit message quality of the OSS projects as they evolve over a period of time. But before that, we look at the differences in levels of the commit message quality in these projects. With the help of box plots, Fig. 1 shows the variation in the commit message quality across the projects. *GnuCash* and *Word-Press* have the best median values (>0.80) for the commit message score. Next is *Firebug* with median commit message score 0.75. The remaining four projects (which includes very popular projects *PostgreSQL* and *Eclipse-CDT*) have median commit message scores less than 0.70.

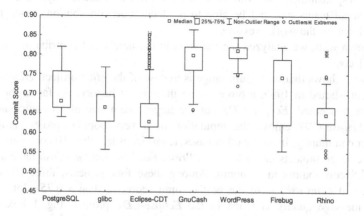

Fig. 1. Variation in commit quality of the OSS projects

Eclipse-CDT has many outliers towards the upper side of the box plot otherwise, the median commit score is the minimum in comparison to other projects.

Next, we analyzed the commit message quality evolution in these projects. Intuitively, commit message quality should improve over the period of time as a project matures as core team of experienced developers is supposed to vet commits submitted by less experienced developers. We can see in Fig. 2a, c (on next page) that commit message quality improves after staying stable for a long period of time. In Fig. 2g, it stays stable throughout. We note from Table 5 that commit message score of these projects follows an increasing trend when analyzed using linear regression [19]. In case of the other three projects (see Fig. 2d–f), it drops down and shows a decreasing trend when analyzed using linear regression. We believe that this behavior may be due to developer dynamics. A detailed explanation of this behavior of the OSS projects is due until discussion of the next section. The in-between variation (e.g. decrease in March 2008 for the *glibc* project) in commit message score of these projects needs further analysis to understand the factors responsible for such behavior. In the next section, we revisit this type of behavior to find the factors that may have affected the commit message score. From the above observations, we can conclude that the commit message quality does not always improve as a software project matures. Some of the projects in this case study point to slender periods when commit message quality goes down.

5.1 Does the Number of Contributors Affect the Commit Message Syntactic Quality?

In OSS projects, developer community plays an important role. Contributors contribute by writing new code and documentation, and also make changes to fix bugs, or to improve the overall quality of a software project. Therefore, it is important to see the relation of contributors' participation in OSS projects with their commit message quality. We want to examine whether an increase in the number of contributors coincides with the increase in the commit message quality of the OSS projects. Intuitively, better commit message quality can be expected as multiple contributors should share the responsibility, and contribute to the project in a better way. Single contributors or small teams may not be able to produce good contributions when they are bogged down by the work pressure.

To begin with, we analyzed the variation in the number of contributors across the OSS projects.

Figure 3 shows that maximum range is in case of the *glibc* project. *glibc* is a very old project, started in 1989, a project with the longest history. As far as the median values are concerned, *Eclipse-CDT* has the largest team size of 15 contributors in a month. *Eclipse-CDT* enjoys the reputation of a very popular project among the developer community. In all the other cases, team size is less than 10 contributors. Four out of the seven projects i.e. *glibc*, *WordPress*, *Firebug*, and *GnuCash* have a median value of 5 contributors in a month. Among these four projects, three (*WordPress*, *Firebug*, and *GnuCash*) have the best commit score (median > 0.75). Interestingly, commit message quality is worst in the *Eclipse-CDT* project (Fig. 1 box plot for commit score). Whereas small teams in four other projects are better in producing good

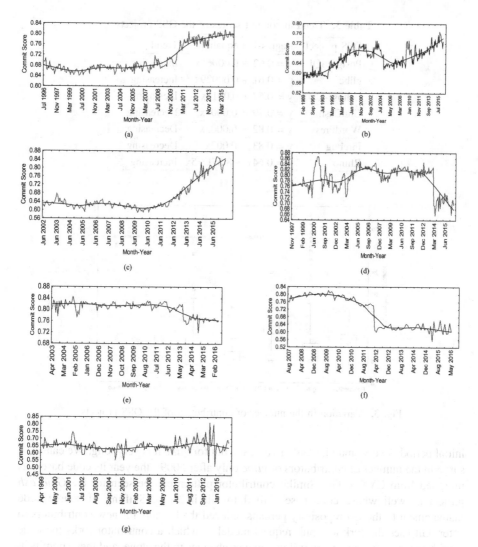

Fig. 2. Average commit message score for *(a)* PostgreSQL, *(b)* glibc, *(c)* Eclipse-CDT, *(d)* GnuCash, *(e)* WordPress, *(f)* Firebug, *(g)* Rhino

quality work. *Eclipse* is a mature project, and such projects also tend to allow contributions from peripheral developers. Therefore, a large team may not ensure better work quality if peripheral (may be untrusted) contributors are allowed to submit changes. It could also be due to if core team does not bother to vet such changes.

Figure 4(a–g) shows contributor churn of the OSS projects over a period of time. In all the OSS projects except *Rhino*, the number of contributors follows an increasing trend over the period of time (see Table 6). We can observe that after initial few years, developer participation has increased manifold notably in the projects *PostgreSQL*, *glibc*, *Eclipse-CDT*, and *WordPress*. However, for the project like *Eclipse-CDT*, this

Table 5. Trend in commit scores of the OSS projects

OSS project	Regression equation	Trend
PostgreSQL	y = 0.62 + 0.00065x	Increasing
glibc	y = 0.61 + 0.00029x	Increasing
Eclipse-CDT	y = 0.57 + 0.0010x	Increasing
GnuCash	y = 0.79 − 0.0001x	Decreasing
WordPress	y = 0.82 − 0.0003x	Decreasing
Firebug	y = 0.83 − 0.002x	Decreasing
Rhino	y = 0.641 + 8.67E−5x	Increasing

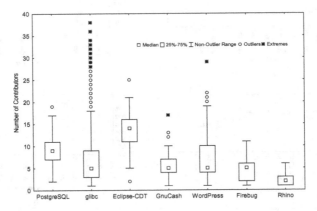

Fig. 3. Variation in the number of contributors of the OSS projects

initial period is very small i.e. only two years, but for *glibc* it is very long. We can see a surge in the number of contributors of *glibc* only after 2009 - the year its code base was migrated from CVS to Git. Similar contributor pattern can be seen for the *GnuCash* project as well whose code base shifted to Git in 2014. Shifting of source code management to the Git repository perhaps reduced the barriers for new contributors to enter. Git uses the fork and pull request model in which a contributor forks the code branch to which it wants to contribute, makes changes to the clone, and then submits it. When accepted, such contributions can be easily merged with the main branch. It suggests that modern tools have improved the process of code contribution.

In case of *Firebug*, the pouring in of contributors stopped around April 2014. An interesting observation is when we relate it to the commit activity of the project; it also dried up around the same time. *Firebug* is an extension of the Mozilla Firefox web browser for debugging and monitoring of the web pages rendered in the browser. Project pages reveal that the *Firebug* project was abandoned during this period of time. People unhappy with this development, as a result, chose Google Chrome over Mozilla Firefox as they had earlier preferred Firefox just because of the *Firebug* plug-in available with it.

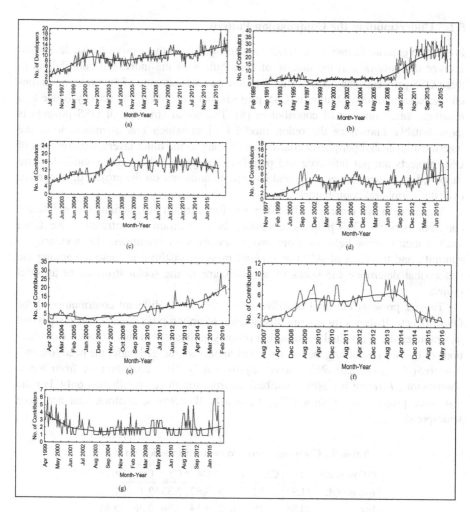

Fig. 4. Average number of contributors per month for *(a)* PostgreSQL, *(b)* glibc, *(c)* Eclipse-CDT, *(d)* GnuCash, *(e)* WordPress, *(f)* Firebug, *(g)* Rhino

Table 6. Trend in number of contributors

OSS project	Regression equation	Trend
PostgreSQL	y = 5.48 + 0.031x	Increasing
glibc	y = 0.064x − 2.05	Increasing
Eclipse-CDT	y = 9.25 + 0.048x	Increasing
GnuCash	y = 2.95 + 0.022x	Increasing
WordPress	y = 0.098x − 0.15	Increasing
Firebug	y = 4.12 + 0.006x	Increasing
Rhino	y = 2.12 − 0.0008x	Decreasing

5.2   Understanding the Contribution Pattern

In order to explore further the commit message quality of these projects, we decided to analyze the volume and the quality of contribution of the individual contributors in these OSS projects. The basis of this decision was the outcome of the previous studies on the patterns of contribution in OSS projects that the bulk of the activity is due to a relatively small number of contributors [8]. The social structure of OSS projects is more notably known as the onion model [10] in which core members form the innermost layer and peripheral contributors belong to the outer layers. Contributors of OSS projects are put into core and periphery categories where core contributors are supposed to possess better skills and have more authority on the project development over the peripheral contributors.

Therefore in this regard, the first step is to find commit distribution among different contributors of the OSS projects to identify the core group of contributors. Next, we analyze their commit behavior from two perspectives – commitment (i.e. regularity to commit), and the level of skill (i.e. commit message quality), as these are among the factors that determine the status of a contributor in the social structure of an OSS project.

Table 7 presents the total contribution (in %) of the different contributors of the OSS projects. It shows the commit distribution of only top six contributors (as beyond this number the individual contribution drops significantly in this dataset). Contributions of the rest (excluding the top six contributors) are merged under the head 'others'. *PostgreSQL*, *glibc*, and *Rhino* have approximately 80% contributions from top 6 contributors. *Firebug* has 80% contributions from top three contributors only. For the rest three projects i.e. *Eclipse-CDT*, *GnuCash*, *WordPress*, contributions are more widespread.

Table 7. Contributor wise commits distribution (in %)

OSS projects	C1	C2	C3	C4	C5	C6	Other
PostgreSQL	34.53	26.52	7.35	3.62	3.33	3.1	21.55
glibc	40.58	24.18	4.72	4.14	3.56	3.36	19.46
Eclipse-CDT	10.11	7.9	6.43	5.64	5.56	5.52	58.84
GnuCash	16.66	14.84	12.65	7.93	7.57	7.57	32.78
WordPress	22.13	7.67	7.4	5.24	4.79	3.82	48.95
Firebug	46.8	19.66	14.37	6.08	2.99	1.29	8.81
Rhino	30.42	20.78	11.82	5.36	4.93	3.35	23.34

We know that, in this data set, *Eclipse-CDT* has the largest (median) number of contributors. The contribution is also quite equally spread among all the contributors of the project as per the data in Table 7. Majority of the *Eclipse-CDT* commits are from non-core (external) contributors. That may be the reason for low commit quality in the project. Though contribution pattern is uniformly spread across different contributors in case of *GnuCash* and *WordPress* projects as well, but they have small team size. At the same time, their commit message quality is good. A small number of contributors are responsible for the commit activity, work distribution is balanced, and commit message quality is also good.

For the commitment or regularity of the commit activity, we tracked their commit activity over the period of time. In Fig. 5(a–g), a horizontal line represents the period when a contributor is active. If there is no contribution in a month, then there is a gap in the line. We can observe in the figure that some of the lines represent continuous activity indicating a regular activity, whereas in some cases there are gaps indicating irregular activity.

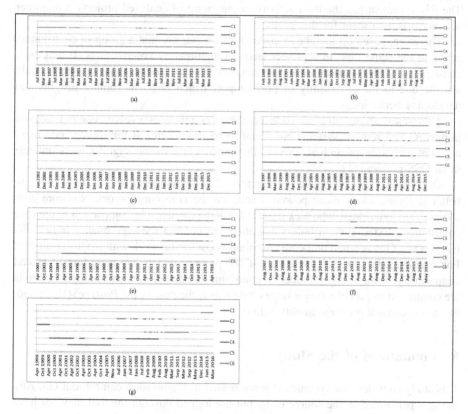

Fig. 5. Committing behavior of the top 6 contributors of *(a)* PostgreSQL, *(b)* glibc, *(c)* Eclipse-CDT, *(d)* GnuCash, *(e)* WordPress, *(f)* Firebug, *(g)* Rhino

It shows that a few contributors are more regular in commit activities. Only a few of them contribute regularly to a repository. The commit activity of different contributors overlaps at several points. Except *Rhino*, all other projects have at least one contributor with regular commit activity of not less than six years. We can see that when multiple contributors are active in a project at the same time, commit quality is better.

For the *PostgreSQL* project, commit quality improves after 2010 (see Fig. 2a). Multiple committers are active around the same time. In case of the *glibc* project, commit quality improves from 1999 to 2004, and after a dip, again from 2009 onwards (see Fig. 2b). Look at the figures for the same time periods, multiple committers are active at the same time. Same is the case for *GnuCash* and *WordPress*. In the *GnuCash* project, commit quality decreases in 2014. At the same time, we can see in the Fig. 5d, the number of active contributors also reduces. There is only one contributor after that time period. In case of the *WordPress* project, commit quality goes down around 2012 (see Fig. 2e). Around the same time period, all the active contributors stop contributing (Fig. 5e). Three new contributors join in, and their commits are perhaps not yet of good quality. *WordPress* project follows a liberal procedure to let people join the project. The *Rhino* project has the least activity in the group of analyzed projects. Committer activeness is also scant for this project.

Therefore, based on the above discussion, we can say that a group of contributors active at the same time in a project leads to high-quality contributions. It may be a consequence of the uniform work distribution among multiple contributors. It could also be due to the availability of peer-support which helps in gaining insights and developing better ideas.

This study shows that as code contribution practices evolve, commit activity improves. Pull request systems are found to be more efficient for source code management. Previous research also shows that process effectiveness ignites users' interest in an OSS project [11].

Open source projects have contributors with diverse skill sets. Individuals with better skills are likely more powerful and, are the core contributors. Non-core contributors are individuals who lack knowledge and experience in comparison to the core contributors. External contributors can affect the commit message quality in two different ways. One is when non-core contributors contribute work with mediocre quality. For example, the case of the *Eclipse-CDT* project, which has a uniformly spread contributions from a large number of contributors. Second is when multiple commits are committed as part of a single large commit as is the case of the *PostgreSQL*. In both the cases, commit message quality suffers.

6   Limitations of the Study

This study considers the commits that are posted in the revision control tool Git. Any changes performed in the source code, but not logged through the tool may not have become part of the study.

Selection of the subject systems is biased towards projects with valid Git repositories.

Though we developed objective measures to capture different aspects of a good commit message, but certain features might have got skipped by both the authors.

7 Conclusions and Future Work

In an OSS community, people are not committed to use or contribute to a particular project regularly. Sometimes, the community support flourishes, and sometimes it dwindles. The major objective of this study was to understand the impact of community dynamics on the quality of contributions submitted to a source code management system of an OSS project. A commit message quality model is proposed to evaluate the syntactic quality of commit meta-data submitted by the developers of an OSS project. *GnuCash* and *WordPress* have very high commit quality throughout in comparison to other five projects analyzed in this study. As per our observation, it is due to the balanced load among core developers of these projects who are active during the same time period. Though *Eclipse-CDT* has the same trait as far as the contribution pattern is concerned, but its commit quality is quiet low. We believe contribution from non-core developers is the reason. Furthermore, choice of source code management for repository management also matters a lot in attracting contributors. We found that as projects (e.g. *glibc*) shifted from traditional SCM systems to modern SCM such as Git, the code contribution process improved. We aim to extend the work further to see the semantic quality of commits. Another proposal is to see the commit message quality of different types of commits such as corrective v/s non-corrective. Future work should also investigate the relevance of commit message quality with quality of the code contributed as part of commits.

References

1. Agrawal, K., Amreen, S., Mockus, A.: Commit quality in five high performance computing projects. In: Proceedings of the 2015 International Workshop on Software Engineering for High Performance Computing in Science, pp. 24–29. IEEE Press (2015)
2. Ahmed, I., Ghorashi, S., Jensen, C.: An exploration of code quality in FOSS projects. In: Corral, L., Sillitti, A., Succi, G., Vlasenko, J., Wasserman, Anthony I. (eds.) OSS 2014. IAICT, vol. 427, pp. 181–190. Springer, Heidelberg (2014). https://doi.org/10.1007/978-3-642-55128-4_26
3. Arafat, O., Riehle, D.: The commit size distribution of open source software. In: Proceedings of the HICSS 2009, Hawaii, USA, 5–8 January 2009, pp. 1–8. IEEE Computer Society Press, New York (2009)
4. Azarbakht, A., Jensen, C.: Drawing the big picture: temporal visualization of dynamic collaboration graphs of OSS software forks. In: Corral, L., Sillitti, A., Succi, G., Vlasenko, J., Wasserman, Anthony I. (eds.) OSS 2014. IAICT, vol. 427, pp. 41–50. Springer, Heidelberg (2014). https://doi.org/10.1007/978-3-642-55128-4_5
5. Beams, C.: How to write a git commit message (2016). http://chris.beams.io/posts/git-commit/. Accessed 26 Mar 2016
6. Berdou, E.: Organization in Open Source Communities: At the Crossroads of the Gift and Market Economies. Routledge, New York (2011)
7. Bird, C., Nagappan, N.: Who? where? what? examining distributed development in two large open source projects. In: Proceedings of the 9th IEEE Working Conference on Mining Software Repositories, pp. 237–246 (2012)

8. Chełkowski, T., Gloor, P., Jemielniak, D.: Inequalities in open source software development: analysis of contributor's commits in apache software foundation projects. PLoS ONE **11**, 4 (2016)
9. Marcolesco, D.J.: Writing good commit messages. https://github.com/erlang/otp/wiki/Writing-good-commit-messages. Accessed 28 July 2016
10. David, P.A., Rullani, F.: Dynamics of innovation in an "open source" collaboration environment: lurking, laboring, and launching FLOSS projects on SourceForge. Ind. Corp. Change **17**(4), 647–710 (2008)
11. Ghapanchi, A.H., Aurum, A., Daneshgar, F.: The impact of process effectiveness on user interest in contributing to the open source software projects. J. Softw. **7**(1), 212–219 (2012)
12. Gonzalez-Barahona, J.M., Robles, G., Herraiz, I., Ortega, F.: Studying the laws of software evolution in a long lived FLOSS project. J. Softw. Evol. Process **26**(7), 589–612 (2014)
13. Kolassa, C., Riehle, D., Salim, M.: The empirical commit frequency distribution of open source projects. In: Proceedings of the 2013 Joint International Symposium on Wikis and Open Collaboration, OpenSym 2013. ACM (2013)
14. Kunegis, J., Sizov, S., Schwagereit, F., Fay, D.: Diversity dynamics in online networks. In: Proceedings of the 23rd ACM Conference on Hypertext and Social Media, USA (2012)
15. Kuechler, V., Gilbertson, C., Jensen, C.: Gender differences in early free and open source software joining process. In: Hammouda, I., Lundell, B., Mikkonen, T., Scacchi, W. (eds.) OSS 2012. IAICT, vol. 378, pp. 78–93. Springer, Heidelberg (2012). https://doi.org/10.1007/978-3-642-33442-9_6
16. Mens, T., Goeminne, M.: Analysing the evolution of social aspects of open source software ecosystems. In: Jansen, S., Bosch, J., Ahmed, F., Campbell, P. (eds.) Proceedings of the Workshop on Software Ecosystems (IWSECO 2011) (2011)
17. Saini, M., Kaur, K.K.: Change profile analysis of open source software systems to understand their evolutionary behavior. Front. Comput. Sci. (2016). https://doi.org/10.1007/s11704-016-6301-0
18. Santos, E., Hindle, A.: Judging a commit by its cover: correlating commit message entropy with build status on travis-CI. In: Proceedings of the 13th International Conference on Mining Software Repositories (MSR 2016), pp. 504–507. ACM, New York (2016)
19. Seber, G., Lee, A.: Linear Regression Analysis, vol. 936. Wiley, Hoboken (2012)
20. Scott, W.R.: Score normalization as a fair grading practice. http://www.ericdigests.org/2003-4/score-normilization.html. Accessed 20 July 2016
21. Souza, R., Silva, B.: Sentiment analysis of travis CI builds. In: 14th International Conference on Mining Software Repositories (2017)
22. Martinez Torres, M.R., Toral, S.L., Perales, M., Barrero, F.: Analysis of the core team role in open source communities. In: 2011 International Conference on Complex, Intelligent and Software Intensive Systems (CISIS), pp. 109–114. IEEE (2011)
23. Levin, S., Yehudai, A.: Boosting automatic commit classification into maintenance activities by utilizing source code changes. In: Proceedings of the 13th International Conference on Predictive Models and Data Analytics in Software Engineering, Toronto, Canada, 8 November 2017, pp. 97–106 (2017)

Mining OSS Data

Process Mining for Process Conformance Checking in an OSS Project: An Empirical Research

Elia Kouzari[✉], Lazaros Sotiriadis, and Ioannis Stamelos

Department of Informatics, Aristotle University of Thessaloniki,
54124 Thessaloniki, Greece
ekouzari@csd.auth.gr

Abstract. With almost 20 years of research, Process Mining can now be considered to be in a mature phase allowing its application to a variety of sectors. In this article, the bug closure process that is followed by a community of an open source software project is investigated in order to perform process conformance checking. Actual data that reveal the process steps have been extracted from the project's Bugzilla database and have been used as input in Disco process mining tool. The data includes extracted information for more than 19,000 bugs for the past 15 years in a csv form, formatted appropriately to construct an event log suitable for process mining. The extracted models have been compared to the process described in the project's blogs and wikis by the community. The same models are also compared to the bug closure process that Bugzilla suggests to be used by the projects using this software for bug tracking purposes. The findings reveal that indeed the process followed in the OSS project is very similar to the declared one but variations do occur under specific circumstances. However, the process is not identical to the one proposed by Bugzilla suggesting that each OSS project can customize its processes in order to better address the needs of the project and the community. This empirical research highlights the importance of process mining in OSS projects in order to investigate the processes followed and identify outliers helping to standardize and improve the processes and enhance the collaboration among the members of the communities.

Keywords: Open source software · Process mining
Open source communities · Software event logs · Process conformance

1 Introduction

Scientific research has been focusing in the field of Process Mining, developing platforms, tools and algorithms for almost 20 years now. Process Mining is extensively applied in a variety of fields and sectors like healthcare, insurances, software etc. [1–5]. Dozens of algorithms can be applied in the context of process mining either on a standalone basis or through the platforms that have been designed to facilitate this.

The majority of applied research in this field focuses on process discovery since this minimizes the cost of understanding the current 'As-is' process [6]. However, a lot of

© IFIP International Federation for Information Processing 2018
Published by Springer International Publishing AG 2018. All Rights Reserved
I. Stamelos et al. (Eds.): OSS 2018, IFIP AICT 525, pp. 79–89, 2018.
https://doi.org/10.1007/978-3-319-92375-8_7

interest arises in the aspect of process conformance as well. According to van der Aalst [7] process discovery is the technique that takes an event log and produces a process map explaining the behavior recorded in the log. On the other hand, process conformance is the procedure where an existing process model is compared with an event log of the same process to indicate whether the reality, as recorded in the log, meets the proposed model and vice versa.

Kouzari and Stamelos [8] suggested that the application of process mining in open source software could reveal not only the variety of processes followed by open source communities but it could also help standardize or improve core activities like the way tasks are shared and bugs are closed. Given the fact that in Open Source Software there is a huge amount of process-relevant data publicly available online, OSS communities are a great opportunity to discover and analyze software processes. These data can be usually extracted from mailing lists, discussion forums, source repositories and binary release sections [9].

In this article, the authors proceed to process conformance checking of the bug reporting and closing process of a large Open Source Software project by examining the documentation of the project and extracting the process model that is believed to be followed against the 'As-is' process that is extracted from the event log. In addition, this process is also compared with the general Bugzilla guidelines for bug reporting and resolution.

The rest of the article is structured as follows: Sect. 2 describes the background of this work and poses the research question. Section 3 explains the methodology followed and Sect. 4 presents the findings of the research. Finally, Sect. 5 contains the discussion, conclusions and future work.

2 Background Work

2.1 Bugzilla

Bugzilla is an open source software system for bug tracking. It is currently the most widely used bug tracking system [10]. This bug tracker allows open source communities to handle the discovered bugs by facilitating the communication of problems effectively throughout the data management chain. This ensures that each reported bug is stored in the project's Bugzilla database along with each detail regarding its state and the steps taken or not towards its resolution.

The lifecycle of a bug in Bugzilla is illustrated in Fig. 1. This workflow can be customized to meet the needs of every community and every project using it as a back-tracking system. In Fig. 1 only the default bug statuses are shown.

The main process followed in Fig. 1 is as follows: When a bug is first reported in the system, its status changes to "UNCONFIRMED". The bug remains in this state until it receives a specific number of votes by community members that is indeed reproduced. By the time the votes are sufficient, the bug status changes to "NEW". A bug can automatically at first be set to "NEW" when the user/developer reporting it has the right to change its status. Following, the bug can be assigned to a specific developer or can be left

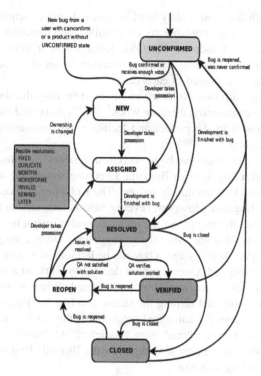

Fig. 1. The lifecycle of a bug in Bugzilla (source: https://wiki.documentfoundation.org/QA/Bugzilla/Fields/Status)

open for anyone to resolve it. At this moment, the status of the bug is set to "ASSIGNED". The developers resolve the bug, and a patch is sent for Quality Assurance (QA). When the QA tests are successful, the bug becomes "RESOLVED" and "VERIFIED". In case QA tests fail, the bug can be set to "REOPEN" and short after this to "ASSIGNED" or "RESOLVED" once again. A bug must be "CLOSED" by the person who first reported it. It is obvious that a lot of variations are also possible depending on the nature of the bug and the authority of the person who first reports it [11].

2.2 Koha Open Source Integrated Library System

Koha is a web-based open source ILS written in Perl and distributed under GNU General Public License[1]. With a very active community of developers around the world, Koha was first released in 2000 and since then it has gained wide acceptance, as it is utilized in hundreds of organizations (both in the governmental and private sector) around the world [12]. Koha interacts with a MySQL database and supports a variety of

---

[1] https://koha-community.org.

library activities with the most widely used being cataloguing, acquisition, circulation and administration [13]. Being able to be installed and function in all Operating Systems (Linux, Unix, Windows, MacOS), Koha offers a very configurable and adaptable user interface, allowing each organization to set it up accordingly to the procedures and policies followed in each case.

For bug tracking purposes, Koha maintains its own Bugzilla database. Since the project has an active community, there are wikis[2], IRC[3] (chats) and blogs[4] that describe the procedures followed in the project and facilitate the communication and coordination of the community.

The Koha blog describes the bugs workflow process as follows: A user or a developer can report a bug through Bugzilla. Everyone should file a bug report, even developers who intend to immediately fix one. The Koha project does not actively use the Priority field in Bugzilla. However, severity field is indicated to be important. For this reason, along with the bug report the user has to also assign the severity of a bug. For unclear situations "normal" severity is suggested. Once a bug is reported it is assigned to a developer. At this stage, a bug can be left idle, if no one takes action on it, and it can also be reassigned. Once a person decides to work on a bug, he has to first accept it and update its status from New to Assigned. When a solution to a bug is available, a patch is submitted turning the status of a bug to "Patch-Sent". The Koha Release Manager evaluates the submitted patch and if the patch works it is marked as "pushed". A resolved bug is altered from "Assigned" to "Resolved - Fixed". Koha Wiki clearly suggests that the user should review the Bugzilla Bug Writing Guidelines prior to submitting a bug to Koha.

Based on all these characteristics and its large and active community of developers and users, Koha is considered at the time as an ideal candidate in the context of this research.

2.3   Research Question

In Sect. 2.2 the Koha bugs workflow is presented as declared in the official pages of Koha project. In terms of process mining, the abovementioned process is considered the "As-Is" process followed. Since Koha is an open source project its data and code are available through the tools used by the community. It would be of great interest to mine the actual process followed to resolve the bugs using data from the project's Bugzilla database and perform process conformance checking. As a result, the research question investigated in this paper is the following:

> RQ: Does the community of Koha Open Source ILS conforms to the bug resolution process described in the project's pages or not? If not, what is the actual process followed?

---

[2] https://wiki.koha-community.org.

[3] https://koha-community.org/get-involved/irc/.

[4] https://www.myacpl.org/koha/.

3 Methodology

Anyone can register in the Bugzilla page for Koha project in order to view all the bugs listed along with the history of each bug. The main Bugzilla page illustrates all current bugs with their current state. In order to get all the actions performed for the resolution of a bug, one must locate a bug and then using the bug id provided he may visit the specific page that illustrates in tabular format the actions taken so far for it.

The methodology shown in Fig. 2 was used to gather all information for all bugs listed in Koha project so far for cleaning/transformation of data for process mining.

Fig. 2. The methodology followed in this article for process conformance check

3.1 Locate Relevant Data

First, the relevant data was located in the Bugzilla database. Using Bash scripting and Wget tool, the data was extracted in html form and appended in a single html file. This procedure gathered historical data for 19,311 bugs between 15/06/2002 and 14/12/2017.

3.2 Data Preparation

Html2text was used to remove any text formatted from the gathered data. In addition, to be able to further format the data in a csv form and to create a tabular representation suitable of an event log for process mining, further scripting was required (grep, icony, recode, sed, tr, cat, uniq, sort, echo). As a result, a csv file with 359,395 records was created containing information for 19,311 bugs.

3.3 Clean Data

For each record, the following columns were present: Event_Id, Bug_Id, Bug_Description, User_Email, Action_datetime, Action_Type and Action_Data. Although this file contained all the required columns to be used as an event log [14], further cleaning of the file had to be performed in order to keep those data that would reveal the process followed for bug resolution. While the first 5 columns reveal their role, columns Action_Type and Action_Data were used to keep the most important information. For every variable mentioned in column Action_Type, a different set of values was used in column Action_Data. After analysis of each variable in the Action_Type column and taking in mind the described process followed for bug resolution in Koha Blogs and Wikis, the csv file was filtered to keep the records for the following variables of Action_Type column: Status, Priority, Severity, Resolution.

Table 1 below presents the Action_Data values per Action_Type selected for filtering.

Table 1. Action_Data values per Action_Type variable

Action_Type variable	Corresponding Action_Data values
Priority	P1, P1-high, P2, P3, P4, P5, P5-low, PATCH-Sent, PATCH-Sent-P5
Resolution	–, DUPLICATE, FIXED, INVALID, LATER, MOVED, REMIND, WISHLIST, WONTFIX, WORKSFORME
Severity	blocker, critical, enhancement, major, minor, newfeature, normal, trivial
Status	ASSIGNED, BLOCKED, CLOSED, REOPENED, RESOLVED, UNCONFIRMED, VERIFIED Failed QA, InDiscussion, Needs Signoff, NEW, Passed QA, Patch doesn't Apply, Pushed by Module Maintainer, Pushed for QA, Pushed to Master, Pushed to Stable, Signed Off

Finally, a csv file with 97,372 records for 19,311 bugs was extracted that was used as an event log for Process Mining. The rest of the steps that concern the process mining and the process conformance check are presented in Sect. 4.

4 Findings

4.1 Process Mining

For Process Mining, Disco[5] process mining tool was used. Initially the event log was used as input to Disco. Prior to the process mining, the columns of the event log had to be assigned as Case_ID (Bug_Id), Resource (User_Email), Timestamp (Action_Date-time), and Activity (Action_Type and Action_Data). Event_ID and Bug_Description were ignored as they had no role in affecting the bug resolution process.

The event log was then used for process mining revealing a "spaghetti model" that it was impossible to highlight useful information regarding the process mined.

The extracted model highlighted the most used statuses but it was hard to analyze and compare to the suggested process. To extract safest conclusions, 47,9% of the most common activities of the diagram were filtered creating a new, clearer process model.

Despite the second process model was significantly more clear than the first one, it was clearly affected by the status of the first 283 bugs in the event log. This was proved by Status/Closed that was shown to be the first step of the process (and the last) for the majority of the cases. With further analysis of the event log, the authors noticed that for the first 283 bugs only a record indicating that a bug's status was set to "CLOSED" existed. This could affect the actual process followed since no history for the resolution process of these bugs was available. In the next session, this is further explained.[6]

---

[5] https://fluxicon.com/disco/.

[6] Additional information on the first process models extracted by the event log and discussed in this section are available online at http://switch.csd.auth.gr/.

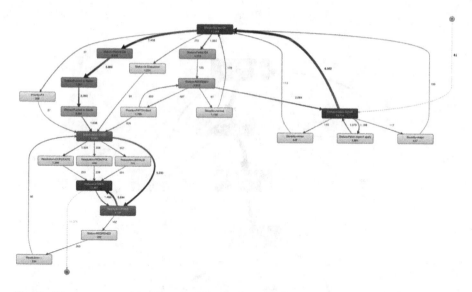

Fig. 3. The process model extracted when the first 283 bugs are removed from the event log

A new event log, ignoring the first 283 bugs was used as a new input with the same parameters in Disco. The process map created for the new event log is shown in Fig. 3.

In the diagram of Fig. 3 a clearer process is extracted. The dark process steps indicate the most common statuses and the darker arrows indicate the most frequent transitions from these process steps. One can identify from this diagram that the most common process path followed is the following:

Needs Sign Off -> Signed Off -> Passed QA -> Pushed to Master -> Pushed to Stable -> Resolved -> Resolution/Fixed -> Closed.

All of the process steps mentioned are associated with the value "Status" of the Action_Type field, except from Fixed that is associated with the value "Resolution" of the Action_Type field.

The same event log was inserted into Disco, keeping only dimensions "Status" and "Resolution" of the column "Action_Type". To extract a more precise model, focused on the resolved bugs, an endpoint filter was applied to the event log. The end event value was set to "FIXED" keeping 10% of the cases and 17% of events. As a result, the process model of Fig. 4 was produced.

In this model, the process is almost identical to Fig. 3 with an exception towards the end of the process. However, the bug resolution process remains unaltered even though a significant number of cases are not included indicating that the community is consistent to the steps taken to resolve a bug.

4.2 Process Conformance Check

By observing Figs. 3 and 4 one can conclude that the discovered process is very similar to the one described in the community's blogs and wikis. By these means we can

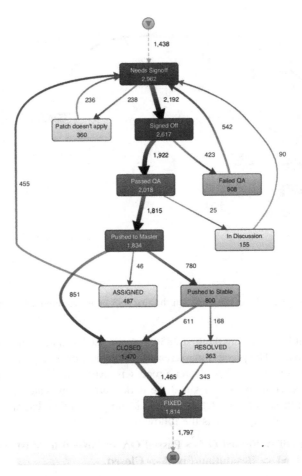

Fig. 4. A process model extracted for all bugs that are FIXED

clearly say that the Koha community does conform to the process suggested for bug resolution.

Focusing on Fig. 3, where the model contains more cases since it includes all the bugs and not just those that have been fixed, it is obvious that there is a main process, identical to the one proposed by the community but this is not exclusive. There are some exceptions, some process variations that are obvious. Disco has the ability to reveal these paths along with their frequency. As a result, Table 2 presents the 5 most frequent process variances that do not follow the proposed guidelines for bug resolution.

4,14% of the time, a bug is automatically Resolved and Closed. This happens either because it is an old bug and no other relevant historical data is available, either because the person who identifies a bug automatically fixes it. However, it is recommended by the community to report each and every bug even if that means the bug is instantly resolved. For this reason, the abovementioned path does not conform to the bug resolution process.

Table 2. The 5 most frequent process variances that do not conform to the process guidelines

Process Variance	Frequency
RESOLVED -> FIXED -> CLOSED	4,14%
PATCH-Sent -> RESOLVED -> FIXED -> CLOSED	1,64%
ASSIGNED -> PATCH-Sent -> RESOLVED -> FIXED -> CLOSED	1,42%
Needs SignOff -> Failed QA	0,37%
ASSIGNED -> RESOLVED -> FIXED -> CLOSED	0,32%

The same seems to happen with the rest of the process variances. In all of the variances, either the bug is not set to Needs SignOff from the beginning of the bug resolution process or several process steps are omitted until the bug is set to Closed.

In the Discussion session below this is further discussed and compared to the Bugzilla suggested process for bug resolution.

5 Discussion and Future Work

The event log created by the Bugzilla database of Koha OSS ILS revealed that the community does follow in practice the bug resolution process described in the official documentation of the project. However, there are some cases where this is not true. It was mentioned earlier that the first 283 bugs did not include any other information rather than a record indicating they were closed. This indicates that 15 years back, when the project was not in a mature phase the community was using another bug resolution process. This might have happened due to a limited number of bugs or due to the lack of mature bug tracking tools. Starting from bug with bugID = 284 there is precise information about the bug and all of its states throughout the resolution process.

At the same time, one can observe that although the community follows a specific process for bug resolution, there are some process variances that do not conform to the proposed guidelines. This illustrates that in an open source software community there is freedom to act and modify procedures that are not as strict as in proprietary software. A developer might decide to act based on his knowledge and experience in a specific situation.

Comparing the bug resolution process of Koha with the proposed guidelines for bug resolution by Bugzilla it is obvious that there are a lot of differences. With a closer look a correlation is identified in some of the states. The RESOLVED status of Bugzilla corresponds to Needs SignOff of Koha and VERIFIED status of Bugzilla corresponds to Signed Off of Koha. This reveals that open source software tools can be freely customized to address the needs of each community of users and developers. At the same time, each OSS community is free to investigate how OSS tools can be modified to be used in favor of their own processes.

As stated earlier, Koha is a very active and serious community that is well organized. In addition, the project contains excellent documentation that the users can address in order to find answers to their questions. For even better communications there are IRC chat rooms where users and developers can further discuss any related issues. The documentation of the project and the good communication between the members of Koha community is illustrated in the process conformance check performed in this article.

However, other communities, less structured and active might face a variety of problems in the management of their processes. Process mining not only can highlight problems in the existing processes followed by OSS communities but it can also use projects like Koha as a benchmark to reveal aspects of processes that can be further improved in other projects. Nonetheless, the extracted process models can be used for predictions regarding the future of a given project in terms of survival, software quality and maturity.

Recently, Bugzilla released newer documentation containing a newer version of the lifecycle of a Bugzilla bug. It would be of great interest to investigate projects following the new guidelines for bug resolution and also see which of the projects currently following the former guidelines will decide to modify their processes and the effect this will bring to process efficiency. Future work includes further empirical research on process conformance for OSS projects. Especially for bug management, the newly released Bugzilla process needs to be taken into account.

References

1. Rojas, E., Munoz-Gama, J., Sepulveda, M., Capurro, D.: Process mining in healthcare: a literature review. J. Biomed. Inf. **61**, 224–236 (2016)
2. Partington, A., Wynn, M.T., Suriadi, S., Ouyang, C., Karnon, J.: Process mining for clinical processes: a comparative analysis of four Australian hospitals. ACM Trans. Manag. Inf. Syst. **5**(4), 1–19 (2015)
3. Delias, P., Doumpos, M., Manolitzas, P., Grigoroudis, E., Matsatsinis, N.: Clustering healthcare processes with a robust approach. In: 26th European Conference on Operational Research, November 2015, pp. 1–6 (2013)
4. De Weerdt, J., Schupp, A., Vanderloock, A., Baesens, B.: Process mining for the multi-faceted analysis of business processes—a case study in a financial services organization. Comput. Ind. **64**(1), 57–67 (2013)
5. Rubin, V.A., Mitsyuk, A.A., Lomazova, I.A., van der Aalst, W.M.: Process mining can be applied to software too! In: Proceedings of the 8th ACM/IEEE International Symposium on Empirical Software Engineering and Measurement, p. 57. ACM, September 2014
6. Rozinat, A., Gunther, C.W.: The added value of process mining. BPTrends (2014). https://www.bptrends.com/the-added-value-of-process-mining/. Accessed 16 Jan 2018
7. Van Der Aalst, W.: Data science in action. Process Mining, 2nd edn, pp. 25–52. Springer, Heidelberg (2016). https://doi.org/10.1007/978-3-662-49851-4_2
8. Kouzari, E., Stamelos, I.: Process mining in software events of open source software projects. In: 2nd International Symposium & 24th National Conference on Operational Research, HELORS 2013, 25–27 September 2013, Athens, Greece (2013)
9. Jensen, C., Scacchi, W.: Data mining for software process discovery in open source software development communities. In: Proceedings of Workshop on Mining Software Repositories, pp. 96–100, May 2004
10. Barnson, M.P., Steenhagen, J., Weissman, T.: The Bugzilla Guide-2.17.5 Development Release. The Bugzilla Team (2003)

11. Akbarinasaji, S., Caglayan, B., Bener, A.: Predicting bug-fixing time: a replication study using an open source software project. J. Syst. Softw. **136**, 173–186 (2018)
12. Kouzari, E., Stamelos, I.: Process Mining applied on library information system usage-A case study (2017). Manuscript submitted for publication
13. Macan, B., Fernandez, V.G., Stojanovski, J.: Open source solutions for libraries: ABCD vs Koha. Program **47**(2), 136–154 (2013)
14. Van Der Aalst, W.M., Dustdar, S.: Process mining put into context. IEEE Internet Comput. **16**(1), 82–86 (2012)

Ranking Source Code Static Analysis Warnings for Continuous Monitoring of FLOSS Repositories

Athos Ribeiro[1]([⊠]), Paulo Meirelles[1,2], Nelson Lago[1], and Fabio Kon[1]

[1] FLOSS Competence Center, University of São Paulo, São Paulo, Brazil
{athoscr,lago,fabio.kon}@ime.usp.br
[2] Department of Health Informatics, Federal University of São Paulo,
São Paulo, Brazil
paulo@softwarelivre.org

Abstract. Performing source code static analysis during the software development cycle is a difficult task. There are different static analyzers available, and each of them usually works better in a small subset of problems, making it hard to choose a single tool. Combining the analysis of different tools solves this problem, but brings about other problems, namely the generated false positives and a large amount of unsorted alarms. This paper presents *kiskadee*, a system to support the usage of static analysis during software development by providing carefully ranked static analysis reports. First, it runs multiple static analyzers on the source code. Then, using a classification model, the potential bugs detected by the static analyzers are ranked based on their importance, with critical flaws ranked first, and potential false positives ranked last. Our experimental results show that, on average, when inspecting warnings ranked by *kiskadee*, one hits 5.2 times less false positives before each bug than when using a randomly sorted warning list.

Keywords: Static analysis · Software quality · False positives
Free software · Open Source Software

1 Introduction

Source code static analysis is a valuable technique to support software assurance. In theory, it can explore abstractions of all possible program behaviors, which is not feasible with software testing [11]. Thus, it can find software bugs using a complementary approach to automated tests.

However, the fundamental problems of static analysis are undecidable [15], so approximations must be made, leading static analyzers to generate false alarms or to miss occurrences of software flaws. *False positives* are produced when a static analyzer processes bug-free code and reports it as buggy code. The tool may also miss actual bugs when it processes buggy code and report it as a

I. Stamelos et al. (Eds.): OSS 2018, IFIP AICT 525, pp. 90–101, 2018.
https://doi.org/10.1007/978-3-319-92375-8_8

bug-free code [5] (*false negatives*). Since static analysis enumerates many execution paths, static analyzer reports frequently contain an excessive amount of information, which often includes a substantial amount of false positives.

The high amount of information generated combined with a significant false alarm rate hinder the inclusion of static analyzers in the software development cycle. Moreover, false positives require manual inspection, which increases the effort of analyzing tool reports [10,17] and may even cause static analyzers to be discarded as irrelevant [14]. Literature suggests that using multiple static analyzers improves static analysis coverage [5] since some tools perform better in specific tasks due to different analysis methods. This practice may decrease the number of false negatives but is likely to generate more false positives as the number of tools used increases.

In this study, we present *kiskadee*, a system designed to support *continuous* static analysis in software repositories using multiple static analyzers to generate reports using a common output language. By running multiple static analyzers on the same code base, kiskadee reduces the number of false negatives in the analysis. To address false positives, kiskadee ranks warnings in the static analysis reports using the AdaBoost algorithm's [8] classification probabilities. Warnings with the highest rank are more likely to indicate real and more critical software flaws and warnings with the lowest rank are more likely to be false positives. In this context, **a warning is a single issue produced by a static analyzer**. Finally, kiskadee stores the ranked static analysis reports in a database. The ranked reports in the database are made available to kiskadee users, providing them with more accurate data and favoring the use of static analysis.

2   Related Work

Muske and Serebrenik [16] provided an overview of different techniques on how to handle static analysis alarms. In this survey, the authors classified part of the techniques as the *automatic post-processing of the alarms*, which includes ranking or classification of alarms. We assessed the studies and techniques under the aforementioned classification to better position the present work.

Previous studies show that the most relevant features for training accurate machine learning models to arbitrate about the positiveness of static analysis alarms are extracted from properties intrinsic to the analyzed project, namely the project change history, function and file names, and even the name of the programmer who introduced the change that triggered the alarm [9,12,13,20,21]. Since these project-specific features are in great part responsible for the high accuracy of the models proposed up to now, a model trained on such features cannot be readily used to query about alarms generated for other projects, hampering the general availability of the model in automated post-analysis tools.

Ruthruff et al. [20] propose a method to predict if a warning is an actionable fault, i.e., if it is not a false positive and if a programmer should fix it. It uses a screening approach for model building that discards metrics with low predictive power. Among the factors used to predict false positives, which happened 85%

of the times in the authors study, are the priority given by the static analyzer, the file length, and code indentation, suggesting that the authors performed additional code analysis to extract factors from the code.

As discussed, related works emphasize that the most important characteristics to arbitrate on static analysis warnings positiveness are internal to the analyzed project. Our study differs from them by assessing static analysis warnings only with the information present in the warnings themselves, therefore, the approach in itself usually produces poor results. To compensate for this, we use multiple static analyzers with kiskadee to generate more information and correlate the information provided by them to assess the correctness of a given warning better. Since this strategy still might result in a low-quality classifier, we turn to ensemble techniques to generate and combine multiple weak classifiers generated this way into a stronger one [19].

3   Continuous Static Analysis with kiskadee

In Free/Libre and Open Source Software (FLOSS) projects, a common source of bug reports are the GNU/Linux distributions. These distributions ship thousands of software projects, which they call packages. Distribution developers refer to the projects that maintain the software they ship in the distribution as *upstream*. It is not unusual for distribution developers to report bugs in upstream projects or to send patches to fix bugs found by their distribution users or during the packaging process.

By continuously running multiple static analyzers in several of these packages, i.e., once for each version of the package, we can create a database of static analysis reports on software projects of different sizes and application domains. Developers can then use the information in this database to find and act on software flaws.

We chose to use GNU/Linux distributions due to the high amount of software packages available and the well-defined and documented interfaces they provide to download the latest versions of these packages. It is also an advantage that the cultural norm for GNU/Linux distribution developers is to report (and often propose fixes for) bugs. Therefore, using their repositories for this work may provide a broader user base for the tools and techniques developed in this research.

To continuously run static analysis on software packages and handle the false alarms generated by these analyses, we developed *kiskadee*. Figure 1 represents kiskadee's architecture overview, where the numbers denote its execution flow. In steps (1) and (2), kiskadee monitors software repositories for new releases. In step (3), kiskadee downloads the source code of each new software version in a repository it monitors and runs a set of predefined static analyzers on it in step (4). In step (5), kiskadee translates each static analyzer report to a common warnings report format. This common format is needed because each static analyzer defines its unique format to report warnings. In step (6), kiskadee ranks the warnings based on their probability of being real bugs, where warnings

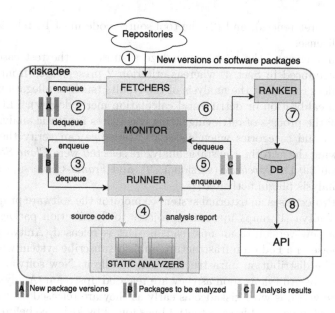

Fig. 1. kiskadee design overview.

on the top have a higher probability of being real bugs and warnings on the bottom are more likely to be false positives. This ranking step is performed with a classification model, described in Sect. 4. The ranked warnings are then saved in a database in step (7), using kiskadee's common warning report format. Finally, in step (8), kiskadee provides an API consumed by a visualization tool to display the ranked warnings filtered by package versions. The information provided can be used either by distribution developers to evaluate and report possible bugs upstream or by upstream developers themselves. Researchers can also use kiskadee's database in different contexts.

FLOSS development communities have been discussing a common static analysis report output format. The Fedora Project Static Analysis Special Interest Group [3] designed a tool to run static analyzers during the package build process [2]. Although the tool itself is in its early development stages and not ready for usage in production, the developers discussed [4] a common report format for the static analyzers in their mailing lists. After a few iterations, with Debian Project developers collaboration, they created *Firehose*, a complete definition of a common warnings report format for static analyzers and a set of tools to generate, parse, and verify this format. We use *Firehose* as kiskadee's common warning report format, eliminating the need to design a new format and to develop the tools to handle it, like parsers and generators.

kiskadee was run with three static analysis tools to generate the warnings data set for our experiments. The Criteria to select the tools were: (1) The tool must be able to examine C/C++ code for security flaws (e.g., buffer overflows, null pointer dereferences); and (2) the tool source code must be released under an FLOSS license.

Criterion 1 ensures the tool can analyze a subset of the test cases in our data set, introduced in Sect. 4, whereas criterion 2 preserves us from disputes by tool vendors regarding the analysis of the results (such as allegations of suboptimal tool calibration or detrimental calculation methodology). FLOSS tools also simplify the process of retrieving string constructs for static analyzer warning messages and categories when necessary, since we can verify their source code. Following the criteria, the static analyzers selected were *Clang Static Analyzer* (version 3.9.1), *Cppcheck* (version 1.79), and *Frama-C* (version 1.14 with the value analysis plugin activated).

Fedora Project uses an external system to monitor the software projects they distribute. Anitya [1] maps upstream projects to distribution package names. Whenever a new version of an upstream project is released, Anitya publishes the new release in a Fedora infrastructure publish-subscribe system where other systems in the distribution infrastructure can handle it. New software versions are published by Anitya as soon as they are released upstream. Analyzing these new software versions with kiskadee as early as they are released allows the distribution developers to address potential bugs found by kiskadee before the software is shipped to final users. Therefore, kiskadee monitors packages by reading information published by Anitya in the Fedora infrastructure publish-subscribe system.

kiskadee can point to other software repositories as well through its plugin architecture (kiskadee's fetchers). Each fetcher must implement functions that define which repository to monitor, how to monitor it, and which static analyzers to run for that repository. Hence, we can extend *kiskadee* to run different static analyzers for different software repositories or GNU/Linux distributions.

4   Ranking Warnings

To create and train a predictive model, before analyzing project repositories, we ran kiskadee on Juliet [6], a publicly available test suite composed of a collection of source code snippets with specific flaws injected in known locations, which facilitates the assessment of static analysis tools. By running kiskadee on Juliet (without the ranking step), we obtained the analysis reports (a set of warnings) in the Firehose format, easing further processing. Then, we checked whether each single warning matched one of the injected flaws in the test suite, labeling them either as true positive or false positive. After the labeling step, we extracted the characteristics used to train our model. These did not include any characteristics from the analyzed source code and project history, which tend to be the most relevant ones when predicting warnings positiveness, as shown in previous works [12,21]. By not using the characteristics aforementioned, we can produce a general model that can be used with any project without prior knowledge about it, eliminating the need to perform the expensive model training step for each project one may want to analyze. This means that the model obtained during the preparation of this paper can be used directly by kiskadee in production to rank warnings in any given project.

To compensate for not using the most relevant characteristics pointed by previous works, we used an ensemble learning method [19] to train several weak classifiers, which were then able to vote about the positiveness of new examples. Finally, instead of just classifying new examples as true and false positives, we ranked the warnings based on their probabilities of being real flaws, where the top entries were more likely to be of interest, and the bottom entries were more likely to be false positives.

The results obtained were auspicious: using three static analyzers with a false positive rate of 0.61 when aggregating all three tool warnings in a single report, we achieved an accuracy of 0.8 over the test set. This accuracy was not too distant from the state of the art (0.85 [20]), which depends on characteristics specific to the project being analyzed to train their model. Since our model does not depend on project-specific features, it may receive any project as input without the need to train a different model for each analyzed project.

The following steps describe the techniques and tools used to collect and prepare the data to train our model, as well as the methodology used to train the model and rank the static analysis warnings.

Step 1: Choosing Data Sources. A data set of labeled static analysis warnings may be obtained by running static analyzers on previously selected source code and matching the triggered warnings with actual software defects, labeling the warnings as true or false positives. The source code used for extracting the data set may consist of real-world software or synthetic test cases, i.e., programs written with intentional defects.

Juliet [6] is a synthetic C/C++ test suite created by the United States National Security Agency (NSA) and distributed by the National Institute of Standards and Technology (NIST) under the public domain. It is composed of 61,387 test cases covering 118 different software flaw categories. Each test case is a code section with an instance of a specific flaw (to capture true positives) and an additional section with a correct, fixed instance of that previous flawed section (to capture false positives). Juliet also includes a user guide with instructions on how to assess and label static analysis tool warnings generated over its test cases. We use Juliet version 1.2 to generate our data set.

Before examining Juliet with kiskadee static analysis tools, we pruned the test suite to prevent analysis of test cases that depend on constructs of specific operating systems or external libraries. Table 1 shows the total number of test cases in Juliet before pruning and the number of test cases after the pruning step for both C and C++. The latter are the tests examined by the static analyzers for alarms generation, consisting of 39,100 C/C++ test cases.

Step 2: Collecting Labeled Warnings from Multiple Static Analyzers. Based on Juliet documentation, we process each file in the remaining test cases to produce a list (L) with information on whether a static analysis warning for a given location should be labeled as true positive or false positive. Then, we run each static analyzer on the pruned test suite to generate the static analyses

Table 1. Number of Juliet test cases.

	Before pruning	After pruning
C	36,078	22,459
C++	25,309	16,641
Total	61,387	39,100

Table 2. Warnings generated per tool.

Tool	Warnings
Clang static analyzer	37,229
Cppcheck	124,025
Frama-C	120,573
Total	281,827

Table 3. Labeled warnings per tool.

Tool	Warnings	TP	FP	FP Rate	Precision
Clang analyzer	6207	984	5223	0.84	0.16
Cppcheck	4035	314	3721	0.92	0.08
Frama-C	15717	8892	6825	0.43	0.57
Aggregated tools	25959	10190	15769	**0.61**	**0.39**

reports. Table 2 shows the total number of warnings generated, before discarding warnings whose labeling step cannot be automated based on Juliet documentation. By matching each warning produced by the static analyzers with the corresponding flaw categories covered by Juliet, we can use the list L to produce labels for each warning.

This set of labeled warnings can finally be examined to extract a training set from it, as discussed next. Table 3 summarizes the findings of the static analyzers on the test cases, including the number of true and false positives generated (TP and FP, respectively), the false positive rates, and the precision for each tool and for the whole kiskadee report, i.e., the aggregated reports composed of the warnings of all tools.

Step 3: Extracting Features from Labeled Warnings. We obtain the features used to train our classifier from the set of labeled warnings. Here, a feature is any characteristic that can be attributed to a warning in the data set. To select relevant features for false and positive alarm classification, we refer to previous studies that also rely on characteristics extracted from alarms and source code to classify alarms [9,12,13,20]. For instance, Kremenek et al. [13] demonstrate that the tool warning positiveness is highly correlated to code locality.

We extract our set of features by processing the aggregated report of labeled warnings. While we can infer the name of the tool that triggered a warning, the programming language analyzed, and the severity of the warning by looking at a single warning at a time, other features require processing the whole aggregated report to be extracted. Namely, these are (1) the number of times the same location was pointed as flawed in the report, (2) the number of warnings triggered around the location of a given warning (e.g., warnings for locations at most 3 lines away from the current warning), (3) the category of the software flaw suggested by the warning, (4) which other static analyzers generated warnings for the same location, and (5) the number of warnings generated for the same file the current warning is pointing to.

Step 4: Training Decision Trees with AdaBoost. Given the data collected, we build a prediction model to classify each triggered warning as being a true positive or a false positive. The classification results may also be used to rank the warnings, as we describe in Step 5.

Since we do not post-analyze the source code nor inspect the project history of the analyzed software projects, which are shown to be the best places to look for features to arbitrate on source code static analysis warnings positiveness, we turn to ensemble learning methods to train several weak classifiers with our feature set. These weak classifiers combined can then arbitrate on new examples together, composing a stronger classifier with lower error [19].

One widely used ensemble learning method is boosting [19], whose main idea is to run a weak learning algorithm several times in different distributions of the training set to generate and combine various weak classifiers into a stronger one. For this study, we use the AdaBoost algorithm [8], a more general version of the original boosting algorithm [18].

The AdaBoost algorithm works with any given base learner. We use a decision tree learning algorithm as our base learner because we have both categorical and non-categorical features in our data set, and decision trees can work with both, without the need to pre-process the data set. Furthermore, as shown in the literature, decision trees perform well with AdaBoost [7].

We divide our data set into a training set and a test set. The training set is built by randomly selecting 75% of the examples labeled as true positives and 75% of the examples labeled as false positives from the features data set. We then proceed to train our predictive model using 10-fold cross-validation with the training set. We perform the 10-fold cross-validation technique with different values for **T** (number of weak classifiers trained) in AdaBoost. We then compare the average performance of the classifiers obtained for each distinct value of **T** validated in this manner and use the best model trained during the cross-validation for that **T** to classify the test set.

Step 5: Ranking Static Analysis Warnings. We use the model trained in Step 4 to rank the warnings in a static analysis report based on the model classification probabilities. We reorder the warnings in a list according to the probability of the warning being a true positive, where warnings with higher probabilities are ranked in the top of the list and warnings with lower probabilities of being true positives are arranged in the bottom of the list. This way, a programmer inspecting the ranked static analysis report may examine only the top warnings in the list up to a given threshold, assuming a certain risk of missing true positives. Alternatively, he/she may stop inspecting warnings when false positives start to abound.

5   Results and Discussion

Although we use a binary classification algorithm to train our model, we do not need to limit ourselves to a direct binary classification; it is also possible to use the trained predictive model to rank warnings according to their expected relevance. Next, we present and discuss the results obtained with kiskadee's ranking approach. While comparing our results with other ranking approaches or, at least, with the ranking order of each tool would be ideal, these would not be feasible. In the first case, we would have to replicate other works with our data set; in the second, it would not make sense to compare the results of a single tool to the aggregate results. Therefore, we chose to compare kiskadee with a random ranking algorithm.

To evaluate our ranking performance over the test set, we refer to the methodology presented by Kremenek et al. [13], which we describe below.

We define $S(R)$ to be the sum of FP_j, the cumulative number of false positive warnings found before reaching the j_{th} true positive warning when navigating a ranked list (starting from the first entry) ordered by a ranking algorithm R.

$$S(R) = \sum_{j=1}^{N_{tp}} FP_j \tag{1}$$

It is worth observing that $S(R) = 0$ for an optimal ranking algorithm and $S(R) = N_{tp} \times N_{fp}$ for the worst ranking algorithm, where N_{tp} and N_{fp} are the total number of true positive warnings and false positive warnings in the list, respectively.

We then define the average of the cumulative number of false positive warnings found before reaching each true positive warning, FP_{avg} (Eq. 2).

$$FP_{avg} = \frac{S(R)}{N_{tp}} \tag{2}$$

Finally, we measure the performance ratio of our ranking algorithm against a random ranking algorithm, which shuffles the list of warnings, with Eq. (3).

$$Performance = \frac{FP_{avg}(random)}{FP_{avg}(\text{AdaBoost ranking})} \tag{3}$$

In a perfect ranking situation, the first false positive occurrence would be positioned after the last true positive occurrence, therefore, $FP_{avg} = 0$. For our test set, in the worst case scenario, one would hit all the false positives before finding the first true positive. Leading to $FP_{avg} = 3942$. When applying a random ranking algorithm, we found $FP_{avg} = 1992$, while, for kiskadee's ranking approach, $FP_{avg} = 380$ over our test set.

The median kiskadee model performance over random, as proposed by Kremenek et al. [13], was 5.2, which indicates that, on average, one hits 5.2 times more false positives before each true positive with a random ranked warning list than one would if using the proposed ranking. Figure 2 shows the number

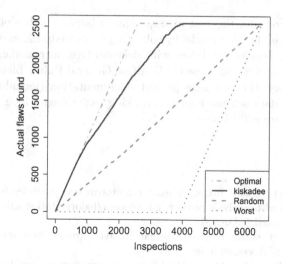

Fig. 2. Number of actual flaws found in top-down inspection of lists ranked with different approaches.

of real flaws found in a ranked list per inspected entries (warnings) for different ranking models applied to the test set: *optimal*, where all the real flaws are in the top of the list; *worst*, where all the false positives are in the top of the list; *random*, where the entries are randomly shuffled in a list; and *model*, which represents the ranking model proposed for kiskadee.

As Fig. 2 shows, kiskadee's model outperforms the random ranking algorithm by presenting all software flaws in the test set after 3990 inspections, while the random ranking algorithm presents software flaws in a linear relation with the number of inspections, where the last few real software flaws in the test set are only presented in the end of the list, after 6486 inspections.

6 Conclusion

Different from related works, kiskadee's ranking approach does not use features based on the analyzed project intrinsic properties for model training, namely, source code change history and code metrics. Consequently, by smoothly decreasing the classification accuracy, the model obtained can be used successfully with any given software project. This is a compelling trade-off to enable kiskadee to analyze and rank any project given as input, allowing the continuous monitoring and analysis of different software repositories, such as the ones provided by GNU/Linux distributions.

kiskadee can be used to reduce the cost of inspecting false alarms by setting a minimum value for the rate in which real flaws are found per inspection in a ranked list (i.e., a confidence level). When the rate of real flaws per inspections drops below that level, one could stop the inspection for that warning list. Interesting future works include studying confidence levels and the trade-off between loss of information and the cost of inspecting a larger number of false alarms, improving the classification model by collecting users feedback, and investigating other algorithms besides AdaBoost with decision trees as classifiers.

kiskadee is licensed under the GNU Affero General Public License. Its development repository, the complete project documentation (including UI screenshots), and the data set used for the ranking experiments here presented are available at pagure.io/kiskadee.

References

1. Anitya project website. https://release-monitoring.org. Accessed 5 Jan 2018
2. Fedora mock-with-analysis project. github.com/fedora-static-analysis/mock-with-analysis. Accessed 5 Jan 2018
3. Fedora project static analysis special interest group. fedoraproject.org/wiki/StaticAnalysis. Accessed 5 Jan 2018
4. Firehose mailing list archives. http://lists.fedoraproject.org/archives/list/firehose-devel@lists.fedoraproject.org. Accessed 5 Jan 2018
5. Black, P.E.: Static analyzers in software engineering. J. Defense Softw. Eng. **22**(3), 16–17 (2009)
6. Boland, T., Black, P.E.: Juliet 1.1 C/C++ and Java test suite. Computer **45**(10), 88–90 (2012)
7. Drucker, H., Cortes, C.: Boosting decision trees. In: Advances in Neural Information Processing Systems, pp. 479–485 (1996)
8. Freund, Y., Schapire, R., Abe, N.: A short introduction to boosting. J. Jpn. Soc. Artif. Intell. **14**(771–780), 1612 (1999)
9. Heckman, S., Williams, L.: A model building process for identifying actionable static analysis alerts. In: International Conference on Software Testing Verification and Validation, ICST 2009, pp. 161–170. IEEE (2009)
10. Heckman, S.S.: Adaptively ranking alerts generated from automated static analysis. Crossroads **14**(1), 7 (2007)
11. Hovemeyer, D., Pugh, W.: Finding bugs is easy. SIGPLAN Not. **39**(12), 92–106 (2004). https://doi.acm.org/10.1145/1052883.1052895
12. Jung, Y., Kim, J., Shin, J., Yi, K.: Taming false alarms from a domain-unaware C analyzer by a Bayesian statistical post analysis. In: Hankin, C., Siveroni, I. (eds.) SAS 2005. LNCS, vol. 3672, pp. 203–217. Springer, Heidelberg (2005). https://doi.org/10.1007/11547662_15
13. Kremenek, T., Ashcraft, K., Yang, J., Engler, D.: Correlation exploitation in error ranking. ACM SIGSOFT Softw. Eng. Notes **29**, 83–93 (2004)
14. Kremenek, T., Engler, D.: Z-ranking: using statistical analysis to counter the impact of static analysis approximations. In: Cousot, R. (ed.) SAS 2003. LNCS, vol. 2694, pp. 295–315. Springer, Heidelberg (2003). https://doi.org/10.1007/3-540-44898-5_16
15. Landi, W.: Undecidability of static analysis. ACM Lett. Prog. Lang. Syst. (LOPLAS) **1**(4), 323–337 (1992). http://dl.acm.org/citation.cfm?id=161494.161501
16. Muske, T., Serebrenik, A.: Survey of approaches for handling static analysis alarms. In: 2016 IEEE 16th International Working Conference on Source Code Analysis and Manipulation (SCAM), pp. 157–166. IEEE (2016)

17. Muske, T.B., Baid, A., Sanas, T.: Review efforts reduction by partitioning of static analysis warnings. In: 2013 IEEE 13th International Working Conference on Source Code Analysis and Manipulation (SCAM), pp. 106–115. IEEE (2013)
18. Polikar, R.: Ensemble based systems in decision making. IEEE Circ. Syst. Mag. **6**(3), 21–45 (2006)
19. Russell, S.J., Norvig, P.: Artificial Intelligence: A Modern Approach, 2 edn. Pearson Education, Upper Saddle River (2003)
20. Ruthruff, J.R., Penix, J., Morgenthaler, J.D., Elbaum, S., Rothermel, G.: Predicting accurate and actionable static analysis warnings: an experimental approach. In: Proceedings of the 30th International Conference on Software Engineering, ICSE 2008, pp. 341–350. ACM, New York (2008). https://doi.acm.org/10.1145/1368088.1368135
21. Yoon, J., Jin, M., Jung, Y.: Reducing false alarms from an industrial-strength static analyzer by SVM. In: 2014 21st Asia-Pacific Software Engineering Conference (APSEC), vol. 2, pp. 3–6. IEEE (2014)

Using PageRank to Reveal Relevant Issues to Support Decision-Making on Open Source Projects

Alessandro Caetano[1]([✉]), Leonardo Leite[2], Paulo Meirelles[2,3], Hilmer Neri[1,4], Fabio Kon[2], and Guilherme Horta Travassos[1]

[1] COPPE, Federal University of Rio de Janeiro, Rio de Janeiro, Brazil
{alessandrocb,gth}@cos.ufrj.br
[2] FLOSS Competence Center, University of São Paulo, São Paulo, Brazil
{leofl,kon}@ime.usp.br
[3] Department of Health Informatics,
Federal University of São Paulo, São Paulo, Brazil
paulo@softwarelivre.org
[4] UnB Faculty in Gama, University of Brasilia, Brasilia, Brazil
hilmer@unb.br

Abstract. Software release planning is crucial to software projects that adopt incremental development. Open source projects depend on their globally distributed maintainers' communities who share project information, usually described in the software project repository as *issues*, to plan the contents and timing of the next releases. This paper introduces an approach based on software *issues* to support decision-making regarding open source software development activities such as release planning and retrospectives. It uses the PageRank algorithm to suggest an importance ranking of the software *issues* based on the *issues* dependencies topology. When based on a highly connected topology, project leaders can use this rank as an input to planning activities. The observation of two open source projects indicates the feasibility of our approach.

Keywords: Open Source Software · Free software
Issue management · Decision-making · PageRank
Empirical software engineering

1 Introduction

The developers' community is responsible for managing the next evolutionary actions in Open Source Software (OSS) projects. Such steps can identify different types of software *issues*, such as new features, artifacts, improvements, comments, bug fixes, among others. Collaborative Development Environments (CDE) [3], such as GitHub and GitLab, provide essential collaboration tools, such as *issue* trackers, in addition to their code repositories. An *issue* tracker

© IFIP International Federation for Information Processing 2018
Published by Springer International Publishing AG 2018. All Rights Reserved
I. Stamelos et al. (Eds.): OSS 2018, IFIP AICT 525, pp. 102–113, 2018.
https://doi.org/10.1007/978-3-319-92375-8_9

supports the community in registering new *issues* and discussing them, keeping track of future work as well as recording the achieved results. Although the concept of "issue" has a broader meaning than the concept of "bug" (a.k.a. software defect), in some contexts, an *issue* tracker can be called a "bug tracker" and its produced report, a "bug report". An *issue* tracker can provide essential data about the software project history and status. Data-driven decisions can contribute to the software development process improvement, helping to the timely delivery of high-quality software [6].

Researchers have conducted investigations on mining software artifacts to provide useful insights for the decision-making process on software projects [1]. Codemine [6], for example, collects and analyzes engineering process data from across a diverse set of Microsoft product teams. Baysal *et al.* inquire Mozilla developers about how qualitative dashboards can support real-time developer decision-making for daily tasks [2]. Robles *et al.* mine commit history to estimate effort spent on a project [14]. Borges *et al.* mine open source GitHub repositories to predict popularity based on repository properties [4]. In our work, *issues* are the software artifacts mined to support decision-making.

An essential input data to planning activities are the history of the project (past *issues*) and the set of opened *issues*. One could consider a set of related *issues* as indicating some relevant theme within an OSS community. Open *issues* can point to essential topics so far neglected and deserving attention. It is also possible to use information regarding closed *issues* to observe where a project community concentrated its efforts. Thus, looking at the history of the *issues* is similar to performing a retrospective study, in which the software development team can learn from the experiences and plan for future improvements [15]. It is possible to use the retrospective based on the history of the *issues* to support decision-making and the prioritization of activities, and also to help identify most energy spent by the team during releases. The relevance of observing previously invested efforts is evident in the research of Robles *et al.*, in which a model estimates the effort on the OpenStack system based on its commit history [14].

Goyal and Sardana explore *issues* mining, comparing techniques for assigning the developer with maximum expertise related to a given bug to resolve it [8]. The match considers various meta-fields of the target bug and the meta-fields of bugs already solved by the developer. The authors also explore the effect of knowledge decay over time, a different meta-field weighting strategy, and developer commits history. Although our analysis target is the same, the bug report, our perspective is different, since we analyze the relevance of *issues* for the community as a whole, and not for specific developers.

Some works handle the summarization of bug reports containing lengthy conversations, so the reader can quickly grasp what matters in a given bug report. He *et al.* focus on summarization improvement based on duplicated bug reports analysis [10]. They apply the PageRank algorithm in a network in which nodes are the sentences of a bug report, and the similarity among them defines the edges, so the rank of sentences defines which ones belong to the summary. Although we also use PageRank to bug reports, our approach is different since we apply PageRank to reveal relevant *issues* from an *issue* set, and not to summarize a single bug report.

From another point of view, Steinmacher *et al.* identified 50 entry barriers faced by new developers in OSS projects [16]. Among them were (i) the lack of a list of project needs and *issues*, (ii) the organization of the backlog in the repository, and (iii) the access to the tasks. Thus, besides supporting planning and retrospective activities, the history of the *issues* is input to newcomers to know the project better and decide where to focus efforts.

A well-organized project may have hundreds or even thousands of *issues*. Considering such significant set of *issues* is hard for decision-making, one should analyze every single software *issue* to produce consistent high-level patterns. For this reason, OSS communities could benefit from automated approaches to extract relevant information from the *issue* tracker to support decision-making activities.

In the *issue* tracker facilities provided by the GitHub and GitLab, users can reference an *issue* from comments or titles on other software *issues*, creating a network of linked *issues* (see Sect. 2). Considering such *issues* network, we propose in this paper an approach to define the top-ranked software *issues* from a given repository, by using the PageRank algorithm [13] to determine the relevance of *issues* based on their network centrality. *Issues* with a large number of references (dependencies) are more likely to be highly relevant, and consequently, those referenced by relevant *issues* are more likely to be also highly relevant. This way, the outcome of the PageRank algorithm (a list of software *issues* ordered by relevance) can support retrospective studies, planning activities, and look for relevant opportunities for newcomers to work out. Therefore, this paper intends to answer the following **research question**: *Can the PageRank algorithm identify relevant issues on OSS projects to support decision-making?*

We used two observational studies with two OSS projects to support the answering of this question. The observed results indicate that the use of PageRank could be somewhat feasible since some ranked relevant *issues* presented terms aligned to the planning documentation, and others were related to effort-consuming activities.

We organized the remaining of this paper as follows. Section 2 describes some basic concepts on the model of software *issues* and the PageRank algorithm. Section 3 presents our proposal to determine the relevance order of software *issues* according to the PageRank algorithm. In Sect. 4 we discuss the evaluation of our approach. Section 5 presents some threats to the validity of this study. Finally, Sect. 6 draws our conclusions and future work.

2   Background

In this section, we present how to build a graph representation of software *issues* extracted from Github and Gitlab platforms. We also discuss the PageRank, a link analysis algorithm that we applied to find the top-ranked software project *issues*.

2.1   The Software *Issue* Model

Software *issues* are used in CDEs such as GitHub and GitLab to organize community activities. Software *issues* can have many purposes, such as discussing new ideas, asking for help, registering desired new features, artifacts improvements, fixes and so forth.

Each software *issue* has a number, a title, a textual description, and commentaries by its contributors. An *issue* title or commentary may refer to another software *issue* through a short link by using the "#" sign followed by the *issue* number. Commit messages can also refer to software *issues* in this style.

A software *issue* starts in the "open" state and finishes in the "closed" state. An *issue* is closed when it is addressed, rejected, or incorporated by another software issue. It may be assigned to a specific member of the software community and linked to a *milestone*. In this context, a *milestone* is a cohesive collection of software *issues*, possibly associated with a due date. A *milestone*, therefore, represents a project goal in a higher level of abstraction than just one issue.

2.2   The PageRank Algorithm

Larry Page and Sergey Brin created the PageRank algorithm in 1999 [13]. It calculates the relative importance of web pages, and it has applications in search engines, traffic estimates, and web browsing. The premise of the PageRank algorithm is that each web page has some outbound and inbound links and that pages with a large number of links are more relevant than pages with fewer links. Besides, the algorithm takes into account the relevance of incoming links to a page: if the web page has an inbound link that has high relevance, that page tends to be more important than another one having several links coming from less relevant pages. The equation used to calculate the rank in the PageRank algorithm is:

$$PR(x) = \alpha \left(\frac{1}{N} \right) + (1 - \alpha) \sum_{y \in L(x)} \frac{PR(y)}{C(y)}, \tag{1}$$

in which x a web page, $PR(x)$ is the page rank of x. $L(x)$ represents the pages with links to x, $C(y)$ is the out-degree of y, α represents the probability of a random jump from one of the links, that is, in a random-surfer model it represents the probability of the surfer restart the algorithm at any given page, preventing the algorithm to be stuck in a node with zero out-degree. N represents the total number of pages analyzed.

3   Using PageRank to Reveal Relevant Software *Issues*

Our approach to analyzing the relevance of *issues* consists in using the PageRank algorithm, i.e., applying Eq. 1 to software *issues* rather than to web pages. So, the first step of our procedure is generating a directed graph based on data retrieved from the software repository. We retrieve such data using the APIs provided by GitHub and GitLab. In the generated graph, a vertex represents a software issue, and a directed edge represents a link from a software *issue* to another one, only issues linked using the "#" sign are considered.

Before applying the PageRank algorithm, two transformations are performed in the graph. The first is to connect all software *issues* within the same milestone. We consider this connection because software *issues* within the same milestone have a semantic bind that means that all of them must be fulfilled so that a higher-level objective is achieved. The second transformation eliminates software *issues* with no links. A software *issue* is kept whether it has at least one inbound link or one outbound link. This transformation is made because software *issues* with no links are irrelevant to the analysis and affect the rank scale, so pruning these software *issues* generates a result that is easier to interpret.

After the graph is prepared, Eq. 1 is applied to the graph with $\alpha = 0.85$, which is the default value used in NetworkX [9], a library for network manipulation we used, and the recommended value from the original Pagerank proposition [5]. The result is the assignment of a real number called "rank" to each software *issue* and a list of software *issues* ordered from the highest to the lowest rank.

Our implementation source code (including data retrieving, graph preparation, and PageRank execution) is available at GitLab[1]. We built the automated solution in Python. The top-ranked libraries we used are Matplotlib for data visualization [11]; Scipy[2] for numerical computing; Pandas[3] for data frame manipulation; NetworkX [9] to generate a digraph and compute the PageRank; and NLTK[4] to find the patterns we were looking for in the *issue* text.

4   Evaluation

We automated an approach to be used by any project that adopts the GitHub or GitLab *issue* trackers to organize the software community activities. We evaluated it by observing two OSS projects: Brazilian Public Software portal[5], with its project repository in its own GitLab instance, and Parliamentary Radar[6], which uses Github.com to host its project repositories. We choose these Brazilian software projects because they documented their roadmaps and backlogs, which enabled us to use this documentation to evaluate the algorithm results. Moreover, the proximity of our research group to the developers of these two software projects helped us to perform qualitative assessments regarding our findings with the project members.

The Brazilian Public Software (SPB) portal is an integrated platform for collaborative software development of OSS projects used by the Brazilian public administration [12]. It includes facilities for social networking, mailing lists,

---

[1] https://gitlab.com/AlessandroCaetano/PageRanking.

[2] https://scipy.org.

[3] http://pandas.pydata.org.

[4] http://nltk.org.

[5] https://softwarepublico.gov.br.

[6] http://radarparlamentar.polignu.org.

version control, and monitoring of source code quality, making it a system-of-systems. The Parliamentary Radar project uses open government data to perform cluster analysis on bill votes of legislative houses of Brazil.

The input to PageRank algorithm is the software *issues* graph. Figures 1 and 2 present the generation of the software *issues* graphs, which is the first step of our approach, for the SPB Portal and Parliamentary Radar projects. In these figures, the tiny red circles (altogether forming an ellipse) represent the software *issues*, whereas the straight lines represent links between them. In short, the graphs use a circular layout, as proposed by Doğrusöz et al. [7].

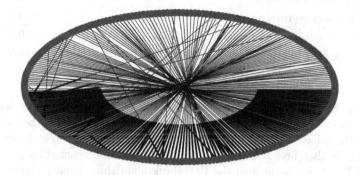

Fig. 1. Software *issues* circular graph of the SPB Portal project.

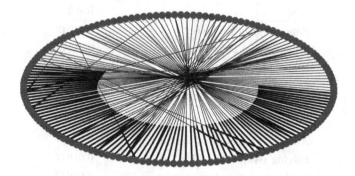

Fig. 2. Software *issues* circular graph of the Parliamentary Radar project.

The SPB graph already contains the transformations to linking the *issues* of the same milestone and pruning those with no links. The Radar Parliamentary graph includes the transformation of pruning software *issues* with no links. However, since the Parliamentary Radar project does not systematically use milestones, we did not perform the linkage of software *issues* of the same milestones to it.

Table 1. The top ten ranked *issues* of the SPB Portal.

Issue	Rank
Moderation of saved resource values of usage report	0.00593
Configure NGINX to serve syslog data	0.00345
Show error message close to the institution field on usage report	0.00345
Run Gitlab 8.5 with the built package	0.00345
Global search improvement	0.00345
White screen on community lateral block edition	0.00345
Portal wiki news import	0.00304
Broken user registration (username: boscojr)	0.00263
Add user e-mail on join community request processing screen	0.00263
Remove SISP question from new institution creation	0.00263

For the SPB portal project, the removal of *issues* with no links decreased from 800 to 127 the number of software *issues* in the graph. After the cut, about 62.5% of them have only one link. Some *issues* appear with two and three links, and there are also three *issues* with four, five and six links each. Using the *issues* graph of Fig. 1, we performed the PageRank algorithm. Table 1 shows the top ten ranked *issues*.

Table 2. The top ten ranked *issues* of the Radar Parlamentar.

Issue	Rank
Import legislative house	0.01242
Controversial polls	0.01242
Highlight party on the chart	0.01242
Duplicated parties and parliamentarians	0.01242
Advanced analysis	0.01242
Filtered polling list refactoring	0.01112
Automatic creation of dumps	0.01047
Solving *issues* 248, 241 e 250	0.01047
Without party voters on cdep in 1997	0.01047
Creation of Executive Chief Importer	0.01047

The removal of Parliamentary Radar project *issues* with no links decreased from 300 to 71 the number of software *issues* in the graph. After the cut, about 50% of them had just one link. Some *issues* appear with two, three and four links, and there is one *issue* with eleven links. Using the *issues* graph of Fig. 2, we performed the PageRank algorithm. Table 2 shows the top-ranked *issues*.

The rank values of SPB project *issues* varied from 0.002 to 0.0172. The median is 0.0028 and the mean 0.0040 with a standard deviation of 0.0018. About half of the *issues* presented the same rank of 0.002. The histogram in Fig. 3 represents the distribution of the generated ranking. For the Parliamentary Radar project *issues*, the ranks values varied in a range from 0.0046 to 0.0124. The median is 0.0059 and the mean 0.0063 with a standard deviation of 0.0020. Figure 4 presents the histogram plot for the Parliamentary Radar.

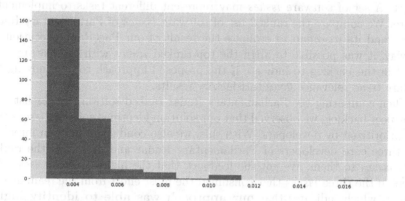

Fig. 3. Histogram of ranks for the SPB Portal *issues*.

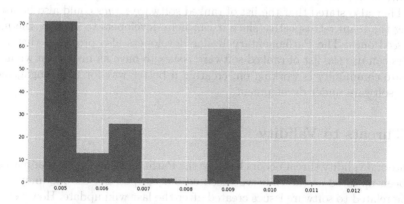

Fig. 4. Histogram of ranks for the Parliamentary Radar *issues*.

We compared the top-ranked software *issues* of the SPB portal project to the planning of the two last releases documented on the SPB wiki. We performed the comparison looking for the terms present in *issue* titles, descriptions, and wiki pages. In the SPB releases documentation, some priority features were "software usage report", "global search improvement", and "general improvements".

These terms align with terms found in the top-ranked software *issues*. We also conducted an open interview with the SPB Portal coordinator presenting the ranked list of *issues* to him, who provided feedback that the ranked list showed the *issues* that consumed the most effort from the team at the project end. It suggests the feasibility of **our approach in capturing some of the relevant *issues* from the management point of view**.

The Parliamentary Radar project maintains its roadmap and backlog organized in the Wiki at its repository. Its backlog[7] describes features desired for the project. A set of software *issues* may represent different tasks to implement a feature. We compare the ranked list of software *issues* of Parliamentary Radar project and its roadmap to evaluate the result of our PageRank execution. In this way, it was possible to align the top-ranked *issues* with the features presented in the backlog to indicate if the proposed approach to determining the software *issue* relevance gives satisfactory results.

When comparing the Parliamentary Radar ranked software *issues* list with the project backlog, we observed that our solution identified software *issues* that were prioritized by developers. With this, we also conducted an open interview with three core developers of Parliamentary Radar and presented the ranked list of *issues* to them. We got the feedback that the highly relevant *issues* list presented the three *issues* that consumed the most effort from the team at that moment, which indicates that **our approach was able to identify highly relevant software *issues* from the developer point of view**.

Moreover, the Parliamentary Radar developers stated that if they had this suggestion when planning the next release, they could have prioritized other software *issues* included in the list instead of some that they preferred to prioritize. They also stated that the list of ranked software *issues* could also be useful during the team retrospective since it can help developers to identify the most discussed ones. The Parliamentary Radar developers also proposed that newcomers can use the list of ranked software *issues* to have an insight on what the software community is working on, creating a better way for their engagement in the software under development.

5   Threats to Validity

An internal validity threat occurs because the Parliamentary Radar roadmap had not been updated at the time we executed our scripts. So, the roadmap could not be related to software issues created after the last wiki update. However, the Parliamentary Radar wiki content had enough information to correlate software issues terms and planning documentation. Moreover, in the SPB Portal project, the wiki content was more reliable, so the sound results for both projects support the applicability of such comparison.

About external validity, we acknowledge that executing our approach with only two OSS projects imposes barriers to a broader generalization regarding our approach applicability. However, at least the positive observations of these

---

[7] https://github.com/radar-parlamentar/radar/wiki/Roadmap.

two projects are encouraging and can motivate other communities to try out our proposal. Our approach is limited by how the developers organize the issue tracker of their projects. Since the algorithm depends on the links of the *issues*, it requires a cultural practice for the community to create these links.

In the evaluation process, the main reproducibility problem is the manual comparison made between terms found on top-ranked software issues and terms present in the planning documentation. An automated process for such comparison would be more suitable. On the other hand, the planning documentation for both SPB Portal and Parliamentary Radar projects are relatively small, so we hope someone trying to reproduce our study might get very similar results.

6   Conclusion

We presented the application of the PageRank algorithm to a network of software issues retrieved from OSS projects. Its use results in a ranking of issues, which can support a software community in decision-making activities, such as the planning of releases, retrospective studies, and helping newcomers to know the project better.

The presented results showed the feasibility of our approach for the Brazilian Public Software portal and Parliamentary Radar projects because some of the top-ranked software issues were also present in their planning documentation. Furthermore, in open interviews with the coordinators and the core developers of the projects, they found the software issues rank insightful in both management and development views. Therefore, we consider that the PageRank algorithm may be used to extract a small set of relevant issues from OSS repositories to support decision-making activities regarding retrospective studies, to support new developers to engage on activities that are currently being worked by the software community, and to track the effort of the team. However, before generalizing its use for all OSS projects, it is vital to understand peculiarities of the software community and project that could affect the results.

Answering the question *"Can the PageRank algorithm identify relevant issues on OSS projects to support decision-making activities?"*, the obtained results indicate that our approach can adequately work for those software projects using the Github or Gitlab software issue trackers and in which **the contributors create a substantial number of links among issues**. The issues should represent activities for the developers, the links between them should represent the relations between two or more activities, that way the algorithm can rank the issues helping the developers prioritize them. Given OSS projects following the specific structures presented in this study, we can answer our research question positively, since the algorithm was able to reveal a set of relevant issues regarding both the software projects. However, since we applied our approach to two OSS projects, more studies are necessary to strengthen this claim.

The adoption of our approach by OSS communities requires a way to integrate the execution and the presentation of results without the need to manually run scripts. To facilitate more studies based on our approach, we shared a package with the scripts used in this study on Gitlab, as described in Sect. 3. Future studies can evaluate the impact of our graph transformations, i.e., linking software issues within the same milestone and pruning those with no links. Finally, structured interviews with adopters of the approach would allow a better evaluation triangulation and broaden its applicability assessment for an extensive range of OSS projects.

References

1. Abdellatif, T.M., Capretz, L.F., Ho, D.: Software analytics to software practice: a systematic literature review. In: Proceedings of the First International Workshop on BIG Data Software Engineering, BIGDSE 2015, pp. 30–36. IEEE (2015)
2. Baysal, O., Holmes, R., Godfrey, M.W.: Developer dashboards: the need for qualitative analytics. IEEE Softw. **30**(4), 46–52 (2013)
3. Booch, G., Brown, A.W.: Collaborative Development Environments. Advances in Computers, vol. 59, pp. 1–27. Elsevier (2003)
4. Borges, H., Hora, A., Valente, M.T.: Predicting the popularity of github repositories. In: Proceedings of the 12th International Conference on Predictive Models and Data Analytics in Software Engineering, PROMISE 2016, pp. 9:1–9:10. ACM (2016)
5. Brin, S., Page, L.: Reprint of: the anatomy of a large-scale hypertextual web search engine. Comput. Netw. **56**(18), 3825–3833 (2012)
6. Czerwonka, J., Nagappan, N., Schulte, W., Murphy, B.: CODEMINE: building a software development data analytics platform at Microsoft. IEEE Softw. **30**(4), 64–71 (2013)
7. Doğrusöz, U., Madden, B., Madden, P.: Circular layout in the Graph Layout toolkit. In: North, S. (ed.) GD 1996. LNCS, vol. 1190, pp. 92–100. Springer, Heidelberg (1997). https://doi.org/10.1007/3-540-62495-3_40
8. Goyal, A., Sardana, N.: Efficient bug triage in issue tracking systems. In: Proceedings of the Doctoral Consortium at the 13th International Conference on Open Source Systems, pp. 15–24 (2017)
9. Hagberg, A.A., Schult, D.A., Swart, P.J.: Exploring network structure, dynamics, and function using NetworkX. In: Proceedings of the 7th Python in Science Conference, SciPy 2008, pp. 11–15 (2008)
10. He, J., Nazar, N., Zhang, J., Zhang, T., Ren, Z.: PRST: a pagerank-based summarization technique for summarizing bug reports with duplicates. Int. J. Softw. Eng. Knowl. Eng. **27**(6), 869–896 (2017)
11. Hunter, J.D.: Matplotlib: a 2D graphics environment. Comput. Sci. Eng. **9**(3), 90–95 (2007)
12. Meirelles, P., Wen, M., Terceiro, A., Siqueira, R., Kanashiro, L., Neri, H.: Brazilian Public Software Portal: an integrated platform for collaborative development. In: Proceedings of the 13th International Symposium on Open Collaboration, OpenSym 2017, pp. 16:1–16:10. ACM (2017)
13. Page, L., Brin, S., Motwani, R., Winograd, T.: The PageRank citation ranking: bringing order to the web. Technical report 1999–66, Stanford InfoLab (1999)
14. Robles, G., González-Barahona, J.M., Cervigón, C., Capiluppi, A., Izquierdo-Cortázar, D.: Estimating development effort in free/open source software projects by mining software repositories: a case study of OpenStack. In: Proceedings of the 11th Working Conference on Mining Software Repositories, MSR 2014, pp. 222–231. ACM (2014)

15. Schwaber, K., Sutherland, J.: Sprint retrospective. In: The Definitive Guide to Scrum: The Rules of the Game. Scrum.Org and ScrumInc (2016). www.scrumguides.org/docs/scrumguide/v2016/2016-Scrum-Guide-US.pdf
16. Steinmacher, I., Chaves, A.P., Conte, T.U., Gerosa, M.A.: Preliminary empirical identification of barriers faced by newcomers to open source software projects. In: 28th Brazilian Symposium on Software Engineering, SBES 2014, pp. 51–60. IEEE (2014)

OSS in Public Administration

Creating and Integrating a FLOSS Product into UK Law Enforcement

Joseph Williams[(✉)]

Department of Computing, Digital Forensics and Cybersecurity,
Canterbury Christ Church University,
North Holmes Road, Canterbury, Kent CT1 1QU, UK
joseph.williams@canterbury.ac.uk

Abstract. Open Source Internet Research Tool (OSIRT) is a free and open source software tool that enables law enforcement officials to conduct online research and obtain artefacts in an evidential and lawful manner. Over the past three years, OSIRT has seen growth from a handful of users within UK law enforcement, to a reach that extends to countries across the globe which also sees usage outside of law enforcement and beyond its original scope.

This paper will reflect upon OSIRT's development, and discusses issues surrounding the development of a FLOSS product for UK law enforcement. With cuts to budgets being made to law enforcement services, FLOSS software like OSIRT has an opportunity to flourish in this sector. To establish OSIRT's and FLOSS' integration into UK law enforcement, interviews, a small case study and questionnaires were conducted with serving police officers, police trainers and an IT administrator; all have experience with OSIRT.

Keywords: Open source research · Open source intelligence
Internet investigations · Law enforcement · Open source software

1 Introduction

With cuts to policing budgets in the UK expected to hit £700 m by 2020 [1], police services are finding themselves needing to reduce expenditure. One of the areas law enforcement can save is by integrating FLOSS. With an ever-increasing rise in cyber-crime, policing is now seeing itself requiring a shift from 'traditional' roles to a digital, online presence with a need for officers to be capable of conducting online investigations.

The Internet plays host to a variety of artefacts law enforcement can also use for intelligence purposes, further extending the need for officers to be able to obtain information using technology. To aid law enforcement in conducting research online, OSIRT, a FLOSS product, was created in collaboration with the UK's College of Policing.

This paper looks at OSIRT's integration and usage within UK law enforcement by looking at, often closed-sourced, tools that were previously used when conducting open source research and why this plethora of different tools was standardized with OSIRT. To support this, views and experiences of law enforcement officials (LEOs) are considered by means of a case study, interviews and questionnaires.

I. Stamelos et al. (Eds.): OSS 2018, IFIP AICT 525, pp. 117–127, 2018.
https://doi.org/10.1007/978-3-319-92375-8_10

2 Background

This section will review how police conduct open source investigations in the UK, including technical limitations and the need for software standardization. This section will also look at how the UK government are encouraging public services to adopt FLOSS.

2.1 Open Source Research

As part of their daily investigative routines, LEOs across the United Kingdom conduct Open Source Research (OSR), which the Association of Chief Police Officers (ACPO) define as "The collection, evaluation and analysis of materials from sources available to the public, whether on payment or otherwise, to use as intelligence or evidence within investigations" [2].

Given a typical OSR workflow, LEOs must manually log any action they have taken. For example, every website visited must be logged with a date and time stamp. If anything tangible is obtained from that website, such as a screenshot or download, it must be hashed using a suitable hashing algorithm and logged with a date and time stamp in tandem with the originating URL. Any artefacts obtained (e.g. screenshots) are then placed into a suitable directory structure, or directly onto the note taking application of choice to complete the audit log. Any extra annotations the investigator wishes to make are also then added.

This only tells part of the story, however, in order to obtain these artefacts, LEOs have to use an exhaustive variety of different tools. These tools differ in quality, usability, and price and will often vary from constabulary to constabulary. Largely, they amount to a web browser, static and dynamic screen capturing tools, a hashing tool and a note taking application for manually maintaining an audit log.

2.2 Toolkit Standardization

To aid digital investigators in conducting OSR, and to help standardize procedures, the UK's College of Policing runs a Researching Identifying and Tracing the Electronic Suspect (RITES) course[1]. The RITES course is a week-long training package aimed at LEOs of all skill levels, with a strong focus around conducting open source investigations and research. As part of this course, trainers provide a standard toolset. However, trainers noted that the introduction of too many tools, and manual audit log entry, overloaded the students.

To establish current practices and tool usage in the working environment, a short questionnaire was distributed to LEOs within the UK who have a range of experience of conducting OSR. The levels of experience ranged from less than one year, to over six years with the participants ranked from Police Constables to Inspectors. Twenty responses were received from twelve constabularies. In addition to establishing current

---

[1] http://www.college.police.uk/What-we-do/Learning/Professional-Training/digital-and-cyber-crime/
Pages/Researching-Identifying-Tracing-Electronic-Suspect.aspx (Last accessed: January 14th 2018).

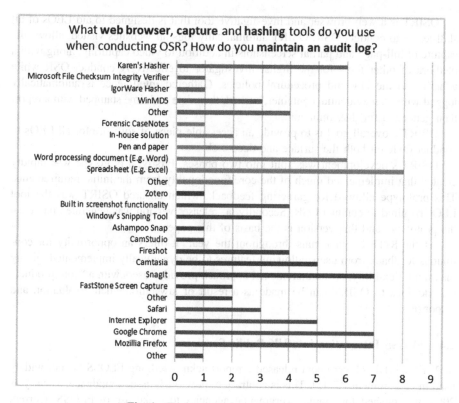

Fig. 1. Tool usage when conducting OSR

tool usage, an exploratory question asked what LEOs would like to see from an all-in-one OSR tool. Figure 1 shows the tool usage results from the questionnaire.

Respondents were also asked "Does the cost of some tools prohibit you from being able to use them?", 13 responded "yes". A question then asked, "I am more inclined to use a tool if it is free of charge.", 12 responded "yes".

Additionally, audit log maintenance was time consuming and prone to unintentional mistakes; such as a digital investigator forgetting to log when action was taken. Given the nature of the potential evidence being obtained, such oversight may compromise a case, and contravenes principle 3 of ACPO guidelines stating the requirement for an audit trail [3]. The trainers at the College of Policing identified these shortcomings, and issued a specification requesting a means to encapsulate the functionality required into a single tool; this prompted the creation of Open Source Internet Research Tool (OSIRT).

2.3   OSIRT

OSIRT is a free and open source C# application available under the MIT license for Windows 7, 8, 8.1 and 10 with a repository available on GitHub at https://github.com/joe-williams-cccu/OSIRTv2. Portable and installable builds are available at http://osirtbrowser.com/get-osirt/, where feedback is highly encouraged by the developer.

OSIRT is a web-browser and investigative tool that is designed to aid LEOs of all skill-levels to conduct OSR. OSIRT automatically logs all websites visited, allows the capture of full-page and partial screenshots in addition to video capturing, along with a plethora of other tools for the digital investigator to effectively conduct OSR while adhering to the law and procedural policies. Gathered intelligence is automatically logged within an evidential container, hashed, then date and time stamped with a report then generated for dissemination.

OSIRT's overall goal is to provide an accessible piece of software for all LEOs to conduct OSR on both the surface and deep web.

OSIRT's development was split into two phases. Firstly, a prototype was rapidly created that implemented much of the core functionality from the initial requirements. This prototype allowed for garnering feedback, which ensured OSIRT was the tool LEOs required to conduct OSR. Secondly, a 'release' version was generated based on the prototype, and this version is the basis of this paper.

As the RITES course runs throughout the year, it offers an opportunity for continuous feedback from users; allowing features to be dynamically implemented, giving maximum flexibility. As an incremental approach provides users with a "core product" [4] additions to OSIRT can be made as a result of law enforcement evaluation and response.

2.4   FLOSS Integration into UK Public Services

In 2012, the UK Government released a report acknowledging FLOSS "is not widely used in Government IT" [5]. This is contrary to previously issued guidance, as early as 2004, that pushed for more governmental agencies to make use of FLOSS. Current policy sees that FLOSS should be "actively and fairly consider[ed]" over its proprietary counterpart [6]. During the UK Government's re-push for FLOSS integration, they released alongside their 2012 report a list of FLOSS alternatives to well-known proprietary systems [5]. In November 2017, the UK Government once again stressed the use of open source "to improve transparency, flexibility and accountability" [7] and provided a 15-point guide to evaluating the use of open source software.

Waring and Maddocks [8] also highlighted that FLOSS was seldom used in the public sector, perhaps due to skills shortages, but those with a "degree of autonomy" may be more able and willing to integrate FLOSS. Law enforcement within the UK are allowed some choice, in which IT decisions, depending upon an officer's skill set, can be made on an individual level. That said, there is little data surrounding what software law enforcement are using and for what purpose.

The potential reason for the slow uptake of FLOSS is that it may bring with it negative perceptions. From personal experience, it is not unusual to receive communications surrounding OSIRT's provenance and why the software is free-of-charge. Questions typically fall in to one of five categories: security, maintenance, technical support, cost and training. These are five points will form the focus of the case study surrounding OSIRT as a FLOSS product.

3 Methodology

3.1 Interviews

Two sets of interviews were conducted, the first were sixteen semi-structured interviews held with LEOs taking the RITES course, along with two interviews from the RITES course trainers and four interviews by officers from UK constabularies. All officers interviewed had experience conducting OSR, and had been in a policing role ranging from 6 to 22 years. These interviews covered their experience of using OSIRT over the RITES course, along with general questions involving their experience conducting OSR and what existing tools they used.

The second batch of interviews looked at OSIRT's integration and the impact of FLOSS into a police force with three participants being interviewed; an Inspector, Detective Constable and IT Administrator. The police service in this case-study has approximately 40 active OSIRT users. The three participants were chosen as they all have a different perspective when integrating or using software. Questions to these participants looked closer at OSIRT's integration as a FLOSS product and how it can make an impact. These questions looked at five key areas: Trust, maintenance, technical support, cost and training.

All interviews lasted from 15 to 45 min.

3.2 General Questionnaires

OSIRT is used extensively during the RITES course, performing a central role where LEOs use it to conduct an open source investigation, capturing evidence for a fabricated case; a task performed throughout the five days of the course. This fictitious investigation provides a robust scenario in which OSIRT can be thoroughly tested by the very users it is intended for. Additionally, each increment of OSIRT is beta tested on the RITES course before general release, and by several LEOs in a live environment. Feedback is sent directly to the author from the LEO, or collated by the lead trainer and passed back.

This study used an opportunity sample to distribute questionnaires to 42 attendees of the RITES course over five courses. The questionnaire focused on OSR, existing tool usage, FLOSS and OSIRT.

4 Results and Discussion

4.1 Case Study Interviews

Trust and Security. A common question received in one form or another is "How can I trust this software?" this is an important question any user should be asking when using software, but it is particularly important on sensitive systems such as policing where evidential artefacts are being obtained. All three interviewees highlighted being able to trust software as being an important factor of usage. The Inspector said "We trust OSIRT because we've spoken to you, and we can contact you. If this was some software made by 'who-knows' then it would be a different story". The IT administrator also highlighted the fact OSIRT being open-source made trusting "easier" and although they are "not an advanced programmer" just the thought of the source code being available provides peace of mind.

Without being a large software distributor, it is, understandably, hard for those to trust a product made by an individual, making OSIRT open source was an attempt to assuage those concerns. OSIRT is both linked to a university and has collaborative links with the College of Policing, aiding in abating trust issues.

Maintenance. Updating is a challenge that is faced by any development team, but as a lone developer working on an FLOSS project, this concern feels amplified by potential consumers. The IT administrator highlighted this initial concern surrounding OSIRT, "We need to ensure our systems are water-tight, so updates are important." The Detective Constable highlighted the dynamic nature of their work and the importance of keeping abreast of current technological advances as a key driver for updates "It feels the nature of my work changes on a yearly basis, who knows what I'll be working on next year, so having a tool that keeps on top of that, like OSIRT has been, is important to me".

The Inspector also noted that updates were "important" but spoke about skills within the police service that may aid in development. Some police services within the UK are adopting 'cyber-specials', a volunteer group with exceptional skills in areas of cybersecurity. The Inspector said that "Given that OSIRT is available [open-source] means we can look at giving the [cyber] specials tasks in updating OSIRT". OSIRT, presently, has no developer community beyond the author so an opportunity to work with volunteers in policing roles provides a good opportunity to extend and maintain OSIRT.

Technical Support. While closely linked to 'maintenance' the ability to provide support and help if needed was an issue raised by all participants. The Detective Constable, who is a daily OSIRT user, highlighted the need to be able to reach out and how "scarce" technical support is, particularly for free tools. "The thing with paid for tools is that, as part of the contract, technical assistance is part of the cost, so we can reach out". This officer felt that was not always the case with free tools, where there is no contact available. "I've had my fingers burnt before where I used some open source tool and it stopped working with an error message, but I had no way of contacting the developer". The Inspector echoed this sentiment, also adding the ability to reach out and get support if needed was "crucial".

The IT administrator agreed with this, too, but said that this is "par-for-the-course" using FLOSS and that expectations of support should be lowered. "To me, this is the sole trade-off. You lower the initial costs, but may face larger ones supporting free software".

Cost. Unsurprisingly, the cost of OSIRT was a driving factor in its implementation within this police services' system. The Inspector said that they had looked at "a couple of other tools", however, the cost of these tools was "too high" with some of the tools being "£60–£150 a user per year." The Inspector also highlighted that buying licenses could be better spent, "If I wanted to roll that out, that would cost me thousands but I have OSIRT for free which means that budget can be spent on other things".

The IT administrator also noted cost and said "money does not necessarily mean better quality". While the administrator said that where proprietary software was used, they were in a position to look at FLOSS alternatives if needed. The administrator said that some forces "may not have this flexibility [to introduce FLOSS] due to policy, but things are changing".

The Detective Constable was, seemingly, least averse to cost and instead highlighted the importance quality software was to deliver the "best service" whether the best software was free "shouldn't decide what's best for the best results, luckily OSIRT for me is the best tool for the job", but they "understood" why management would be forced to look at free alternatives.

Software where there is no immediate charge may invoke a 'try before you buy' response as there is not a commitment to integrate the product if it does not work out.

Monetary costs are not the only considerations to any implementation of, or change to alternative, software. Further considerations include costs in time, deployment and training.

Training. One issue surrounding the use of more FLOSS products was the need to provide training on the new technology. This is not particularly a FLOSS issue, as any piece of software will require familiarization. The Detective Constable spoke about the "comfort zone" and changing an officer's workflow may cause them to "resent" the new software; highlighting the need for a robust training plan to abate those concerns.

The Inspector highlighted additional training as a cost/benefit trade-off "Of course you get the software for free, but we have things in place already and replacing software means training, it means time, and we have to trade-off the cost of licenses versus the cost of training".

OSIRT is fortunate in that it is used as the tool on the RITES course, providing officer's hands-on use over the five-days as part of a wider training package. Additionally, as part of OSIRT's development, usability tests have been conducted by means of observations, SUS questionnaires [9] and cognitive walkthroughs [10]. Conducting these usability tests, arguably, enhance OSIRT's ease-of-use which may then lead to require less training for OSIRT itself.

Summary. While this short case-study is not necessarily, nor does it claim to be, representative it does highlight experiences, thought-processes and issues faced by those using and making decisions when integrating software into systems. These interviews are reflective of the conversations had with several police services within the past, and while anecdotal in nature, does support the need for, and successful implementation of, OSIRT in law enforcement systems.

4.2 OSIRT Interviews and Questionnaires

This section looks at the 22 interviews and 42 questionnaires conducted with various LEOs and trainers. The topics covered OSIRT and how, if applicable, the participants conduct OSR.

OSIRT as Part of LEO Training. Interviews and discussions with the lead trainer for the RITES course have shown that OSIRT has had a positive impact. The lead trainer noted that before OSIRT, the audit log was all maintained within a spreadsheet. "[Spreadsheets] were so time consuming, and you've noticed on the course we have people with different skill bases, so if you add the complexity of trying to operate a spreadsheet, trying to fit an image inside a cell on top of all the tools they have to use, you can imagine how complex that is. OSIRT pulled that all together, and streamlined the process".

Since OSIRT has been introduced on the course, there has been a "large increase" in the number of students who fully complete the 'live' open source investigation, where previously auditing and reporting were identified as issues.

OSIRT Integration into Workflow. Respondents were asked in the general questionnaire "Can you see OSIRT being integrated into your current role?" thirty-six out of forty-two responded "Yes". During the interviews, participants from the RITES course were asked about how they could see OSIRT's integration into their roles, with thirteen participants making positive comments that it would be "simple" or "easy" to do so. A response from a Detective Sergeant noted "It's quite a simple sort of transition to move away from our current system, which is to use pen and paper to record things, and straight into using OSIRT", another noted that their procedure involved a spreadsheet and a notebook, and while they would not stop hand writing notes, OSIRT's automated logging of actions was "a God send". Those that could not see OSIRT being integrated either said their current IT infrastructure makes it too burdensome (two), or that OSIRT could not integrate into their role at all (one).

The four officers interviewed from the constabularies, who have been using OSIRT as part of their investigations, all noted OSIRT has saved them time. "Its [OSIRT] at least halved, probably more actually, how long it takes me to conduct [open source] research", noted one interviewee.

Automated Logging and Reporting. The end product after an investigation is crucial for LEOs with all respondents noting the report output by OSIRT was in their top three features. An interviewee noted that reporting "[…] can be a complete pain, so anything that can do it for me is fantastic", a sentiment largely echoed by nine other interviewees. While the report generation was popular amongst respondents, seven interviewees did mention that the report could do with some cosmetic changes.

The automated logging of actions was another popular choice, with thirteen LEOs acknowledging during the interviews that logging every minute action as not possible. An interviewee noted that "Seeing my audit in OSIRT surprised me, […] I performed a lot of actions that I wouldn't really think twice about. Opening Google, performing a search and clicking a link are actually three [actions], but I've always considered [it] just one". The majority of interviewees all explicitly mentioned how the automated log was a time saver.

Respondents to the questionnaire shed some light as to why the automated logging and reporting is an ideal feature, as when asked in the questionnaire "How do you maintain an audit log when conducting OSR?" all respondents used some manual means for logging. Table 1 summarizes their results. Multiple answers were selectable; hence the responses exceeding 42.

Table 1. How LEOs maintain their audit log

How do you maintain and audit log when conducting OSR? (Select all that are relevant)	
Spreadsheet (E.g. Excel)	26
Word processing document (E.g. Word)	17
Pen and paper	10
In-house solution	4
Zotero (or other bookmarking app)	2
Web browser's inbuilt bookmarking functionality	8
Forensic CaseNotes	3
Notepad/++	2
I don't maintain an audit log	0
Other	4

OSIRT's automated logging and report generation were very popular amongst interviewees and questionnaire respondents. It was not unusual to hear an officer criticize the monotony of having to manually maintain an audit log, and how an automated system is better not only to save time but to also ensure guidelines and policies are enforced.

Screen Capturing. The ability to capture screenshots and screen recordings was also favorable among respondents. Interviewees frequently commented that having this functionality for free is good, as they do not necessarily have the budget to afford the licenses for some tools. "Screen recording tools can be very expensive, or have an upper limit of how much you can record if they are free. The inbuilt video capture in OSIRT does not impose limits, plus it's free". One interviewee said, when asked about what screen capturing tools they use, "Anything I can find and is free. I used to use *FastStone Capture* but the free trial run out, and I cannot obtain a license." A similar story was raised by six other interviewees.

Ten interviewees commented that being able to take full-page screenshots of large pages, such as Facebook, was beneficial to them. An interviewee noted "We have to take small screenshots, then stitch them back together. So OSIRT is going to be extremely useful."

5   Reflection

Developing OSIRT has been a highly rewarding experience and has provided opportunities to deliver a useful tool for law enforcement. OSIRT's growth has seen it shift from a simple training tool to use across the globe, with a user base ranging from Barbados to Israel. While OSIRT's growth is exciting, it has brought with it additional challenges. OSIRT was written only with UK law enforcement in mind, and as such is British-centric in its design. Obviously, the nature of the Internet makes nothing localized and purposeful software will disseminate to wherever it finds a use, and this brings with it a need for internationalization.

Being an academic, sometimes it is easy to forget that software must be shipped and that people are going to be using it, and will need support. Thankfully, OSIRT is buoyed in the policing community with many questions answered before being contacted. That said, if OSIRT did not have that internal support it would be considerably harder to manage as an individual.

6 Conclusion

Over the past three years, OSIRT has gone from a prototype used on the College of Policing's RITES training course to a fully-fledged piece of software used by various law enforcement agencies and individuals across the globe. OSIRT has been well received, with responses pointing to its rich feature integration and time saving through automation as a significant reason for this positive reaction.

Feedback is continually given and encouraged, with this avenue providing feedback which enhances OSIRT's trust and offers an opportunity for growth. The case-study highlighted the balance OSIRT must straddle with being FLOSS, and the importance that trust, support, maintenance, cost and training have. There is a conscious need to ensure pros of the software outweigh both the imagined and potential cons. Only by being aware of and managing those expectations can FLOSS flourish.

By receiving both positive responses and suggestions for improvement, OSIRT is perpetually evolving along a path dictated by the very people who comprise its target audience. Having such direction will be crucial in OSIRT's continued development.

References

1. Dodd, V.: Britain's police budgets to lose £700 m by 2020, amid rising crime (2017). http://www.theguardian.com/uk-news/2017/nov/09/britains-police-budgets-to-lose-700m-by-2020-amid-rising
2. Association of Chief Police Officers: Online Research and Investigation (2013). http://library.college.police.uk/docs/appref/online-research-and-investigation-guidance.pdf
3. Association of Chief Police Officers: ACPO Good Practice Guide for Digital Evidence (2012). http://www.digital-detective.net/digital-forensics-documents/ACPO_Good_Practice_Guide_for_Digital_Evidence_v5.pdf
4. Pressman, R.S.: Software Engineering: A Practitioner's Approach. McGraw-Hill Higher Education, New York (2014)
5. Cabinet Office, Home Office: Open Source Software Options for Government (2012)
6. Cabinet Office, Home Office: All About Open Source - An Introduction to Open Source Software for Government IT (2012). https://assets.publishing.service.gov.uk/government/uploads/system/uploads/attachment_data/file/61962/open_source.pdf
7. UK Government Digital Service: Be open and use open source - GOV.UK. https://www.gov.uk/guidance/be-open-and-use-open-source

8. Waring, T., Maddocks, P.: Open Source Software implementation in the UK public sector: evidence from the field and implications for the future. Int. J. Inf. Manag. **25**, 411–428 (2005)
9. Brooke, J.: SUS-A quick and dirty usability scale. Usability Eval. Ind. **189**, 4–7 (1996)
10. Wharton, C., Rieman, J., Lewis, C., Polson, P.: Usability Inspection Methods. Wiley, New York (1994)

Possibilities of Use of Free and Open Source Software in the Greek Local Authorities

Stavros Koloniaris$^{(\boxtimes)}$, George Kousiouris, and Mara Nikolaidou

Department of Informatics and Telematics, Harokopio University of Athens,
9, Omirou Street, 177 78 Athens, Greece
skoloniaris@gmail.com, {gkousiou,mara}@hua.gr

Abstract. Use of Free and Open Source software has started to get an increased level of functionality and trust, following the existence of a variety of solutions and supporting communities across the Web. In this paper, the current penetration and usage of Free and Open Source Software in the municipalities of Greece was recorded, as well as its potential especially when compared with the current state of computerization and hardware level. Conclusions were drawn on whether the municipalities will benefit from the usage of Free and Open Source Software, in technical and financial terms, as well as proposals are submitted in how the municipalities can benefit from an uptake in technology (especially Cloud computing), given their existing IT staffing and municipality organization. The possibility of improving the provided services to the citizens by using this software is also examined as well as cost aspects that can be improved.

Keywords: Free and open source software · Adoption · Municipalities
Government · Survey · Cost analysis

1 Introduction

The municipalities of Greece provide a variety of services to their citizens and perform different processes within their responsibilities and obligations. All their processes involve and use an IT sector in order to provide the required services. Although the computerization of the Greek municipalities and the usage of IT infrastructure to perform their operations is not something new, most of them fail to use modern technologies and are bind to proprietary software and high specification hardware. This leads them to have an increased operational cost, which eventually bounces to the citizens.

Furthermore, because of the ongoing economical crisis, the budgets of the municipalities are decreased and the available funds that can be invested in IT are cut-off to minimum. Many local authorities are forced to operate with old infrastructure and abolished or near end of life cycle software. This situation puts them in high risk, since they become vulnerable to hacking operations and exploits, risking to lose funds and data of their citizens.

In the year 2009 the total budget of all 325 Greek municipalities for IT expenses, including both hardware and software, was 22,409 million euro for buying new equipment and software plus another 5,985 million euro for service and updating purposes of the existing software. Those amounts are no longer available thus it

I. Stamelos et al. (Eds.): OSS 2018, IFIP AICT 525, pp. 128–143, 2018.
https://doi.org/10.1007/978-3-319-92375-8_11

became essential to find a way to continue providing the same, or even better quality of services to the citizens, by using late software but in decreased cost. Another goal is to increase the life time of the existing hardware so that it will not need an upgrade or replacement for a longer period of time.

The use of Free and Open Source Software may be the answer to this quest and the purpose of the current research is to evaluate the benefits and profits that the municipalities will enjoy from the usage of FOSS in relation to the risks that they must take and the dangers that they may encounter [1, 2]. By following the example of other European municipalities, such as Munich in Germany, and great organization, such as NASAs, or even Governments, such as China, the Greek municipalities may become able to save resources for using them in more crucial sectors [3, 7, 9, 12–14].

2 Information Gathering and Computational Details

2.1 Questionnaire Creation

There are no official records on each municipality's existing infrastructure, since they were free to call for offers and choose the winner on their own, according to their needs and pursuits. This happens for both hardware and software, so the municipalities may perform the same operations in different ways, using totally unique compilation of hardware and software.

In order to gather and organize such kind of information, a questionnaire was created that was directed to each municipalities IT department. The purpose of this questionnaire was to gather information on the existing hardware infrastructure of each municipality, the existing software in use as well as the reason it is used for, the knowledge that the IT department's employees have on modern technologies and the ability they could have on deploying those technologies and support its usage.

2.2 Questionnaire Creation

The questionnaire that was created was intended to be anonymous and the participants were all invited to participate via personal telephone communication with the head of each municipality IT department. There was a field were the participant was asked to reveal the municipality where he is employed but that was just to ensure that there are no double answers to the questionnaire from the same municipality.

The questionnaire had six sections:

Section 1, Utilized Hardware: In the first section the participant was invited to list the hardware specifications of the personal computers that are used in the municipality. The speed of the structured network wiring was answered in this section as well. The purpose of those questions was to estimate the remaining lifetime of the hardware and to check the probability of extending its lifetime through the use of free and open source software. The network speed that the cabling could offer would help to check the probability of using network or cloud services.

Section 2, Utilized Software: Information about the installed operating systems and the proprietary software that it is being used was gathered in this section. The information gathered was used to check if there is free and open source software that could provide the same usability whilst being less resource consuming than the proprietary software.

Section 3, Provided Services: The third section had questions about the backbone of the municipality's infrastructure. The participants gave information about the servers their municipality has and the services that they offer to the rest of the departments. The purpose was to check the estimated life span of the servers hardware and the probability of using free and open software to expand their usability. This section also helped to check if the municipalities use centralized services and services provided through network in any of their activities.

Section 4, Cloud: The questions of this section were about cloud based services and technologies. The purpose was to check the degree of penetration of cloud computing in the municipalities and to identify the difficulties that occur when trying to implement cloud based solutions in the municipalities.

Section 5, Support Plan: In this section were gathered information about each municipalities IT support plan and the cost of it. The purpose was the see if there are possibilities of lowering the support cost by providing network or cloud based services and by using free and open source software.

Section 6, FOSS: The last section of the questionnaire was intended the check if the IT departments employees of each municipality have the knowledge and the ability to learn, deploy, use and support free and open source software. Some opinions on what are the factors of success or failure in using free and open source software were gathered in this section.

The questionnaire itself was accessible online and created by using a free and open source platform (Lime Survey). All questions were optional while partially completed questionnaires were also acceptable.

2.3   Contact Establishment

Greece has 325 municipalities. The participants were contacted via telephone and a link to the questionnaire was sent to each one of them to the e-mail address that they provided. The contact period was from early to end of June 2017, while the questionnaire was online and accepting answers up to the end of July 2017.

There was no success in communicating with 55 of the municipalities IT department. In those cases, a link of the questionnaire was sent to the main e-mail address of the municipality, with a kind request to be forwarded to the IT department.

There were also 99 municipalities that stated they do not have an IT department and the support comes completely from an external associate.

3   Results and Discussion

3.1   Participation and Statistics

The goal was to gather at least 30 participations in the questionnaire. When the answering period ended there were 61 full answers to the questionnaire plus additional

59 incomplete answers. The above accomplishment gave the possibility to continue the research by taking in mind only the completed answers, while the incomplete were studied in some cases to gather additional information but mostly for statistic reasons.

From the 61 complete answers there were 7 that the participant did not share the name of the municipality to which they are employed. The remaining 54 municipalities have a combined population of 2.554.332 citizens which is the 23,62% of the total population of Greece. Furthermore, the total number of computers that those municipalities have deployed in their departments is 8.750 PCs.

99 of the municipalities that were contacted stated that they do not have an IT department which means that at least 30% of Greece's local authorities are depended on an external partner to provide them with IT support (Table 1).

Table 1. Contact and answer details

Contacted	Complete answers	Municipality percentage (complete answers)	Population coverage
325	61	18,7%	23,62%

3.2 Absolute Numbers and Cost Calculations for Workstations

The 61 IT departments declared that their municipalities have a total of 8.750 computers deployed. About 1.108 of those are running on an Intel Pentium or a corresponding to that generation AMD processor, which means that they are over 15 years old. Another 3.066 computers are equipped with an Intel Core, Core 2, Core 2 duo processor or an equivalent AMD processor, aged at about or over 10 years.

When checking the installed memory on each of those computers, there are 2.386 computers than have 2 GB or less RAM installed, and another 1.229 computers that have 1 GB or less installed.

It is the logical continuity of the above computer specification, that there are 2.003 computers that their operation is based on Microsoft's Windows XP or Microsoft's Windows Vista, which operating systems are already been abandoned and not supported or updated any more. Furthermore, there are 2.738 computers that operate on Microsoft's Windows 7 or Microsoft's Windows 8/8.1, which operating systems are closing to their end of life cycle, since their mainstream support has ended and they are closing to the end of their extended support (Fig. 1).

All the above conclude that over half of the existing workstations need an urgent upgrade or will soon need an upgrade, on either their hardware, their operating system or both.

The upgrading cost for hardware is estimated to be over 1.500.000 euro and the cost of new licenses for the later operating system would be another 784.500 euro (Table 2).

Furthermore, most of the computers of the local authorities have installed proprietary software that serves the needs of their day-to-day operation. Almost all IT departments mentioned that their computers have an office suite installed, with Microsoft's Office in all of its versions being the most popular, while there are some municipalities that use a mix of proprietary and FOSS suite having Microsoft's Office

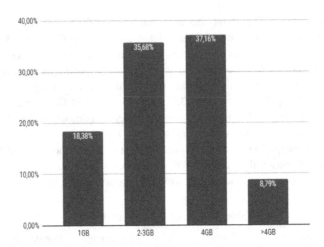

Fig. 1. The percentage of RAM availability in municipality workstations

Table 2. Number and upgrade cost of workstations

#Workstations	10 years and older	Cost of H/W upgrade	Cost of OS S/W upgrade	Cost of Other S/W (estimated)
8750	4741 (54,18%)	1.500.000E	784.500E	3.512.650E

and Libre/OpenOffice simultaneously. Other proprietary software that it is used includes but is not limited to client-based antivirus program, from vendors such as ESET, Kaspersky, Panda and Symantec, a file compression manager, mostly WinRAR, a PDF creator and manipulation tool and a CAD suite, mostly Autodesk's AutoCAD.

The number of computers that have the above mentioned software installed is not clearly declared, but it could be assumed that at least half of those computers have a Microsoft's Office Suite and a client-based antivirus. It could be also assumed that 25% of those computers have a proprietary PDF creator/manipulation program and a proprietary file compression manager. Lastly, it could be assumed that an average of 3 computers per municipality have a CAD suite installed. Under all the above assumptions, the estimated cost of the installed proprietary software raises up to 3.512.650 euro, which is the cumulative amount that will need to be spent over time when these programs need to be upgraded. It should be mentioned that some of those programs, such as the CAD suite and the antivirus suite, operate on yearly subscription and a continuous renewal of a 5 year period was assumed in order to calculate the cost of those programs (Fig. 2).

Besides the above, a series of more purposeful software where mentioned. Those included programs that served the needs of warehouse management and logistics, financial management, civilian communication and complaints recording, e-protocol, HR and payroll, public works monitoring. The cost of this software is unclear since they are offered as "by request", according to the needs of each organization, the components that should be bundled to it and the support plan that will accompany it.

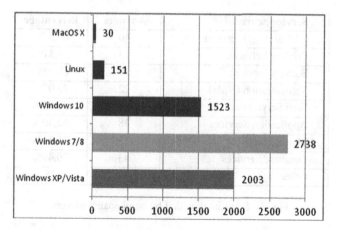

Fig. 2. Operating System usage in workstations (no longer supported versions in red, near end of life versions in yellow) (Color figure online)

However, even though an estimation of their cost cannot be accurate, it cannot be considered negligible and proposals on alternatives should be made for these programs as well.

3.3   Absolute Numbers and Cost Calculations for Backbone Infrastructure

Besides workstations, the questionnaire asked for information about the backbone infrastructure of the municipalities. In the municipalities that answered the questionnaire there are 312 servers offering services to the workstations.

There are 6 of the 61 municipalities that still use a server which operates on Microsoft Windows NT/2000 server edition and another 33 that operate on Microsoft Windows Server 2003, including all of its versions. The support for those operating systems has already ended and no service packs or updates of any kind have been released for them in many years, which render them vulnerable to modern security and operational dangers.

Furthermore, there are 40 municipalities that still have servers operating on Microsoft Windows Server 2008, an operating system that in most of its versions is not supported any more, while the versions that are still supported are closing to their extended support end date.

Of the municipalities that answered, 21 have deployed servers running Microsoft Windows 2012 server, including all versions, and only 3 have servers running Microsoft Windows 2016 server. Lastly there are 15 municipalities that have deployed servers running a Linux Server distribution.

The servers are used to provide various services to the departments of the municipality and to the citizens in some cases. Some of those services are file (storage) services, backup services, database and other application services (Fig. 3).

Service provided	Answers	Percentage
File (Storage) services	40	65,57%
Printing Services	13	21,31%
Backup Services	39	63,93%
Virtualization (VMs)	22	36,07%
Web Services	31	50,82%
Application Services	38	62,30%
Mail Services	13	21,31%
Database Services	43	70,49%
Other	2	3,28%

Fig. 3. Services provided by municipality servers

By assuming that one third of the servers are operating with an older operating system that needs replacement, the cumulative cost of the licenses is estimated to be at 99.088 euro, which does not take into account the extra cost of the required service packages that are needed in each case or the hardware upgrades that should be done beforehand (Fig. 4).

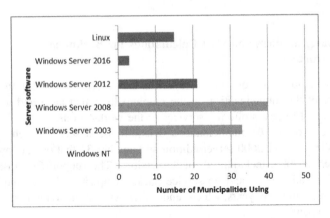

Fig. 4. Used OS on Municipality Servers (in red the no longer supported versions) (Color figure online)

On examining the existing structured network installation, most of the municipalities have a 1000BASE-TX (Gigabit Ethernet) infrastructure and only 12 of them, mostly small in population and coverage area or near the borders and island municipalities, are still operating on 100BASE-TX (Fast Ethernet) network infrastructure. In most use cases the Fast Ethernet infrastructure could be considered to be sufficient, but surely an upgrade of this infrastructure would be needed if a complete server-based or cloud-based implementation would be deployed in the future. In this scenario the largest municipalities would need to upgrade their Gigabit Ethernet infrastructure to fiber optics in order to not suffer from network delays and bottleneck phenomena.

3.4   Cloud Computing in the Municipalities

The survey also examined the knowledge and the familiarity that the IT department's employees have with the concepts of cloud computing, as well as the existence of any such a service in their municipality.

The answer to the question of knowledge and familiarity was unanimously affirmative but the deployment statistics are discouraging. Only 4 of the municipalities provide public cloud services to their departments and another 11 that provide private cloud services. Most of these implementation are used for file sharing through remote departments of the municipality.

Nevertheless, the majority of the respondents believe that cloud services could and should be offered in order to achieve lower operational costs and take advantage of the benefits that this technology has to offer, such as scalability and operating system independency. However, there are still concerns about the data safety that a cloud implementation could provide and the fact that a device has to be online in order to operate on cloud basis (Fig. 5).

Cloud services offered	Answers	Percentage
Yes, via public cloud	4	9,84%
Yes, via private cloud	12	21,31%
No	37	60,66%

Fig. 5. The percentage of municipalities that offer cloud based services

3.5   Free and Open Source Software (FOSS) in the Municipalities

The main purpose of the current research was to determine if it is possible to reduce the cumulative cost of computerization of a municipality by using Free and Open Source Software. So it was essential to check the experience that the IT department's employees have on FOSS. As in the cloud section, all the respondents replied that have knowledge of what is FOSS but only 34 of them stated that there is some familiarization of IT department's employees with FOSS.

Only 35 of them stated that they use some kind of FOSS in their organization and that is mainly limited to the use of a FOSS office suite such as Libre/OpenOffice. Some of them use a FOSS mail client (Mozilla Thunderbird), alternative internet browsers (Google Chrome, Mozilla Firefox) and a CMS (Joomla, Wordpress). Once again it is clear that the penetration of FOSS in the Greek municipalities is at an early stage and that they are bind to proprietary software in order to operate.

When asked if the change from proprietary to Free and Open Source Software would be possible and would have positive effects to their organization, only 22 of the respondents replied positively. Even worse is the belief that a change to the use of FOSS will not be accepted by the end users (resistance to change phenomena) since only 10 participants though that this is likely to happen without the occurrence of any major problem (Fig. 6).

Advantages of using FOSS		
	Answers	Percentage
Small or no cost	37	60,66%
Lower hardware requirements and greater durability	11	18,03%
Existence of active communities that support and evolve the available software	28	45,90%
Faster incorporation of software innovations	10	16,39%
They are easily customizable and can be optimized to the individual needs of each user	9	14,75%
Easy functionality expansion by adding modules	17	27,87%
Plaethora of available tutorials as well as online community support	14	22,95%

Fig. 6. Believed advantages of deploying and using FOSS

On the more technical and financial side the most favored factors that would lead FOSS to be successfully accepted in a municipality was considered to be the low or no cost of acquisition and maintenance of this software and the continuous upgrades that those software obtain through their supporting companies or the user communities. On the contrary, the main reasons that would lead such an attempt to failure where considered to be that FOSS software does not provide out of the box full functionality and that there are is insufficient training in usage of FOSS since there are not known certification programs that provide such kind of training. High favored reasons of failure where also the belief that support of FOSS is often insufficient and that the communities that develop and maintain FOSS cannot provide the same degree of security that a commercial company does at all levels of software support.

Through the communication that was made with the IT departments that eventually involved in the current research and answered the questionnaire, there was another conclusion made, that beyond the resistance to change phenomena, which includes the end users, there is also a fear of the unknown, which concerns the IT departments employees. Most of them have been skeptical and doubtful about the possibility of a radical change in the way they work and support their departments and the possibility that they would be requested to learn and support something totally new (Fig. 7).

Disadvantages of using FOSS	Answers	Percentage
Inadequate support	19	31,15%
Insufficient documentation	14	22,95%
They do not provide full functionality	25	40,98%
Insufficient training in FOSS and lack of certifications	21	34,43%
Does not integrate innovations and is evolutionarily behind commercial competition	10	16,39%
User communities do not provide the security provided by a commercial company at all levels of software support	19	31,15%

Fig. 7. Believed disadvantages of deploying and using FOSS

3.6 Software Support Plans

Lastly, the cost of the existing software support plans was examined as well as the involvement of external supporters. Apart from the 99 municipalities that do not have an in house IT department and are totally dependent on support from external partners, all of the municipalities that have such a department and answered the questionnaire have a support plan that involves someone from outside the municipality itself. 48 of them gave an estimation of the current financial year budget for software support and the sum is over 1.650.000 euro.

The majority of the municipalities have a maintenance/support contract with an external partner concerning the provided software. Since the involvement of the IT departments in supporting the proprietary software seems to be minimal, it is no surprise that there are no complaints concerning the functionality of the used software. Only 13 are concerned about the reduced functionality that the software in use provides, compared to the required one, and even fewer state that the current software cannot be upgraded due to its high cost

4 Proposals that Include Foss and Usage of Modern Technologies

4.1 Operating Systems and Commonly Used Software

About half of the computers that exist in the participating municipalities are over aged and unable to run the modern proprietary operating systems and software efficiently. Although the minimum requirements of modern proprietary operating systems are relatively low, they still require more resources than the available modern free operating systems [4]. In addition, the cost difference makes the free operating systems a fine choice.

There are some choices of free operating systems, with the Linux family being the most popular and better supported, while BSD and Solaris are yet excellent choices [5]. Linux has been around for over two decades now and has dominated as an operating system for web servers, mainframes and supercomputers, but still its acceptance for desktop, workstations and everyday use computers is relatively low [6]. Nevertheless it

Hardware requirements comparison	
Windows 10	**Lubuntu 17.10**
1 GHz processor or faster, 32 or 64 bit;	512 MHz processor or faster, 32 or 64 bit;
1 GB of RAM for the 32 bits version, or at least 2 for the 64 bit version;	512 MB of RAM;
16 GB of hard drive (32 bit) or 20 GB (64 bit);	6 GB hard drive;
Graphics card that supports DirectX 9 with WDDM 1.0 controler or superior	no fancy graphics

Fig. 8. Hardware requirements comparison between Windows 10 and the later Ubuntu Linux with LXDE desktop environment

makes an excellent choice for public sectors workstation since some of the most popular distributions have very low hardware requirements making it ideal for use in older computers. Modern distributions deployed with an LXDE or XFCE desktop environment can be efficiently used in a 20 year old, Pentium 4 era, computer with as low as 256 MB of RAM. Furthermore, the most popular distributions offer long term support (LTS) versions of their operating systems that are actively supported with updates for up to five years (Fig. 8).

Most of Linux distributions come with preinstalled packages that serve the everyday use needs while there is a plethora of alternative software to be freely obtained and used through its public repositories.

A more precise approach that could cover most use cases that where proposed from the respondents is the use of an Ubuntu Linux distribution with a lightweight LXDE graphical environment (Lubuntu) loaded with LibreOffice as an office suite and PDF editor, Peazip as an archive manager, LibreCAD as a CAD suite and ClamAV as an antivirus suite, although an antivirus is probably not needed at all. There are many more alternative programs that can be used to serve the same purposes and that makes the current proposal to be one of the many available choices. There is also proprietary software available for Linux operating systems that may offer a different use experience than the free ones and are usually offered in affordable prices.

The majority of these programs are compatible with their proprietary rivals and the exchange of produced files between them rarely produce problems that cannot be easily addressed. Furthermore, the modern look of the graphical environment can be modified and disguised in such a way that the end user will not easily realize the difference, making it easier to bend their resistance to change.

The implementation of the current proposal can lead to savings, counted in millions of euro, amounts of funds that can be utilized in other areas of the municipality's activities [8].

4.2   Purposeful Software

User communities that are involved in software development have produced a huge variety of programs that serve the needs of practically every user and organization. Most of them are given s open source which means that they can be freely altered and adjusted to the needs of the organization.

There are free and open source programs that can cover the needs of all areas of activity of a municipality. In context of the current research it was considered to be inappropriate to directly compare the used software with FOSS, since there were no records on specific usage that each of the proprietary software served and the way it is utilized and used in each municipality. A more thorough research would be needed in order to determine the true intended usage of this software in order to safely propose alternatives.

Nevertheless, honorable mentions should be made on free and open source software that serve the generic needs that where discussed. Those include but are not limited to OrangeHRM as an HR management software, Scriptum as an e-protocol, OpenWMS as an warehouse management, GnuCash and Eqonomize as a financial and accounting software, SuiteCRM, OpenBravo as an ERP solution. There are many more available options that can be freely obtained, examined, altered and used, whilst many of them can be utilized in server-client or even cloud basis and used through a web browser, making it unnecessary to install them separately on each workstation while its maintenance would be easier [10].

4.3   Server Operating Systems and Software

As already mentioned, Linux is the dominating operating system used in web servers, mainframes and supercomputers worldwide. Obviously, it is considered to be the most secure and stable choice for such a purpose and there are major companies that have their Linux server releases available offering alongside with them support plans on demand.

The hardware requirements for Linux servers are so low that it can even be deployed on a 20 year old PC, so the existing hardware could be used as is without the urgent need of any upgrade. The basics services that a server should offer are easily triggered, including file (storage) services, backup services, mail services, printing services and web services. Other services can be deployed as well, including those that were mentioned as purposeful software and can be offered in a server-client basis. Virtual machines can also be deployed, using FOSS such as KVM or Xen.

Furthermore, the existing server infrastructure can be used to deploy private cloud and offer remote services to the municipalities departments. There are tools available that can help deploying and managing cloud services such as the OpenStack, Kubernetes, Juju etc. There are also new technologies emerging, such as containerization, that are even more lightweight and help provide more services without the need of new and powerful hardware. The use of a FOSS tool such as Docker for this purpose will help even more in keeping the current hardware operational without the need for its upgrade or replacement.

Server OS comparison		
	Windows	**Linux**
Cost	Per user license	Free with support plans available
User interface	Graphical	Command line
Remote access	Not available by default, needs to be installed	Integrated (terminal & shell)
Software availability	Popular proprietary software is supported	Most proprietary software are not ported to Linux but there is a big amount of FOSS available
Hardware support	Usually supported by OS	There is a latency in porting drivers for newer devices
Safety	Open to users, very prone to errors, very likely to be attacked	Users do not have access to system settings, security holes and vulnerabilities are corrected immediately
Support	Long term support available	Varies depending on distribution and version
Documentation	Well documented	Complete source code of the system, API, libraries, and applications available: MAN and Info pages

Fig. 9. Server OS feature comparison

Most of the servers maintenance procedures can be executed remotely, so even if the municipality does not have an IT department or its employees do not have the ability to operate in a Linux server environment, those procedures can be executed from a far from a cooperating department of another municipality (Fig. 9).

4.4   Cloud Computing Utilization Possibilities

Cloud technologies are far from known to the Greek municipalities. None has implemented a cloud based approach and the only usage of commercial cloud services seems to be for file sharing purposes. Through the questionnaire it became clear that there is confusion between the concepts of server-client basis services and cloud services.

However, there is a prospect for the development and usage of cloud services in the Greek Municipalities [11]. A prospect that would lead to a technological leap and would dramatically reduce the need for powerful and expensive hardware, cost-effective software and continuous on-site support. Since the services would be offered remotely there will be only a need for internet-connected hardware. Most services could be offered as web-based services, so the need for purposeful software will be also reduced since a simple web browser will be enough to do the work.

There can be two possible scenarios for adopting the cloud computing technologies. The first is that every municipality deploys its own cloud network using the existing hardware and the available software that has already been proposed. In this case, each municipality would be free to adopt a plan differently from the others, having the ability to differentiate its implementation according to the specific needs it may have.

A team of able IT specialist would be needed in order to work on the project, a team that would have to be outsourced, if there are no available and adequately qualified human resources from within the municipality's IT department. According to this plan there would be a need to deploy up to 325 private cloud networks, one for each municipality, and up to the same number of IT supporting teams would be needed in order to ensure its continuous operation. The cost for such an approach would be discouraging for the smaller municipalities that luck the funding or do not have capable teams for working on such a project.

The second scenario would involve higher authorities from the municipalities, in order to create a centralized cloud infrastructure that would serve the needs of all municipalities in the same distinct way, with little choices of differentiation.

The local authorities in Greece are divided into two levels. The first level includes the municipalities themselves and the administrative body of the Central Union of Municipalities of Greece. The second level includes the thirteen administrative regions of Greece, that each includes regional units which are further subdivided into the municipalities.

A cloud network could be created in each of the administrative regions, serving the needs of its municipalities. In this way the need for hardware and specialized personnel for the implementation of the cloud infrastructure would be decreased to 13 and only a small supporting team would be needed in each municipality. Furthermore, a totally centralized cloud infrastructure could be implemented under the responsibility of the Central Union of Municipalities, an infrastructure that could be based in the Unions headquarters and from there to serve the needs of all municipalities all over Greece.

In this way all municipalities would benefit since they all would be able to use new technologies, to unify, consolidate and automate their processes and offer the same services to all citizens. There would be a need for a team in charge of assuring the central cloud infrastructure operation and care for its maintenance. There will be no need for large support teams in the municipalities since most of the operations would be held and executed on the cloud. It is even possible under certain circumstances for only a team of supporters per administrative region to be enough.

An estimation of the cost for such an infrastructure would be around 800.000 euro, a cost that is very small considering the annual spent of the municipalities towards their existing infrastructure. The annual operational cost of the cloud would be around 150.000 euro, including the power and cooling costs. The municipalities themselves would only need active internet connections and hardware able to connect to it, making most of the existing hardware enough for the purpose. The cost for software could be reduced down to zero, with the exception of some software that may not have alternatives on FOSS repositories. A support plan for the software is not calculated in the above estimation, and if one is needed its cost would probably not exceed the sum of 25.000 euro annually.

Furthermore, the cloud can offer increased levels of security, reliability scalability, manageability and immediate upgrades for all municipalities simultaneously [16]. Also, such an attempt would offer possibilities of centralized management of request and processes as well as more efficient gathering of data necessary for analysis, statistics and future planning.

The whole plan implies the agreement of all municipalities and the definition of a joint action plan with a view to create a cloud computing infrastructure that will operate according to the overall needs of all municipalities and that will eventually benefit them all equally, with the ultimate goal being the citizens satisfaction from providing cost effective and more efficient services to them.

5 Conclusions

The computerization of the Greek municipalities is still in a stage that can be characterized as "early", while the used hardware and software resources are considerably out of date. There is a need of adopting new technologies that will raise the quality of the provided services to the citizens while lowering its operational and maintenance costs.

The usage of Free and Open Source Software locally is the first step to such an attempt, while the creation of a cloud infrastructure that would serve the needs of all municipalities is the ultimate goal. Especially for the latter, it could also hide the performance drawback of the ageing workstations as well as act as a centralized point of security given their vulnerabilities due to no longer supported software versions. Based on the municipalities characteristics and available IT resources, two separate proposals were considered, one based on the overall regional administrative areas and a centralized one.

For the FOSS case, except for the obvious cases of OSs, Office suites and anti-viruses, the use can be easily extended to more advanced software such as CAD, HR, ERP, CRM and e-protocol based solutions, whose commercial licensing costs equivalents are also considerably higher.

The combination of FOSS and Cloud technologies would give to the municipalities bleeding – due to the continuous crisis - economy a surplus of about 5 million euros that can be used in other areas of competence. Setting a common goal and the cooperation of all stakeholders is essential in order for this to succeed, and if it succeeds it would benefit them all and mostly the citizens.

References

1. Rosen, L.: Open Source Licensing, Software Freedom and Intellectual Property Law. Prentice Hall, Upper Saddle River (2004)
2. Wong, K., Sayo, P.: FOSS A General Introduction. International Open Source Network (2004)
3. Hall, A.J.: Open Source Business Models: Making Money by Giving It Away. The Linux Foundation (2015)
4. Raymond, E.: The Cathedral & the Bazaar: Musings on Linux and Open Source by an Accidental Revolutionary. O'Reilly Media, Sebastopol (2009)
5. DiBona, C., Ockman, S.: Open Sources: Voices from the Open Source Revolution. O'Reilly Media, Sebastopol (2008)
6. Pintscher, L.: Open Advice: FOSS: What We Wish We Had Known When We Started. Lulu (2012)

7. The National IT and Telecom Agency of Denmark: Open Source Software and the Public Sector. The National IT and Telecom Agency (2009)
8. Ghosh, R.A.: CODE: Collaborative Ownership and the Digital Economy. The MIT Press, Cambridge (2005)
9. Busquets, J.P.: El Ayuntamiento de Barcelona rompe con el 'software' de Microsoft, El Pais, 4 December 2017
10. Wheeler, D.A.: Why Open Source Software/Free Software (OSS/FS, FLOSS, or FOSS)? Look at the Numbers! (2015). https://www.dwheeler.com/oss_fs_why.html
11. Stallman, R.M.: Free Software, Free Society: Selected Essays of Richard M. Stallman. GNU Press, Boston (2002)
12. Dua, A.: Linux is Running in Almost all of the Supercomputers. TechFAE (2017). https://www.techfae.com/linux-running-almost-supercomputers/. Accessed 25 June 2017
13. Jim Gruen: Linux in space. The Linux Foundation (2012)
14. CERN: Linux @ CERN. http://linux.web.cern.ch/linux/install/
15. Bouras, C., Kokkinos, V., Tseliou, G.: Methodology for Public Administrators for selecting between open source and proprietary software. Telematics Inform. J. (2011). www.elsevier.com
16. Blackduck: The 7 Myths of IP Risk: The Real Exposure Issues with Free and Open Source Software. Black Duck Software White Paper (2012)

Mining and Linking Open Economic Data from Governmental Communities

Michalis Vafopoulos[1]([✉]), Stylianos Rallis[2],
Ioannis Anagnostopoulos[3], Vassilios Peristeras[4], Dimitrios Negkas[1],
Ilias Skaros[1], and Aggelos Tzani[1]

[1] Software and Knowledge Engineering Laboratory, IIT,
NCSR-"Demokritos", Athens, Greece
vaf@aegean.gr, dimneg@gmail.com,
skaros.ilias@gmail.com, tzaniaggelos@hotmail.com
[2] School of Engineering, Department of Production and Management
Engineering, Democritus University of Thrace, Xanthi, Greece
strallis@gmail.com
[3] School of Sciences, Department of Computer Science and Biomedical
Informatics, University of Thessaly, Lamia, Greece
janag@dib.uth.gr
[4] School of Science and Technology, International Hellenic University,
Thessaloniki, Greece
v.peristeras@ihu.edu.gr

Abstract. In this paper, we propose a model conceptualization (Linked Open Economy - LOE) capable of exploiting the massive amount and variety of open economic data that are gradually becoming available by governments and open source communities. The main aim is to unleash the power of open data and open source systems and create a common ground to serve as a catalyst in providing more efficient answers in important economic activities.

Keywords: Open data · Open systems · Government · Economy

1 Introduction

In order to ensure transparency and provide valuable means of innovation, many governments demand from their public authorities to open their data (e.g. data.gov.uk), as well as to support their provision and maintenance with crowd-source independent repositories and open-source systems (like CKAN[1] etc.). Towards this end, there are also many organized initiatives and projects. To name a few, the IBP[2] promotes public access to accountable budget systems, thus allowing citizens to investigate whether central governments manage properly procedures in respect to public finances. Similarly, the Open Budgets[3], the Big Data Europe[4] and the Your Data Stories[5] H2020

---

[1] ckan.org.
[2] internationalbudget.org/.
[3] OpenBudgets.eu.
[4] BigDataEurope.eu.
[5] YourDataStories.eu.

© IFIP International Federation for Information Processing 2018
Published by Springer International Publishing AG 2018. All Rights Reserved
I. Stamelos et al. (Eds.): OSS 2018, IFIP AICT 525, pp. 144–148, 2018.
https://doi.org/10.1007/978-3-319-92375-8_12

projects provide a scalable platform for public administrations to publish and preserve open economic data under open-source support (e.g. GitHub). A comprehensive review of other similar initiatives can be found in [1].

2 Our Proposed Model

There are several standards, controlled vocabularies and ontological schemes for achieving semantic linking between open data. In the economy domain, the most important are: (i) the GoodRelations ontology [2], (ii) the Public Contracts ontology [3], (iii) the Organization ontology, and (iv) the vCard ontology. All above ontologies and schemas are cross-linked with several domain-independent controlled-vocabularies such as FOAF, DC Terms, SKOS [4], and DBpedia.

Based on the above (data and interoperability standards), we propose the Linked Open Economy (LOE) model (see Fig. 1), which is an economy-driven rather than a data- or statistics-driven approach. The model has been designed to better balance the trade-off of, being as generic as to be scalable to future open data categories, and as specific as to be compatible with existing initiatives. Furthermore, its top-level conceptualization interlinks the main publicly available data for the economy, as well as it models the flows incorporated in public budgeting, procurement and subsidies/aid. Detailed information about LOE modeling, as well as its main classes and properties can be found at https://github.com/LinkedEcon/LinkedEconomyOntology-ELOD.

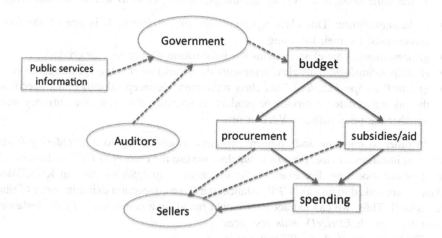

Fig. 1. The Linked Open Economy (LOE) model.

3 Application Case Study: Greek Public Procurement

The Central Electronic Registry of Public Procurement (KHMDHS) (eprocurement. gov.gr) is the official procurement portal of the Greek government which contains information on all public contracts for goods, services, and public works worth more than €1,000. It was established to reinforce transparency and effective management of public procurement. According to the Linked Economy Ontology (hereafter under the *elod* prefix), the basic model consist of:

elod:DecisionDomain

In this dataset the "tenders" concept is available. In order to model this part of the LOE flow, we use the *pc:Contract* class. The main parts are the following:

- the contracting authority which issues a contract,
- the CPV code which characterizes the products or services,
- the specified price of the contract including the currency specification, and
- the tender to whom a contract is awarded.

elod:SpendingDomain

The main components are:

- the authority which pays for the products or services,
- the sponsor who is paid for the offered products or services,
- the CPV code which characterizes the products or services, and
- the expense amount including the currency specification.

Organization Classes

The essential elements of the organization are given by the vat Id, the name, the vat Id type, and the country registered at.

elod:PriceDomain

In the same sense as above, we use the *gr:Offering* class as well as the following:

- *gr:BusinessEntity:* This class represents the organizations. It is one of the four classes used for their modeling.
- *gr:SomeItems:* This class contains the information of a service or product.
- *elod:SpendingItem:* This class represents decisions that involve spending actions.
- *gr:UnitPriceSpecification:* This class represents a conceptual entity that specifies the price asked for a service or product. It specifies the price, the currency and whether the price includes VAT or not.

In order to combine and compare products which belong to a *gr:Offering* from different instances of *elod:PriceDomain* class we use the class *elod:CPV* in the second level of our modeling. For example the instances of *gr:Offering* class in KHMDHS Data set are linked to an *elod:CPV* instance, the same connection exists in eprices Data set as well. Thus, we can extract information based on a common *elod:CPV* instance from different *elod:PriceDomain* resources.

The basic part of *elod:CPV* instance is:

- The unique code of cpv and the property which specifies it is *elod:cpvCode*.
- The Greek and English name of this category by using the properties *elod: cpvGreekSubject* and *elod:cpvEnglisSubject*.

4   Conclusions

LOE can be used to (i) enable information exchange between open source systems, (ii) integrate open data from heterogeneous sources and (iii) publish semantic and linked data related to economic activities. It can also be connected to market processes as analytically described in [1] where the generic LOE model is introduced. At the end of this short paper, we depict a SPARQL query for an open API endpoint (http://143. 233.226.49:8890/sparql). This query asks for retail tomato prices from the official Greek Price Observatory and compares them with wholesale prices provided by the Central Market of Thessaloniki/ KATH (in three different qualities) for a specific day. Retail stores with the highest and the lowest prices are also provided. Finally, the query returns the price paid for a specific public contract for tomatoes, thus combining information from governmental communities and market itself.

Beyond government and public authorities, we do believe that LOE can provide high valuable insights to other domain stakeholders (e.g. citizens, developers, researchers, journalists, companies etc.), who can use it as an establish and compact common ground to get and compile valuable economic information.

Endpoint: http://143.233.226.49:8890/sparql
PREFIX pc: <http://purl.org/procurement/public-contracts#>
PREFIX elod: <http://linkedeconomy.org/ontology#>
PREFIX gr: <http://purl.org/goodrelations/v1#>
PREFIX vcard: <http://www.w3.org/2006/vcard/ns#>
SELECT DISTINCT ?signatureDate ?buyer (str(?buyerLegalName) as ?buyerName)
(str(?sellerLegalName) as ?sellerName)
?cpvEnglishSubject ?amountOfThisGood
(xsd:decimal((1+?vatPercentage/100)?amount) AS ?amountInclVat)*
?minPriceWholesail ?maxPriceWholesail
FROM <http://linkedeconomy.org/EprocurementProper>
FROM <http://linkedeconomy.org/Organizations>
FROM <http://linkedeconomy.org/KATH>
FROM <http://publicspending.net/Diavgeia1/CPV>
WHERE {
<http://linkedeconomy.org/resource/Contract/15PAY002574748> elod:buyer ?buyer ;
pc:item ?offering ;
elod:signatureDate ?signatureDate .
?offering gr:includesObject ?tqn ;
gr:hasPriceSpecification ?ups ;
elod:seller ?seller .
?tqn gr:typeOfGood ?someItems ;
gr:amountOfThisGood ?amountOfThisGood .
?ups elod:hasVat ?vat ;
gr:hasCurrencyValue ?amount ;
gr:valueAddedTaxIncluded ?taxIncluded .

```
?vat elod:vatPercentage ?vatPercentage .
?someItems elod:productCategory <http://linkedeconomy.org/resource/CPV/03221240-0> ;
    gr:description ?description .
OPTIONAL {
?someItems elod:producedAt ?producedAt } .
<http://linkedeconomy.org/resource/CPV/03221240-0> elod:cpvEnglishSubject
?cpvEnglishSubject .
OPTIONAL {
?buyer gr:legalName ?buyerLegalName .
}.
OPTIONAL {
?buyer vcard:hasAddress ?address .
?address vcard:postal-code "55337"^^xsd:string .
}
OPTIONAL {
?seller gr:legalName ?sellerLegalName .
}
#KATH
?offerWholesail gr:includesObject ?tqnWholesail; gr:hasPriceSpecification ?upsWholesail ;
elod:year <http://linkedeconomy.org/resource/Year/2015> .
?upsWholesail gr:hasMinCurrencyValue ?minPriceWholesail ; gr:hasMaxCurrencyValue
?maxPriceWholesail;
gr:validThrough "2015-02-11T00:00:00"^^xsd:dateTime ;
rdfs:label "Category II"^^xsd:string. ?tqnWholesail gr:typeOfGood ?someItemsWholesail.
?someItemsWholesail elod:hasCpv <http://linkedeconomy.org/resource/CPV/03221240-0> ;
elod:productEnglishName ?nameProductWholesail .
}
```

Acknowledgments. This paper is supported by the project "Open Journalism – OpJ", which has received funding from the Digital News Initiative (DNI) Innovation Fund.

References

1. Vafopoulos, M., Vafeiadis, G., Razis, G., Anagnostopoulos, I., Negkas, D., Galanos, L.: Linked Open Economy: Take Full Advantage of Economic Data (2016). https://doi.org/10.2139/ssrn.2732218
2. Hepp, M.: GoodRelations: an ontology for describing products and services offers on the web. In: Gangemi, A., Euzenat, J. (eds.) EKAW 2008. LNCS (LNAI), vol. 5268, pp. 329–346. Springer, Heidelberg (2008). https://doi.org/10.1007/978-3-540-87696-0_29
3. Nečaský, M., Klímek, J., Mynarz, J., Knap, T., Svátek, V., Stárka, J.: Linked data support for filing public contracts. Comput. Ind. **65**(5), 862–877 (2014)
4. Miles, A., Matthews, B., Wilson, M., Brickley, D.: SKOS core: simple knowledge organisation for the web. In: International Conference on Dublin Core and Metadata Applications, pp. 3–10 (2005)

OSS Governance

Understanding Industry Requirements for FLOSS Governance Tools

Nikolay Harutyunyan[✉], Andreas Bauer, and Dirk Riehle

Friedrich-Alexander University Erlangen-Nürnberg, 91058 Erlangen, Germany
{nikolay.harutyunyan,andi.bauer}@fau.de,
dirk@riehle.org

Abstract. Almost all software products today incorporate free/libre, and open source software (FLOSS) components. Companies must govern their FLOSS use to avoid potential risks to their intellectual property resulting from the use of FLOSS components. A particular challenge is license compliance. To manage the complexity of license compliance, companies should use tools and well-defined processes to perform these tasks time and cost efficiently. This paper investigates and presents common industry requirements for FLOSS governance tools, followed by an evaluation of the suggested requirements by matching them with the features of existing tools.

We chose 10 industry leading companies through polar theoretical sampling and interviewed their FLOSS governance experts to derive a theory of industry needs and requirements for tooling. We then analyzed the features of a governance tools sample and used this analysis to evaluate two categories of our theory: FLOSS license scanning and FLOSS in product bills of materials. The result is a list of FLOSS governance requirements based on our qualitative study of the industry, evaluated using the existing governance tool features. For higher practical relevance, we cast our theory as a requirements specification for FLOSS governance tools.

Keywords: Open source software · FLOSS · FOSS · Open source governance
FLOSS governance tools · Company requirements for FLOSS tools

1 Introduction

Commercial use of FLOSS is on the rise as more companies realize the benefits of using FLOSS components in their products, going beyond the commonplace use of FLOSS development tools [9, 12, 19, 25, 34, 35]. In 2017 a report by the European Commission estimated that using FLOSS saves the European economy an estimated EUR 114 billion per year directly and up to EUR 399 billion per year overall [11]. However, companies also need to govern and regulate their use of FLOSS components to avoid common threats, such as FLOSS license non-compliance, copyright and patent infringement, that can result in litigation, cease and desist claims or product recalls [2, 33, 37, 39]. In the context of this paper, we define FLOSS governance as the set of processes, best practices and tools employed by companies to use FLOSS components as part of their commercial products while minimizing their risks and maximizing their benefit from such use.

© IFIP International Federation for Information Processing 2018
Published by Springer International Publishing AG 2018. All Rights Reserved
I. Stamelos et al. (Eds.): OSS 2018, IFIP AICT 525, pp. 151–167, 2018.
https://doi.org/10.1007/978-3-319-92375-8_13

FLOSS governance processes and tools can apply to the commercial use, contribution or leadership of FLOSS projects. We limited the scope of this paper only to the commercial use of FLOSS components, intentionally excluding governance considerations of FLOSS contribution or leadership by companies. This is in line with our earlier definition of FLOSS governance. Such focus allowed us to generate an in-depth theory covering the earliest maturity phase of industry involvement with open source that is of highest practical relevance to most companies today and novel to the growing open source research [20].

Despite the practical relevance of the issue, research has been slow to address the use of FLOSS in products. The existing literature is limited to general FLOSS governance research [1, 3, 4], to research of the governance of open source communities and their development practices [26, 28, 36, 40], and to FLOSS license compliance related governance [10, 13–17, 31, 42, 46]. However, past research has not comprehensively addressed FLOSS governance requirements and best practices in industry. A particularly practical aspect of FLOSS governance is its automation through tooling, which ensures increased efficiency and better integration into the development process. Focusing on the specific aspect of FLOSS governance tooling, we addressed this gap by asking the following research question:

RQ: *What are the core industry requirements for FLOSS governance tools needed to facilitate the use of FLOSS components in commercial products?*

The research method employed is an adaptation of the grounded theory method [5, 6] called the QDAcity RE method for structural domain modeling using qualitative data analysis [23]. We chose this novel, yet promising research method because it enables using qualitative data analysis (QDA) to develop a theory that can be specifically cast as a requirements specification. Answering our research question, we aimed to cast our theory as a list of common industry requirements for FLOSS governance tools. This format is well-understood in the industry and can, therefore, ensure a high practical value of our research results. Data gathering and analysis were performed using formal semi-structured interviews, researcher notes, and materials review. We interviewed 15 FLOSS governance and compliance experts from 10 diverse companies chosen through theoretical sampling of more than 140 companies.

There are few reports on commercial adoption of FLOSS that are cast as lists of requirements focusing on technical and managerial aspects of using FLOSS in proprietary products [46]. However, neither academic nor practitioner literature offers a detailed list of industry requirements for FLOSS governance or its tooling that goes beyond a high-level of abstraction [30]. In this paper, we addressed this research gap with our main contribution – the theory of industry requirements for FLOSS governance tools. Our theory indicated four key categories of FLOSS governance tool requirements in no particular order:

- Tracking and Reuse of FLOSS components
- License Compliance of FLOSS components
- Search and Selection of FLOSS components
- Other requirements (security, education, etc.)

We then broke down each of these categories into detailed requirements and sub-requirements.

To evaluate our theory, we analyzed marketing materials and demos of 6 widely used and representative FLOSS governance tools. We compared the key tool features with our suggested theory and evaluated our proposed requirements confirming many of them. In future publications, we also plan to address other aspects of FLOSS governance in high detail, including industry best practices for FLOSS supply chain management and license compliance.

2 Related Work

The early research on FLOSS governance in companies was part of the broader research on the commercial use of FLOSS development tools and components [1, 20]. In a systematic literature review on FLOSS adoption in industry, Hauge et al. identified only a limited amount of research focusing on FLOSS component selection by companies [7, 8, 22, 45] and knowledge sharing within FLOSS communities [24, 27, 43]. Hauge et al. [20] did not identify any academic studies focused on the actual industry practice of using FLOSS components in products, thus suggesting that further research is needed on this topic. Our literature review confirmed this research gap prompting us to conduct this study of 10 industry-representative companies.

We set our research scope and that of the related work review to the commercial use of FLOSS components in products and industry requirements for FLOSS governance tooling. We explicitly excluded FLOSS governance related to industry contribution to or leadership of FLOSS projects. We did not identify literature explicitly focused on FLOSS governance tool requirements. However, we found indirect references to the topic that we used as a starting point for our research. We derived three key categories of FLOSS governance requirements that can be addressed through tooling:

- Tracking and Reuse of FLOSS components [21, 32, 44]
- License Compliance of FLOSS components [10, 13–17, 31, 42, 46]
- Search and Selection of FLOSS components [7, 8, 22, 41, 45]

Tracking and Reuse. With the growing availability of high-quality FLOSS components, software developers increasingly use FLOSS components in commercial products. FLOSS governance policies in many companies require developers to track and document such FLOSS use [21, 32]. This enables the well-structured management and reuse of FLOSS components that have been added into product software. Umarji et al. [45] suggest using FLOSS governance tools to create and maintain libraries of reusable FLOSS components. Our findings confirm this as one of the industry requirements for FLOSS governance tools.

Other requirements focus on supply chain management [30], automated management of bill of materials [42], maintenance of FLOSS component metadata in product architecture models [38], etc. Our theory confirms and captures these requirements.

License Compliance. Wang and Wang present a number of requirements for industry adoption of FLOSS. Some of these requirements can be translated into industry requirements for FLOSS governance tools. The authors suggest a managerial requirement for license compliance that includes understanding different FLOSS licenses and documenting their terms [46]. Our theory suggests that industry requires the use of FLOSS governance tools for documenting company interpretation of most common and used FLOSS licenses and their implications. This requirement is also confirmed by industry associations, such as *The Open Source Automation Development Lab eG*, which in 2017 attempted to standardize FLOSS license obligations through checklists and own license describing language that can eventually be used in a FLOSS governance tool [10].

Other industry requirements for compliance tools include automated FLOSS license scanning [14, 15], automated FLOSS code detection in company's codebase and in its supply chain using source code and binary scans [16, 31, 42], checking FLOSS license compatibility when mixing licenses [17] etc. We confirm all these requirements through expert interviews and formalize them in our theory, while recognizing the technological complexity of fulfilling these requirements by the currently existing tooling.

Search and Selection. Umarji et al. [45] surveyed a sample of 69 programmers. Their research suggested that software developers require and use tools for the search and selection of FLOSS components. The majority of the survey respondents said they used general-purpose search engines with some also using project hosting sites and code-specific search engines. Our expert interviews confirmed the requirement for search and selection of FLOSS components. A requirement in our proposed theory formalizes this industry need.

Other industry requirements for search and selection of FLOSS components focus on the automated identification of software families and types of FLOSS communities [41]. Our theory did not confirm the industry requirement for the tool-assisted software family identification, but did confirm the need for the tool-assisted identification and evaluation of FLOSS communities.

Many other requirements are suggested in both academic literature and practitioner white papers. However, in this section, we combined and presented the literature related to only several key requirements due to our narrow scope.

3   Research Method

We conducted a two-step study that consists of:

1. Deriving a theory based on our understanding of key industry requirements for FLOSS governance tools through expert interviews
2. Evaluating our understanding of industry requirements through marketing materials and demos of existing FLOSS governance tools

Our research approach is represented in Fig. 1 and explained below.

For theory building, we conducted 15 interviews with ten industry-leading companies to understand their requirements for FLOSS governance tools.

We employed an adaptation of the grounded theory [5, 6] method called the QDAcity RE method for structural domain modeling using qualitative data analysis [23]. Corbin and Strauss [6] or Charmaz [5] define the grounded theory method as one that consists of systematic, yet flexible guidelines for collecting and analyzing qualitative data to construct a theory from that data. Kaufmann and Riehle [23] accept this definition, but extend the method to a more structured, traceable and iterative one providing guidelines for data collection, creation and application of a code system. This enabled us to use the QDAcity-RE method for requirements engineering based on our industry expert interviews. The result is a partial theory of industry requirements for FLOSS governance tools cast as a requirements specification.

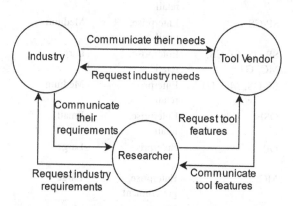

For theory evaluation, we reviewed marketing materials and demos of 6 widely used FLOSS governance tools. We used the QDAcity RE method and qualitative data analysis to derive the common features they offer to meet industry needs for automating FLOSS governance.

Assuming that the tool vendors as a whole understand industry needs and offer tools that address these needs, we compared the common tool features to our

Fig. 1. Theory Building using Industry Requirements and Theory Evaluation using Tool Features

partial theory of industry requirements. We evaluated which tool features match the industry requirements in our proposed theory and which ones do not. We used this evaluation to demonstrate that our theory represents the current state of industry requirements for FLOSS governance tools. To the extent that our theory agrees with tool features, we put the work of industry product managers onto a sound scientific base of theory development based on the user's perspective.

3.1   Theoretical Sampling

For theory building, we chose ten companies sampled from our industry network of about 140 companies with advanced FLOSS governance practices. The companies in our sample have advanced understanding of FLOSS governance and use internal and/or external governance tools. We conducted polar theoretical sampling to cover a diverse and representative set of companies. Polar sampling aims to choose companies with highly varying characteristics. We considered diverse dimensions including types of business models, customer types, company size, market position and company maturity. The resulting sample of companies includes small, medium and large companies with both enterprise and retail customers and varying business models. The list of companies and their essential characteristics are presented in Table 1. Company names are anonymized per their request.

Table 1. Theoretical sample of companies

Company	Company domain	By business model	By type of customer	By size (employees)
Company 1	Consulting	SP-OS, SDS	Enterprise	Medium
Company 2	Automotive	SDS	Enterprise	Small
Company 3	Automotive	SDS	Enterprise	Large
Company 4	Enterprise Software	SP-OS	Enterprise, retail	Medium
Company 5	Enterprise Software	SP-CS	Enterprise, retail	Medium
Company 6	Enterprise Software	SP-OS, SP-CS, MC, GT	Enterprise, retail	Large
Company 7	Enterprise Software	SP-OS, MC, GT	Enterprise, retail	Medium
Company 8	FLOSS Foundation	OSF	Enterprise, retail	Small
Company 9	Hardware and Software	OP	Enterprise	Large
Company 10	Legal	MC	Enterprise, government	Large

Legend for Table 1: SDS= Software development service, SP-OS= Software product vendor for open source software,
SP-CS = Software product vendor for closed source software, GT = Governance tool providers,
MC = Management consulting,
OSF = Open source foundation, OP = Other products incorporating software

For theory evaluation, we chose 6 widely used and prominent FLOSS governance tools that represent the broader spectrum of FLOSS governance tools [44]. Not all tools compete but have some overlap in their functionalities, like support for license scanning or component repository management. To reduce bias, we made sure that our selection differs in these dimensions:

- By the **license** under which a vendor makes its tool available. The sampling contains tools that are licensed under permissive and copyleft type open source licenses, and proprietary closed source licenses.
- By the **delivery model** of a tool. A critical factor for companies is the ability to choose whether a software tool is available as cloud-based service or can be used on-premise, depending on aspects like costs, customization, and security.
- By the **scannable artifacts**. For scanning of license information, tools can analyze source code or binary artifacts. Scanning of binary artifacts is necessary if the source code of dependent components is not available. In contrast scanning of source code artifacts provide better results.

We also consider other dimensions for the theoretical sampling (maturity of a tool, automation and integration into the development process, and additional audit service by experts), but to offer more depth we focus on the three key dimensions presented above. The list of tools and their key characteristics are presented in Table 2.

Table 2. Sampling of governance tools

Tool	Tool provider	By license	By delivery model	By scannable artifacts
Black Duck Hub	Black Duck Software by Synopsys	Proprietary	Cloud-based	Source and binary code
DejaCode	nexB	Apache 2.0	Cloud-based, on premise	Source and binary code
FOSSology	FOSSology FLOSS project	GPL-2.0	On premise	Source and binary code
FOSSA	FOSSA	Proprietary	Cloud-based, on premise	Source code
OSS-Review-Toolkit	OSS-Review-Toolkit (ORT) FLOSS project	Apache 2.0	On premise	Source code
WhiteSource	WhiteSource Software	Proprietary	Cloud-based, on premise	Source and binary code

3.2 Data Gathering and Analysis

For data gathering, we mainly used semi-structured interviews conducted by one or two researchers with FLOSS governance experts or responsible coworkers from the sampled companies. In seven companies we interviewed one expert, in one company we interviewed two experts, and in two companies we interviewed three experts. In total, we conducted 15 interviews. When possible, we recorded and transcribed the interviews. In three cases we took notes. We also studied additional materials both public and private about these companies and their FLOSS governance practices.

We developed key questions and an interview guideline for the semi-structured interviews and kept them stable, except for few iterative adjustments from company to company, throughout the whole data gathering process. The interviews were exploratory in line with our grounded-theory-based research method.

For data analysis, we followed the QDAcity-RE method performing iterative and incremental qualitative data analysis (QDA) supported by the MaxQDA software. We developed two separate coding systems for the theory building using expert interviews and for the theory evaluation using tool marketing materials and demos.

During the QDA coding process, we iteratively refined the code system. Reaching theoretical saturation [23], the code system became the basis for our theory. Individual codes correspond to low-level tool requirements in our requirements specification. Both for theory building and evaluation, our code systems consist of hierarchical codes. We did not apply the top category codes in our QDA. We followed the QDAcity-RE method's QDA process as follows:

- *Open coding.* We created a basic set of codes from which the hierarchy is built. Open codes are direct annotations of primary materials and link to them for data-theory traceability.
- *Axial coding.* We built a code system by deriving more abstract concepts and categories from open codes, thus developing the axes of the code system.

- *Selective coding*. We applied the codes to the gathered data and chose which codes are important and which are not. We adjusted the coding system by removing the irrelevant codes and by adding the ones that emerged when applying the axial codes.

4 Research Results

This section presents our partial theory of industry requirements for FLOSS governance tools, followed by the evaluation of the suggested theory through feature analysis of existing FLOSS governance tools. Section 4.1 presents our theory cast as a requirements specification for high practical relevance. Section 4.2 presents our evaluation of the theory.

4.1 Theory of Industry Requirements for FLOSS Governance Tools

We limited our scope to FLOSS governance tools related to the commercial use of FLOSS components, explicitly excluding companies' contribution to or leadership of FLOSS projects. We only present the requirements that have been directly derived or inferred from our data, thus excluding the ones that have been presented in the literature, but not confirmed by our industry study. The result is a partial theory that covers the key requirement categories and requirements based on our sample. Analyzing 15 expert interviews, researcher notes and company materials, we derived the following high-level industry requirements for FLOSS governance tools:

1. **Tracking and Reuse of FLOSS components**
   1.1. The tool should help users **identify the use of FLOSS components in their code base**.
   1.2. The tool should help users **report the use of FLOSS components in a product architecture model**.
   1.3. The tool should help users **update FLOSS components and their metadata**.
   1.4. The tool should help users **maintain a bill of materials of the FLOSS components used in a product**.
   1.5. The tool should help users **reuse FLOSS components that have already been used in a product**.

Virtually all companies track their use of FLOSS components in order to efficiently manage FLOSS integration into their products, as well as to enable cost-saving reuse of FLOSS components already used by the company's other developers. Efficient FLOSS component management ensures a company's ability to maintain and produce upon customer request an up-to-date bill of materials. One interview partner mentions this requirement for this use case *(Requirement 1.4)*:

> *"So, we do have tools to keep track of different components or licenses we're using. If you get requests or requirements from customers to provide a list of used [FLOSS] components and licenses, we use this tool to track those and push those requirements into our [development] process." (Company 7)*

Another expert suggests a requirement to enable tracking and reusing FLOSS components *(Requirement 1.5)*:

> *"What we have there at the moment is that [for] half of the company we have essential database or half of the company uses that central database of components and their licenses." (Company 2)*

2. License Compliance of FLOSS components

    2.1. The tool should help users **interpret open source licenses**.

    2.2. The tool should help users **document the identified licenses of the used FLOSS components in the company's open source license repository or license handbook**.

    2.3. The tool should help users **find and document the unidentified licenses of the used FLOSS components in the company's open source license repository or license handbook**.

    2.4. The tool should help users **approve the use of a FLOSS component in a product based on FLOSS license compliance guidelines**.

    2.5. The tool should help users **distribute a product that is compliant with the FLOSS licenses of the FLOSS components used in that product**.

FLOSS license compliance is a central aspect and key tool requirement category to the companies we studied. Companies strive to automate license compliance, license scanning and license management. Some companies employ continuous integration/deployment and thus require appropriate license compliance tools that can be integrated in their development process. Tool requirements for license compliance go on to encompass automated license interpretation, license identification and documentation, etc.

An expert from Company 7 mentions the tool requirement for automating FLOSS license scanning and identification of other FLOSS component metadata *(Requirement 2.2)*, as well as the requirement for automating component approval *(Requirement 2.4)*:

> *"We have a full toolset that goes through and scans the code, that pulls out all the license information, the authorship [copyright] information, and runs that through our process for verification, for compliance, for compatibility and so forth." (Company 7)*

Another expert talks about the need to find and document the unidentified FLOSS components and licenses *(Requirement 2.3)*:

> *"We need this [license scanning] tool to re-check if any of the developers are not handling [FLOSS components] in the way [the management] wants, to better do it because we have no possibility to check it in a clear way if you have no tool." (Company 3)*

3. Search and Selection of FLOSS components

    3.1. The tool should help users **search for FLOSS components**.

    3.2. The tool should help users **select best FLOSS components**.

    3.3. The tool should help users **estimate the cost of using an FLOSS component**.

Companies need to FLOSS governance tools to efficiently search and select the right FLOSS components, which translates into tool requirements on evaluating different component candidates and estimating the cost of their usage. One interviewee talks about the role of tools in FLOSS component selection process *(Requirement 3.2)*:

> *"When you move on from a strategic decision to component selection like with components of open source projects to be used, then we have a process that we require the projects to name all the open source components to assess that they want to use, that they assess the license, that they check the license, and that they document that and that again this assessment is communicated to upper management and signed off that." (Company 2)*

4. Other requirements

4.1. The tool should help users **detect and prevent security vulnerabilities in product's FLOSS components**.

4.2. The tool should help users **document and communicate company's FLOSS governance strategy, policies and best practices**.

4.3. The tool should help users get **training on FLOSS governance and compliance when using open source software in products and contributing to open source projects**.

The detailed subcategories of requirements for Tracking and Reuse of FLOSS components are demonstrated in Table 3. The detailed subcategories of requirements for License Compliance of FLOSS components are demonstrated in Table 4. The detailed subcategories of requirements for Search and Selection of FLOSS components are demonstrated in Table 5.

4.2   Evaluation

This section presents the evaluation of our suggested theory using the feature analysis of existing FLOSS governance tools. We analyzed marketing materials and demos of six widely used FLOSS governance tools. The analysis resulted in the following list of common key features related to FLOSS use in products:

- *Component Tracking & Reporting*: support for bill of materials, component inventory, knowledge base (external inventory), license obligation reporting, and commonly accepted data exchange standard support;
- *Scanning/License Checking*: support for licenses identification, copyright identification, code origin identification, and license management;
- *Policies*: support for applying/ensuring FLOSS policies;
- *Security*: support for security vulnerability detection;
- *Development Integration & Automation*: support for integration into continuous integration and deployment.

To ensure the depth of evaluation, we focus on two main requirement categories: **Tracking and Reuse of FLOSS components** and **License Compliance of FLOSS components**. We chose these categories because these requirements are fundamental to any software company according to the analysis of the industry interviews and tools support of these requirements as base functionalities.

Table 3. Tracking and Reuse of FLOSS components requirements

---

1. The tool should help users **identify the use of FLOSS components in their code base**.
   a. The tool should allow reading in an existing code base.
   b. The tool should allow automated finding of open source licenses in an existing code base.
   c. The tool should allow automated finding of open source software checked-in and used by a company developer.
   d. The tool should allow automated finding of open source software not checked-in, but used by a company developer.
   e. The tool should allow automated finding of open source software that is part of the supplied proprietary software using commonly accepted data exchange standards (such as SPDX).
   f. The tool should allow automated finding of open source software that is part of the supplied proprietary software using binary or source code scanning.

---

2. The tool should help users **report the use of FLOSS components in a product architecture model**.
   a. The tool should allow creating a product architecture model to systematically record use of FLOSS components, their metadata and component dependencies.
   b. The tool should allow manual recording of metadata of the used FLOSS components.
   c. The tool should allow confirming the metadata of FLOSS components identified automatically.
   d. The tool should allow modifying the metadata of FLOSS components identified automatically.
   e. The tool should allow removing the metadata of FLOSS components identified automatically.
   f. The tool should allow automated reporting of a newly used FLOSS component within the build process and/or continuous integration process.
   g. The tool should allow reporting undeclared use of FLOSS components and their metadata.

---

3. The tool should help users **update FLOSS components and their metadata**.
   a. The tool should allow automated updates of FLOSS components to their newest available versions.
   b. The tool should allow to back up the current versions of FLOSS components before updating them.
   c. The tool should allow automated identification of changed metadata including FLOSS component license and copyright information.
   d. The tool should allow automated history recording of FLOSS components and their metadata.

---

4. The tool should help users **maintain bill of materials of the FLOSS components used in a product**.
   a. The tool should allow creating a formal bill of material using a commonly accepted data exchange standard (such as SPDX).
   b. The tool should allow automated generation of a formal bill of materials using company's product architecture model.
   c. The tool should allow developers to add identified and reported metadata on used FLOSS components into the formal bill of materials.
   d. The tool should allow developers to update the formal bill of materials.
   e. The tool should allow automated generation of a bill of materials instance in a structured textual format.
   f. The tool should allow automated generation of a bill of materials instance in a commonly accepted data exchange standard (such as SPDX) format.

---

5. The tool should help users **reuse FLOSS components that have already been used in a product**.
   a. The tool should allow creating a centralized and company-wide accessible FLOSS component repository.
   b. The tool should allow automated adding of FLOSS components and their metadata into the repository using the product architecture model.
   c. The tool should allow automated updating of FLOSS components repository using the product architecture model.
   d. The tool should allow all company developers to access the FLOSS components repository.
   e. The tool should allow searching in the FLOSS component repository.
   f. The tool should allow finding the company developers who used an FLOSS component from the repository.

Tracking and Reuse of FLOSS components. The identification of FLOSS components and their licenses in a given software product or component is a core functionality of all sampled tools. All the high-level requirements of the category 1 in the proposed theory are matched by the features of the sampled tools. For example, Black Duck Software enables its users to identify the used FLOSS components *(Requirement 1.1)* in both the source code and in binaries (with lesser precision):

> *"[Black Duck Hub enables to] fully discover all open source in your code" (Black Duck Hub)*

Table 4. License Compliance of FLOSS components requirements

---

1. The tool should help users **interpret open source licenses**.
   a. The tool should allow user to document open source license interpretations using a formal language or notation supported by the tool.
   b. The tool should provide automated standard interpretation of the most common FLOSS licenses in company's license repository or license handbook.
   c. The tool should allow users to modify license interpretation of the most common FLOSS licenses in company's license repository or license handbook.
   d. The tool should allow users to add license interpretation of the FLOSS licenses of the used FLOSS components to company's license repository or license handbook.
   e. The tool should allow users to change license interpretation in the license repository or license handbook.
   f. The tool should allow developers to request license interpretation of a FLOSS license of an FLOSS component s/he wants to use in a product.
   g. The tool should allow open source program office to discuss license interpretation requests.
   h. The tool should allow open source program office to fulfill license interpretation requests.

---

2. The tool should help users **document the identified licenses of the used FLOSS components in the company's open source license repository or license handbook**.
   a. The tool should allow creating an open source license repository.
   b. The tool should allow developers, lawyers and managers to read the open source license repository.
   c. The tool should allow automated inventorying of known open source licenses from the product architecture model.
   d. The tool should allow users to add new open source licenses into the open source license repository.
   e. The tool should allow users to remove obsolete open source licenses from the open source license repository.
   f. The tool should support the commonly accepted data exchange standards (such as SPDX).
   g. The tool should allow users to search open source license information in the open source license.

---

3. The tool should help users **find and document the unidentified licenses of the used FLOSS components in company's open source license repository or license handbook**.
   a. The tool should allow software package scanning to find the open source licenses unidentified previously through product architecture model.
   b. The tool should allow source code scanning for the internally developed code to find the origin of used, but unidentified open source code and its license.
   c. The tool should allow source code scanning for the FLOSS components taken from FLOSS projects to find the origin of used, but unidentified open source code and its license.
   d. The tool should allow binary scanning for the FLOSS components that are part of the supplied proprietary software components to find the origin of used, but unidentified open source code and its license.
   e. The tool should allow automated inventorying of the open source licenses identified because of binary and source code scanning.
   f. The tool should allow manual changing the automatically identified open source licenses.
   g. The tool should allow removing the automatically identified open source licenses.
   h. The tool should support binary and source code scanning integration into the build process and/or continuous integration process.
   i. The tool should allow finding and documenting copyright notices, export restriction information and other compliance-related metadata for FLOSS components used in a product.

---

4. The tool should help users **approve the use of a FLOSS component in a product based on FLOSS license compliance guidelines**.
   a. The tool should allow creating white lists of company-approved FLOSS licenses according to company policy.
   b. The tool should allow creating black lists of company-blocked FLOSS licenses according to company policy.
   c. The tool should allow updating white and black lists of FLOSS licenses.
   d. The tool should allow creating license interpretation-based rules for automated recommendation on component use approval according to company policy.
   e. The tool should allow developers to request approval of FLOSS components with previously unassessed licenses.
   f. The tool should allow lawyers to approve or block use of FLOSS components due to license incompatibility with company policy.
   g. The tool should allow automated recording of FLOSS license approval decisions in company's open source license repository.

---

5. The tool should help users **distribute a product that is compliant with the FLOSS licenses of the FLOSS components used in that product**.
   a. The tool should allow automated generating of FLOSS license obligations for each product using product architecture model and open source license repository.
   b. The tool should allow automated assignment of tasks that will ensure compliance with FLOSS license obligations.
   c. The tool should allow automated audit of product's bill of materials before distribution.
   d. The tool should allow manual audit of product's bill of materials before distribution.
   e. The tool should allow adjusting product's bill of materials before distribution.

Table 5. Search and Selection of FLOSS components requirements

---

1. The tool should help users **search for FLOSS components**.
   a. The tool should allow automated search of available FLOSS components using publicly available data.
   b. The tool should allow automated comparison of available FLOSS components using publicly available data.

---

2. The tool should help users **select best FLOSS components**.
   a. The tool should allow automated health assessment of open source communities using publicly available data.
   b. The tool should allow automated maturity assessment of open source communities using publicly available data.
   c. The tool should allow automated corporate dependence assessment of open source communities using publicly available data.
   d. The tool should allow automated maturity assessment of open source communities using publicly available data.
   e. The tool should allow automated responsiveness assessment of open source communities using publicly available data.

---

3. The tool should help users **estimate the cost of using an FLOSS component**.
   a. The tool should allow automated cost estimation of FLOSS component integration and maintenance in a product.
   b. The tool should allow automated risk assessment of FLOSS community discontinuing its development of the FLOSS component and automated cost estimation of internal maintenance of the FLOSS component.
   c. The tool should allow users semi-automated estimation of the benefit of using an FLOSS component compared to proprietary and in-house development alternatives.

FOSSA helps explore and report relationships between modules incl. the open source ones *(Requirement 1.2)*:

> *"[FOSSA allows its user to] explore relationships between modules and if/how dependencies are included in your build" (FOSSA)*

Black Duck Hub also has features for BOM maintenance *(Requirement 1.4)* and for FLOSS component reuse *(Requirement 1.5)*:

> *"We provide a license obligation report, including an easily consumable bill of materials (BOM) that you can deliver to your customers and/or internal stakeholders." (Black Duck Hub)*

> *"[Black Duck Hub enables to] eliminate uncertainty and promote reuse [of FLOSS]" (Black Duck Hub)*

However, not all detailed (low-level) requirements from the proposed theory are supported by existing tool features. *Requirement 1.1.d*, for example requires tools to allow automated finding of open source software not checked-in but used by a company developer. This requirement is not entirely supported by any of the studied tool because of its technological complexity.

License Compliance of FLOSS components. All the studied tools support FLOSS license compliance features. They fulfill offer fulfilling requirements, such as license interpretation, license identification and documentation, FLOSS component approval etc.

FOSSology covers several requirements related to FLOSS license compliance *(Requirement 2.2, 2.3)* [18]:

> *"FOSSology is an open source license compliance software system and toolkit. As a toolkit you can run license, copyright and export control scans from the command line. As a system, a database and web UI are provided to give you a compliance workflow. License, copyright and export scanners are tools available to help with your compliance activities." (FOSSology)*

However, none of our studied tools completely fulfill some of the following low-level requirements: *Requirement 2.1.b* (automated standard interpretation of common FLOSS licenses), *Requirement 2.3.h* (automated license checking within continuous integration), *Requirement 2.5.b* (automated assignment of FLOSS compliance tasks), *Requirement 2.5.c* (automated audit of product's bill of materials before distribution). One reason is the complex computational nature of the complete automation of compliance tasks. An empirical study by German et al. [16] showed that a deeper understanding of licensing issues requires human expertise, which limits the automation of some license compliance tasks. Moreover, most companies don't allow complete automation of compliance as they require a human actor to be responsible for legal matters, even if they use semi-automated tooling.

Our limited evaluation demonstrates that the high-level requirements of our theory do match the features offered by industry leading FLOSS governance tools. The evaluation shows that existing tools satisfy most of the low-level requirements by the industry, but not others, such as requirements of complete automation.

5   Discussion

Our main contribution is the requirements specification presented in Sect. 4.1 and its evaluation in Sect. 4.2.

We recognize that our research results are limited, but novel and practice relevant. They present only a partial theory on the issue. However, we lay groundwork for future studies into FLOSS governance tool requirements, that will hopefully expand our requirements specification theory. Our work leads us to propose the following research questions for future research:

RQ1: *What are other detailed FLOSS governance tool requirements beyond Tracking and Reuse of FLOSS components, License Compliance of FLOSS components and Search and Selection of FLOSS components?*

RQ2: *How can FLOSS governance tool requirement theories be better evaluated or validated?*

RQ3: *How to engineer FLOSS governance tool requirements of the future addressing missing features and industry needs before companies become aware of them?*

6   Research Limitations

The study faces several limitations including those to internal validity and to external validity:

Internal validity. Qualitative data research realized by one researcher has inherent subjectivity and bias. Even though we followed the research method constructs carefully, there is bias associated with method interpretation and application to our specific context. To address this limitation, we had a second coder analyze our data and improved our original QDA coding with that of the second coder. The high inter-coder agreement between the original coding and the second coder coding suggests an adequate quality of our code system and by extension an adequate quality of the derived theory [29].

External validity. The resulting theory is based on the data gathered from the experts of the ten companies we interviewed. We cannot claim broad generalizability of the findings, even though we followed a careful theoretical sampling to ensure the applicability of our results. This limitation can be tested with further validation studies.

7 Conclusion

This paper presents a study of ten industry companies with advanced FLOSS governance practices. Our study concluded in a partial theory of FLOSS governance tool requirements by the industry. Also, we provide a detailed hierarchical list of these industry relevant requirements. As such it offers unique insight into industry understanding of FLOSS governance tools and their expectations from them, alongside existing tools and their features.

The data gathered through semi-structured interviews and materials collection was analyzed using the novel adoption of grounded theory method – the QDAcity-RE method. We cast our theory as a requirements specification making it applicable and practice relevant to the companies willing to employ these requirements. Finally, we evaluated our findings using six industry leading FLOSS governance tools and the analysis of their features matched with the requirements of the suggested theory.

The study of the missing features of existing tools is out of scope of this paper but it can be a valuable part of further research. Further research can also focus on the reasons why tool providers do not fulfill the unsatisfied requirements of our theory (e.g. full automation of compliance) and how such problems can be solved.

Acknowledgments. We would like to thank Hannes Dohrn, Michael Dorner, Maximilian Capraro, Andreas Kaufmann and Shushanik Hakobyan for their generous feedback that helped us improve our paper. We would also like to thank our industry partners that provided their valuable time and expertise for this research project.

References

1. Aksulu, A., Wade, M.: A comprehensive review and synthesis of open source research. J. Assoc. Inf. Syst. **11**(11), 576 (2010)
2. Black Duck Software: 2017 Open Source Security and risk analysis. Center for Open Source Research & Innovation. In: (self-published white paper) (2017)
3. Bonaccorsi, A., Rossi, C.: Why open source software can succeed. Res. Policy **32**(7), 1243–1258 (2003)
4. Capra, E., Francalanci, C., Merlo, F.: An empirical study on the relationship between software design quality, development effort and governance in open source projects. IEEE Trans. Softw. Eng. **34**(6), 765–782 (2008)
5. Charmaz, K.: Constructing Grounded Theory. Sage, Thousand Oaks (2014)

6. Corbin, J., Strauss, A.: Basics of Qualitative Research: Techniques and Procedures for Developing Grounded Theory. Sage Publications, Thousand Oaks (2014)
7. Cruz, D., Wieland, T., Ziegler, A.: Evaluation criteria for free/open source software products based on project analysis. Softw. Process Improv. Pract. **11**(2), 107–122 (2006)
8. Deprez, J.-C., Alexandre, S.: Comparing assessment methodologies for free/open source software: OpenBRR and QSOS. In: Jedlitschka, A., Salo, O. (eds.) PROFES 2008. LNCS, vol. 5089, pp. 189–203. Springer, Heidelberg (2008). https://doi.org/10.1007/978-3-540-69566-0_17
9. Deshpande, A., Riehle, D.: The total growth of open source. In: Russo, B., Damiani, E., Hissam, S., Lundell, B., Succi, G. (eds.) OSS 2008. ITIFIP, vol. 275, pp. 197–209. Springer, Boston, MA (2008). https://doi.org/10.1007/978-0-387-09684-1_16
10. Emde, C., Jaeger, T.: Open source license obligations checklists (version 5). In: Open Source Automation Development Lab (self-published white paper) (2017)
11. European Commission: The economic and social impact of software & services on competitiveness and innovation (SMART 2015/0015). Publications Office of the European Union, Luxembourg, pp. 197–198 (2017)
12. Fitzgerald, B.: The transformation of open source software. MIS Q. **30**(3), 587–598 (2006)
13. Gangadharan, G.R., De Paoli, S., D'Andrea, V., Weiss, M.: License compliance issues in free and open source software. In: MCIS 2008 Proceedings, vol. 2 (2008)
14. Gangadharan, G.R., D'andrea, V., De Paoli, S., Weiss, M.: Managing license compliance in free and open source software development. Inf. Syst. Front. **14**(2), 143–154 (2012)
15. German, D.M., Hassan, A.E.: License integration patterns: Addressing license mismatches in component-based development. In: Proceedings of the 31st International Conference on Software Engineering, pp. 188–198. IEEE Computer Society, May 2009
16. German, D.M., Di Penta, M., Davies, J.: Understanding and auditing the licensing of open source software distributions. In: 2010 IEEE 18th International Conference on Program Comprehension (ICPC), pp. 84–93. IEEE, June 2010
17. German, D.M., Manabe, Y., Inoue, K.: A sentence-matching method for automatic license identification of source code files. In: Proceedings of the IEEE/ACM International Conference on Automated Software Engineering, pp. 437–446. ACM, September 2010
18. Gobeille, R.: The fossology project. In: Proceedings of the 2008 International Working Conference on Mining Software Repositories, pp. 47–50. ACM, May 2008
19. Hammond, J., Santinelli, P., Billings, J.J., Ledingham, B.: The tenth annual future of open source survey. In: Black Duck Software (2016). (self-published presentation)
20. Hauge, Ø., Ayala, C., Conradi, R.: Adoption of open source software in software-intensive organizations–A systematic literature review. Inf. Softw. Technol. **52**(11), 1133–1154 (2010)
21. Helmreich, M.: Best practices of adopting open source software in closed source software products. In: (Doctoral dissertation, Diplomarbeit, Friedrich-Alexander-Universität Erlangen-Nürnberg) (2011)
22. Hummel, O., Janjic, W., Atkinson, C.: Code conjurer: pulling reusable software out of thin air. IEEE Softw. **25**(5), 45–52 (2008)
23. Kaufmann, A., Riehle, D.: The QDAcity-RE method for structural domain modeling using qualitative data analysis. Requirements Eng. 1–18 (2017)
24. von Krogh, G., Spaeth, S., Haefliger, S.: Knowledge reuse in open source software: An exploratory study of 15 open source projects. In: 2005 Proceedings of the 38th Annual Hawaii International Conference on System Sciences, HICSS 2005 p. 198b. IEEE, January 2005
25. Von Krogh, G., Von Hippel, E.: The promise of research on open source software. Manage. Sci. **52**(7), 975–983 (2006)

26. De Laat, P.B.: Governance of open source software: state of the art. J. Manage. Governance **11**(2), 165–177 (2007)
27. Lakhani, K.R., Von Hippel, E.: How open source software works:"free" user-to-user assistance. Res. Policy **32**(6), 923–943 (2003)
28. Lattemann, C., Stieglitz, S.: Framework for governance in open source communities. In: 2005 Proceedings of the 38th Annual Hawaii International Conference on System Sciences, HICSS 2005, p. 192a. IEEE, January 2005
29. Lombard, M., Snyder-Duch, J., Bracken, C.C.: Content analysis in mass communication: assessment and reporting of intercoder reliability. Hum. Commun. Res. **28**(4), 587–604 (2002)
30. OpenChain Specification (2018). https://www.openchainproject.org/spec
31. Di Penta, M., German, D.M., Antoniol, G.: Identifying licensing of jar archives using a code-search approach. In: 2010 7th IEEE Working Conference on Mining Software Repositories (MSR), pp. 151–160. IEEE, May 2010
32. Popp, K.M.: Best practices for commercial use of open source software. In: Business Models, Processes and Tools for Managing Open Source Software. BoD–Books on Demand (2015)
33. Radcliffe, M., Odence, P.: The 2017 open source year in review. Black Duck Software, DLA Piper. (self-published presentation) (2017)
34. Riehle, D.: The economic motivation of open source software: stakeholder perspectives. Computer **40**(4), 25–32 (2007)
35. Riehle, D.: The commercial open source business model. In: Nelson, M.L., Shaw, M.J., Strader, T.J. (eds.) AMCIS 2009. LNBIP, vol. 36, pp. 18–30. Springer, Heidelberg (2009). https://doi.org/10.1007/978-3-642-03132-8_2
36. Riehle, D.: Controlling and steering open source projects. IEEE Comput. **44**(7), 93–96 (2011)
37. Riehle, D., Lempetzeder, B.: Erfolgsmethoden der Open-Source-Governance und-Compliance. In: Friedrich-Alexander-Universität Erlangen-Nürnberg (FAU) (2014)
38. Riehle, D., Harutyunyan, N.: License clearance in software product governance. In: NII Shonan (2017)
39. Ruffin, C., Ebert, C.: Using open source software in product development: a primer. IEEE Softw. **21**(1), 82–86 (2004)
40. Sadowski, B.M., Sadowski-Rasters, G., Duysters, G.: Transition of governance in a mature open software source community: Evidence from the debian case. Inf. Econ. Policy **20**(4), 323–332 (2008)
41. Semeteys, R.: Method for qualification and selection of open source software. In: Open Source Business Resource, May 2008
42. Software Package Data Exchange (SPDX) (2018). https://spdx.org/
43. Sowe, S.K., Stamelos, I., Angelis, L.: Understanding knowledge sharing activities in free/open source software projects: an empirical study. J. Syst. Softw. **81**(3), 431–446 (2008)
44. Tools for Managing Open Source Programs (2018). https://www.linuxfoundation.org/tools-managing-open-source-programs/
45. Umarji, M., Sim, S.E., Lopes, C.: Archetypal internet-scale source code searching. In: Russo, B., Damiani, E., Hissam, S., Lundell, B., Succi, G. (eds.) OSS 2008. ITIFIP, vol. 275, pp. 257–263. Springer, Boston, MA (2008). https://doi.org/10.1007/978-0-387-09684-1_21
46. Wang, H., Wang, C.: Open source software adoption: a status report. IEEE Softw. **18**(2), 90–95 (2001)

OSS Reusability

Building a Social Platform Using FLOSS
to Support Collaborative Communities:
The ReWeee Case Study

Ioannis Routis[✉], Anargyros Tsadimas, and Mara Nikolaidou

Harokopio University of Athens, 70, El. Venizelou Str, 17671 Kallithea, Greece
{i.routis,tsadimas,mara}@hua.gr

Abstract. In this paper we present the development of a collaborative community using exclusively open source software. After the definition of the functional requirements of the project, we focus on finding specific software components to satisfy these requirements. The intention was to minimize the development effort and labor, relying on open source software. As a result, the platform was developed writing less than 10% of the required code and reusing more than 20 software components, not counting the software dependencies. The new components developed form our contribution to the community.

Keywords: Collaborative communities
Open source software development · Social networks
Component-based development

1   Introduction

Social networks have influenced the way that modern web applications are operating. A large number of them have adopted many characteristics of social networks, such as user profiles, real time notifications, instant messages, definition of users relationships, history of user actions, etc. Moreover, social network technology has been established as a prominent way of communication between members of an organization or enterprise [3]. Smart Communities as these are defined in [5], understand the potential of Internet technology, and make a conscious decision to adopt this technology to transform life and work in significant and positive ways [7]. Social software systems aim at the production of specific artifacts, thereby inviting users to participate in goal-oriented activities [4]. The user to user interaction is a major feature of collaborative communities.

In collaborative communities, leadership is decentralized and structured horizontally, a feature that makes communication on those groups more personal and more conversational than in other traditional groups. For that reason, in environments like those described above, the workflow and processes in general need to be highly adaptive and loosely structured in order to make ideas cross-fertilized and generate rich opportunities for innovation [6].

© IFIP International Federation for Information Processing 2018
Published by Springer International Publishing AG 2018. All Rights Reserved
I. Stamelos et al. (Eds.): OSS 2018, IFIP AICT 525, pp. 171–180, 2018.
https://doi.org/10.1007/978-3-319-92375-8_14

Such an adaptive process lies within the framework of the LIFE ReWeee Project, which aims to facilitate and promote Electrical and Electronic Equipment exchange and donation among households or households and public/private bodies so as to prevent the creation of Waste Electrical and Electronic Equipment (WEEE) [8].

Reuse of electrical and electronic equipment is among the top priorities in the EU waste hierarchy. In order to enhance the public perception towards the reuse of electric appliances and the prevention of WEEE generation, an initiative has been undertaken by a group of partners, which is implemented via the LIFE+ ReWeee project[1]. ReWeee Project includes a major action which is the development of a web-based collaborative platform for donating and exchanging Electrical and Electronic Equipment (EEE). That platform is used by households, companies and public services and its success lies within the social communication between volunteers and their collaboration in order to achieve the best possible result.

The challenge was to build the ReWeee platform using FLOSS and reuse as many software components as possible. Due to the previous experience of building applications with social characteristics, the development team decided to build the platform using the Django framework[2].

The remainder of this paper is organized as follows. In Sect. 2, the project requirements are presented alongside with the collaborative platform perspective. Section 3 highlights how FLOSS could satisfy the above presented platform requirements by not only using as-is or extending existing Django applications, but also by developing new ones. The final section refers to the conclusion that can be drawn for FLOSS adoption in web application development, while the contribution of this work is presented as well.

2   Project Requirements

In ReWeee Platform, users are categorized in three main types. These are guest users, registered users and administrators, that differentiate themselves as far as their granted permissions upon the use of the platform is concerned. More analytically, registered users are divided in two categories: a regular user, called civilian and an NGO user, indicating a representative of an Non Government Organization, while administrators include two different role types. The first one, the manager, which is responsible to validate a NGO through a provided official document (e.g., statute) and update the terms and conditions document for the platform and the second one the administrator whose responsibilities include user management, product categories management etc.

As far as the platform user authentication is concerned, when any unregistered user visits the web platform for the first time, he gets prompted to register into it, by creating a user account. The platform can authenticate users either as usual, namely, via an email and a password or from the most popular social

---

[1] ReWeee Project. https://www.reweee.gr/en.
[2] Django Project. https://www.djangoproject.com/.

networks (i.e., Twitter, Facebook and Google Plus). This account can be created by giving to the platform the necessary permissions for using personal user data. For NGOs there is a second level of validation when a new NGO user subscribes to the ReWeee platform.

After a successful registration, the, from now on, registered platform user, is able to submit an advertisement donating or exchanging an item, to declare interest for an existing product and propose an offer to acquire it, as well as to communicate with any other user who owns a desirable electric device. Products are categorized in a multilevel hierarchy which was provided by the committee of the ReWeee project. A product belongs to a lower level of hierarchy.

ReWeee platform enables messaging and notifications for its users so as to enhance communication and collaboration for product exchange. Namely, whenever user expresses interest on a product, the owner of the product is notified via email and through a notification inside the platform. In this product exchange process the involved role interaction can either be civilian-to-civilian and civilian-to-NGO.

Moreover, a registered user is not only able to search a product but also to has a profile with information about his/her location, products, and rating in which he can activate or deactivate an uploaded product. A registered platform user can also comment in any advertisement that he had made use of. That way, either the platform administrators or the appropriate users will be notified for either the category change proposal or the commenting in an advertisement.

Finally, the stakeholders of the ReWeee project would like to view some statistics about the products exchanged in specific periods of time, how many users have been registered and are active etc. These reports are produced at any time through the administration environment of the platform.

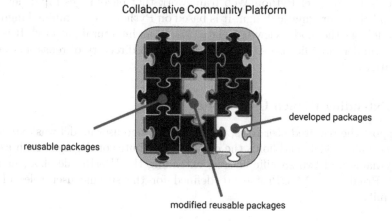

Collaborative Community Platform

reusable packages

developed packages

modified reusable packages

Fig. 1. Collaborative platform perspective

For the development of the collaborative platform and the satisfaction of its requirements described above, an implementation strategy should be adopted.

More specifically, as it is projected in Fig. 1, firstly, a set of already existing packages should be reused in order to reduce coding effort and testing. Secondly, some existing packages could undergone minor changes so as to adapt in project development requirements. Thirdly, several new packages should be developed for the satisfaction of requirements that the reuse of existing packages could not satisfy.

3   Satisfying Project Requirements with FLOSS

The collaborative platform architecture is illustrated in Fig. 2. The operating system of all servers is Debian Linux. The platform is a multi-layered application, where the user interface is based on bootstrap front-end framework (forming the django views), the data are kept in a Postgres database and the business logic is implemented using django framework. A number of reusable software components, called django packages or django applications were used in order to provide the required functionality. Users management is relying on python-social-auth and registration applications, while users interaction/communication is based on django-messages and notification applications. The products definition and exchange mechanism is based on the product application, which was developed because there was not available any related application. Table 1 summarizes the reused django applications and the reusability level of each one. Moreover, some new django packages were developed to support the complete set of functional requirements.

3.1   Django Framework

Django is a high-level Python Web framework that encourages rapid development and clean, pragmatic design. It is based on Python programming language. Django follows the model-view-template (MVT) architectural pattern[3]. It is distributed under BSD license. Django-packages[4] is a directory of reusable django applications.

3.2   Extending Django User Model

To support the required user roles, the default django user model was extended. A UserProfile model class holds the common attributes of the users such as the display name and two specific classes, extending the UserProfile class, namely CivilianProfile and NGOProfile are defined for the specific user roles of the community.

---

[3] The Model-View-Controller design pattern. https://djangobook.com/model-view-controller-design-pattern/.

[4] Django-packages. https://djangopackages.org/.

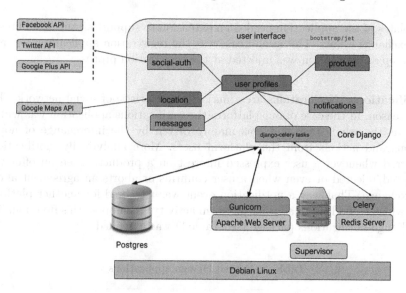

Fig. 2. ReWeee platform architecture

3.3 Supporting Periodic Tasks

To satisfy specific functional requirements, such as constraints about the amount of products that are exchanged between the users, it was necessary to periodically check the amount of products exchanged per user. Moreover, for optimal process completion control, it is required to check whether an exchange is completed on time.

More specifically, reminders are being sent to user for completing a product exchange/donation on time. An asynchronous task manager software could satisfy these requirements. Celery[5] is an asynchronous task queue/job queue based on distributed message passing . It is focused on real-time operation, but supports scheduling as well. Due to the fact that it is written in Python, it is easy to integrate with django. Celery uses "brokers" to pass messages between a Django Project and the Celery workers. Redis is an open source (BSD licensed), in-memory data structure store, used as a database, cache and message broker. Redis can serve as the message broker for the Celery. Supervisor[6] was used in order to run the celery worker and scheduler as daemon processes.

3.4 Reusable Applications with Minor Changes

Although the plenty of the reusable django application were exploited, in two specific cases there was a need to modify some of them to feet the requirements of the platform. The first case is the notification mechanism, where the html

---

[5] Celery. http://www.celeryproject.org/.
[6] Supervisor. A process control system. http://supervisord.org/.

templates of the application needed an extension to support all the attributes of the exchange events. The second case was the registration application, where a new step of verification was injected at the registration process.

Notifications. Notifications are a major characteristic of social networks. For that reason, in the case of our platform the notifications application was widely used as the whole task flow was mainly driven by the interchange of notifications and actions from the platform users. More analytically, notifications occurred whenever a user expressed interest on a product, when an offer was accepted/rejected or even when a user confirms or aborts an agreement about an exchange. That way a notification event was triggered for another platform user which could lead to another platform activity. To support this functionality, the django-notifications package (see Table 1) was extended.

Table 1. Reused Django applications

Operation	Library name	Reusability
Messaging	django-messages	as is
Notifications	django-notifications	modified
Categories	django-categories	as is
Import/Export	django-import-export	as is
Rating	django-star-ratings	as is
Autocomplete	django-autocomplete-light	as is
Upload multiple files	django-multiupload	as is
Avatar	django-avatar	as is
Pagination	django-endless-pagination	as is
Captcha	django-recaptcha	as is
Terms and conditions	django-termsandconditions	as is
Cookies disclaimer	django-cookie-law	as is
Contact form	django-envelope	as is
Notify on model changes	django-fieldsignals	as is
Bootstrap forms	django-forms-bootstrap	as is
Registration	django-registration	modified
Social network authentication	python-social-auth	as is
Model translation	django-modeltranslation	as is
Admin ui	django-jet	as is
Task manager	celery	as is
Message broker	django-redis	as is

Registration. Due to the platform user requirement analysis and the categorization of roles that are involved, an extension was made to the default Django Registration application. More specifically, on the one hand, for the NGO user, an advanced authentication method was implemented as it was mentioned above. Registration process was the same as with the plain users but its complexity involved, a formal document inspection (organization statute) from one of the administrator roles, the Platform Manager. The NGO user was inactive unless its statute was verified. On the verification, an email informs the user of the successful registration. On the other hand, for all the user types, it was planned to provide the functionality of signing in the platform using a social network choosing from the major ones (i.e. Facebook, Twitter, Google Plus). For the implementation of this platform feature, the appropriate APIs were used. During the authentication on each social network, the user defined which information platform could use (email, username, etc.).

3.5 Developed Applications

User Profiles. A civilian has a private profile (Fig. 3a), which is accessible only from logged in users. An NGO user has a public profile, where basic info are presented such as the name of the organization, the location (only area/city, no specific location), the document that certifies the fact that this organization is an NGO. For all user profiles rating information, along with comments from other users are presented. Moreover some statistics about the products that this individual has received and provided. Moreover a products list link and a send message link are provided.

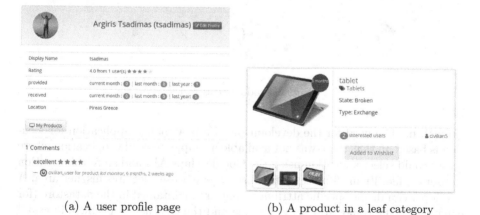

(a) A user profile page   (b) A product in a leaf category

Fig. 3. A user profile and product view

Product. A user can create products that he/she would like to exchange. For each product a name, a state, a description and some images can be used to characterize the product (Fig. 3b). Also the date that the product was added is kept. Moreover, a user can express interest on acquiring a product. Upon each interest declaration a user can define if he/she wants to provide some of his/her products to support the specific exchange. Every time a uses expressed interest on a product, the owner of the product is notified via email and by a notification inside the platform. Here he/she can review the details of the exchange and he/she can accept or decline the exchange. On the acceptance, the users are physically exchanging the products and one last step is that the user that acquires the product(s) is responsible to verify the exchange and has the ability to rate the acquired products.

Products are categorized to leaf categories and a user can check the number of products in each category hierarchy, as shown in Fig. 4. To effectively categorize the products, the django-categories application was exploited. Django-categories relies on django-mptt package[7] [1], which provides utilities for implementing Modified Preorder Tree Traversal with Django Models and working with trees of Model instances.

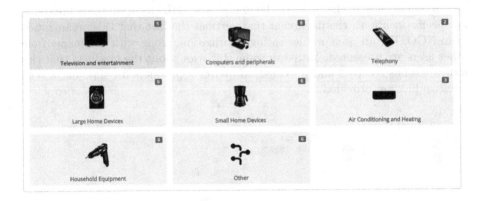

Fig. 4. Products categories

Location. The need for the development of a new django application for location is based on that there was not available a simple, reusable application where a user could select a location using the Google Maps API and store this location to user profile. Figure 5 presents the form where a user declares his/her area. A developer can define specific attributes that are maintained in the datastore (for example he/she could store only the area and the city, not a specific address).

---

[7] django-mptt. Modified preorder tree traversal with django models. https://github .com/django-mptt/django-mptt/.

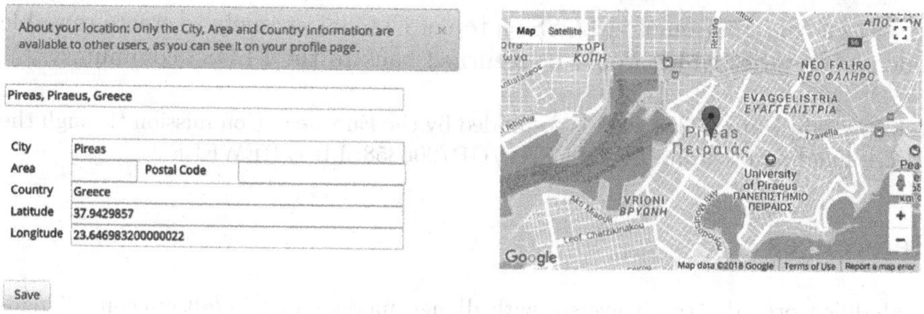

Fig. 5. User location definition

3.6 Discussion

What was obtained throughout this development process was mainly the inspiration not only to reuse but also to contribute to the FLOSS community. Using existing software components from other developers promotes the interoperability and applicability of software components as the result of minor modifications ending in code refactoring and optimization. As an observation, in our case, the development phase was decreased by around 70%, since the developed -from scratch- code represented less than 10% of the total project. The remainder of the development phase was used to test and integrate the adopted code, to make the appropriate modifications and integrate the feedback of the final users in order to ensure the platform acceptance. Obviously, the developed software components are planned to return to the open source community as our contribution in building a collaborative community. The ReWeee platform is currently in internal testing mode from the participants. We are currently refactoring the code and developing integration tests in order to ensure the interoperability with the Django underlying environment.

4 Conclusions

Open source software developers reuse code because they want to integrate functionality quickly, because they operate under limited resources in terms of time and skills, and because they can mitigate development costs through code reuse [2]. Although there is a large number of reusable software components available, the reusability, the customization and the development of new components is not a straightforward process. The documentation, the code quality and the tests included in a software repository are some of the criteria that a developer could rely on in order to select the appropriate software.

However, using existing software, it helps the maintainability of the software, software bugs are resolved and refactoring is performed in order optimize the performance and the security. Our contribution was two-fold, as it primarily aimed to minimizing labor through the reuse of existing work and secondly to be set as a contribution of "FLOSS on top of FLOSS", namely to create reusable code and libraries which would be returned back to the FLOSS community.

Acknowledgment. This work is co-funded by the European Commission through the LIFE+ Funding program, LIFE14 ENV/GR/000858: LIFE REWEEE.

References

1. Modified preorder tree traversal with django models. https://github.com/django-mptt/django-mptt/. Accessed 29 Jan 2018
2. Haefliger, S., Von Krogh, G., Spaeth, S.: Code reuse in open source software. Manage. Sci. **54**(1), 180–193 (2008)
3. Hatzi, O., Meletakis, G., Katsivelis, P., Kapouranis, A., Nikolaidou, M., Anagnostopoulos, D.: Extending the social network interaction model to facilitate collaboration through service provision. In: Bider, I., Gaaloul, K., Krogstie, J., Nurcan, S., Proper, H.A., Schmidt, R., Soffer, P. (eds.) BPMDS/EMMSAD -2014. LNBIP, vol. 175, pp. 94–108. Springer, Heidelberg (2014). https://doi.org/10.1007/978-3-662-43745-2_7
4. Johannesson, P., Andersson, B., Wohed, P.: Business process management with social software systems – a new paradigm for work organisation. In: Ardagna, D., Mecella, M., Yang, J. (eds.) BPM 2008. LNBIP, vol. 17, pp. 659–665. Springer, Heidelberg (2009). https://doi.org/10.1007/978-3-642-00328-8_66
5. Lindskog, H.: Smart communities initiatives. In: Proceedings of the 3rd ISOneWorld Conference, vol. 16 (2004)
6. London, S.: Building collaborative communities. On Collaboration. Tate, London (2012)
7. Meletakis, G., Hatzi, R., Katsivelis, P., Nikolaidou, M., Anagnostopoulos, D., Anastasiou, C.A., Karfopoulou, E., Yannakoulia, M.: MedWeight smart community: a social approach. In: Ismail, L., Zhang, L. (eds.) Information Innovation Technology in Smart Cities, pp. 151–162. Springer, Singapore (2018). https://doi.org/10.1007/978-981-10-1741-4_11
8. Routis, I., Nikolaidou, M., Anagnostopoulos, D.: Using CMMN to model social processes. In: Teniente, E., Weidlich, M. (eds.) BPM 2017. LNBIP, vol. 308, pp. 335–347. Springer, Cham (2018). https://doi.org/10.1007/978-3-319-74030-0_25

Improving C/C++ Open Source Software Discoverability by Utilizing Rust and Node.js Ecosystems

Kyriakos-Ioannis D. Kyriakou[1], Nikolaos D. Tselikas[1(✉)], and Georgia M. Kapitsaki[2]

[1] Communication Networks and Applications Laboratory,
Department of Informatics and Telecommunications, University of Peloponnese,
End of Karaiskaki Street, 22 100 Tripolis, Greece
{kyriakou, ntsel}@uop.gr
[2] Department of Computer Science, University of Cyprus,
75 Kallipoleos Street, P.O. Box 20537, 1678 Nicosia, Cyprus
gkapi@cs.ucy.ac.cy

Abstract. Discovering Open Source Software (OSS) components efficiently is not always an easy task. Node.js is a popular JavaScript runtime environment, whereas Rust is widely used for system programming, and both can be utilized for OSS discovery purposes. In this work, we examine whether Rust and Node.js can be used, along with their respective tooling and package repositories, in order to achieve improved discoverability of existing OSS implemented in C/C++. The paper describes how the capabilities of Rust in C/C++ interoperability can be combined with novel compilation techniques of low-level code to asm.js and WebAssembly, in order to harness JavaScript's popularity as the medium to publicize hard to discover C/C++ OSS. A proposed incremental methodology is presented and the main, as well as the collateral, effects of enforcing the proposed methodology in a proof-of-concept situation are examined. Our findings indicate potential increase in discoverability, code quality, portability, along with viable performance degradation of portable binaries, demonstrating 8.7 times slower execution compared to machine code, in a worst-case scenario.

Keywords: Free open source software · Software discoverability
Software performance evaluation · Software convergence
Software interoperability · C/C++ · WebAssembly · Node.js · Rust

1 Introduction

Node.js [1] is an open source JavaScript (JS) runtime built around V8 [2], the JS engine used in Chromium, the base for Google's Web browser. It has gained massive adoption by developers and organizations around the world, because of its ease of development, as well as the efficient, event-driven and non-blocking input/output (I/O) model. According to the results of the 2017 annual survey conducted by Stack Overflow, JS

I. Stamelos et al. (Eds.): OSS 2018, IFIP AICT 525, pp. 181–192, 2018.
https://doi.org/10.1007/978-3-319-92375-8_15

has been declared as the most popular programming language for the fifth consecutive time [3]. The overall shifts in popularity throughout the years the survey has been conducted, displays both JS and Node.js as technologies with the greatest gain in traction among all popular choices; thus, representing the ubiquity of JS as a programming language of choice, in both server and client infrastructures. JS as part of the Web standard specifications, has enabled the production of complex applications that require no installation or upgrades, enable real-time communications, provide access to device-specific hardware and foster portability and accessibility, due to the prevalence of Web browsers.

One key advantage that can be attributed to the success of JS based systems is Node.js' package manager, npm [4], which houses the largest distribution of open source libraries in the world, counting over 570,000 individual modules [5]. Publicly available modules provide ease in the discovery of building blocks, that enable rapid prototyping of systems with minimal effort, through code reuse maximization [6].

Although Node.js applications are most commonly written in pure JS, the underlying interoperability with foreign compiled code is abstracted. According to Node.js' announcement for version 8.0.0 of the platform, 30% of all modules rely indirectly on native modules [7]. Node.js developers can provide their own bindings to C/C++ libraries, in order to extend the platform's capabilities and optimize performance, but in doing so, new challenges related to the application's integrity arise. Furthermore, re-purposing such modules to the Web platform has been largely impossible, due to the fact that the only recognized programming language in such environments is JS. Recent advancements have made compilation of lower-level languages to JS, or the WebAssembly portable binary format, possible. Whereas these novel technologies enable components to be written in C/C++, the long-studied challenges related to memory-safety and language misuse, propagate towards the higher layer, where the presumed safe JS code executes. In addition, the absence of a modules' system and of a common mechanism to package, document, discover and distribute libraries written in C/C++ hinders the discovery of existing libraries.

Rust is a systems programming language designed to prevent common C/C++ pitfalls, while at the same time it incorporates contemporary development methods, encouraging collaboration in OSS. Having the above as starting points, we observed an opportunity to study whether Rust's capabilities of providing safe interfaces to existing libraries, can be combined with the proliferation of the npm ecosystem, in order to enhance the discoverability and reuse potential of open source projects, and evaluate the side effects of such a coupling. This work describes the process we have followed, in order to perform the above investigation, and how this approach can positively affect discoverability, as well as quality aspects.

The rest of the paper is structured as follows. Section 2 introduces the background of this work describing the current state of JavaScript and C/C++ OSS, along with open challenges. The main contribution of our work with its architecture are presented in Sect. 3, and evaluated and discussed in Sect. 4. Finally, Sect. 5 concludes the paper outlining directions of future work.

2   Background and Motivation

Translation of programs written in C/C++ for the Web has been a recent topic of interest in various fields of research. Compilation of audio tools has been examined by Letz et al. and Zbyszyński et al. [8, 9], whereas a distributed evolutionary algorithm has been investigated by Leclerc et al. [10]. Furthermore, the potential of using Rust instead of other systems programming languages is another emerging recent topic. Rust has been shown to produce efficient code for the implementation of garbage collectors reducing at the same time the programmer error surface [11, 12]. Combination of both is possible, and we were motivated to examine the application of these technologies in junction with modern development trends in OSS, in order to improve the state of C/C++ software discoverability. The rest of this section provides the background information in order to justify our thought process, as well as the technologies chosen.

2.1   JavaScript in Open Source Projects

JS is one of the most popular programming languages intended to facilitate interaction with the user in web applications [3]. More recently, it has been employed in server-side infrastructure for distributed services, in cross-platform applications targeting stationary and mobile users alike, but has also been used as a compilation target for a plethora of programming languages [13]. In our previous work, we have examined the aforementioned aspects of JS by implementing a full-featured high-performance cross-platform social application and distributed service, with only OSS components, and evaluated the benefits and implications of our choices [14–16]. This endeavor was only made possible due to the wide spectrum of focused OSS modules, easily accessible via the npm repository. The word "module" is used to describe building blocks, usually performing a single task, leading to composable, instead of monolithic, design patterns. According to Modulecounts [5], a service monitoring language for module repositories, npm averages 697 new modules/day, followed by Packagist (PHP) with 136 modules/day and Maven Central (Java) with 100 modules/day. It is noteworthy, that npm module submissions follow an exponential growth curve, clearly outpacing all the other repositories. Furthermore, TF Bissyandé et al. have studied 100,000 OSS projects hosted on GitHub [17]. Their findings exhibited that JS was the programming language that appeared the most frequently in multi-language projects. The Node.js platform is such a multi-language project, where its components are written in both JS and C/C++.

Node.js Architecture. The "Applications/Modules" space is where all JS project files reside. They may make either direct, or indirect use of precompiled foreign code. Additionally, required external dependencies, which are reused in the application's logic, belong in this space as well. Although JS has positive aspects, Node.js has to rely upon compiled code to perform I/O operations [18]. The runtime's garbage collector (GC) abstracts the, potentially error prone, manual dynamic memory management, but there is no thread-safety mechanism present when performing I/O, making memory related faults, and race conditions possible [19]. Furthermore, failure points may be present in the underlying foreign compiled code, propagating to the higher levels, and leading to unexpected behaviors and faults. Node.js utilizes C/C++ libraries internally, in order to provide access to the operating system resources. Such libraries provide efficient solutions to all I/O related operations included as core functionalities. For instance, the libuv project provides event-loop and asynchronous I/O access [20]. Other examples of libraries used internally by Node.js are c-ares, zlib, and OpenSSL. The "C/C++ Bindings" space is where the functionality of such libraries is exposed via the core JS Application Programming Interface (API). Some examples in this space are the os, fs, net and http modules.

Addons in Node.js refer to libraries and their corresponding bindings, which are not included in the core modules [21]. They are usually written in C/C++, in order to extend Node.js' functionality, or provide performance gains, when a JS implementation is found to be lacking. For instance, µWebSockets is a popular WebSocket protocol implementation for Node.js, which out-performs all known pure JS implementations [22]. Moreover, libxmljs provides bindings to the popular XML parsing C library, libxml, fulfilling Node.js lack of XML support [23].

Although addons have capabilities to extend Node.js, they require knowledge of how the V8 engine works and their implementations must be fine-tuned, in order to avoid locking the main thread JS executes, duplication of memory allocations, data races, memory faults, etc. Another method of interfacing shared objects with Node.js is via the ffi module. It involves no elaborate setup, at the cost of highly reduced performance on high Input/Output systems. We theorize that writing and publishing Node.js bindings, may pose an opportunity for undiscoverable C/C++ OSS to receive exposure and be collaboratively improved, due to the massive reuse potential in Node. js projects. Unfortunately, their implementation is connected to a performance-productivity trade-off.

2.2 Challenges in C/C++ OSS

OSS implemented in the popular systems programming languages C and C++ predates the proliferation of cloud computing, which enabled OSS to flourish. There is evidence of the inherent inflexible codebase componentization in the amount of build systems available. Some well-known examples are CMake [24], qmake [25], SCons [26], and GYP [27], with the latter being used by Node.js. Legacy codebases that are not using such systems gradually degrade in maintainability, as observed by Dayani-Fard et al. [28]. In contrast, most prevalent programming languages in OSS implement some form of enforced conventions, as well as a queryable directory or repository, containing the corresponding metadata for every published project, e.g. via mvn for Java [29], npm for JS [4], gem for Ruby [30], pip for Python [31], etc. Those enforced conventions serve as guidelines to interact with code repositories, document, license, test, build, distribute, etc., features which may exist for C/C++ in the form of various third-party tools, but are incapable of providing the cohesion needed across OSS. The lack of advocated methodology in C/C++ OSS is more apparent in legacy projects, with many of them accessible only through manual pursuit via web search-engines. Downloading arbitrary dependencies by-hand, extracting, copying-and-pasting, figuring out the right compiler flags, are not uncommon practices.

Finally, inconsistent dynamic memory management is common in even mainstream utilities. For example, the GNU tool ls, has been known to leak memory, and is considered as a non-issue by its maintainers [32]. Although in its intended use, the operating system would handle the leak, using the library unknowingly of that issue in a persistent system, e.g. a server, would pose a threat to robustness. Moreover, lack of C/C++ programming experience may cause integer overflow/underflow leading to "undefined behavior". Type safety is not guaranteed by C/C++, and although programs may not exhibit type errors, undefined behaviors are incorporated in the standard specification, leading compilers to produce unspecified results and also to allow the program to do practically anything. A simple example of iterator invalidation, leading to undefined behavior is demonstrated in the following listing.

```
std::vector v;

v.push_back(MyObject);

for (auto x : v) {

    v.clear();

    x->whatever(); // results in undefined behavior

}
```

If the contents of a container that is being iterated over are destroyed, the program is led into undefined behavior. This is an example of a perfectly valid code from a C++ compiler's perspective, capable of halting the project using it. Such cases of undefined behavior have already been investigated in depth [33]. Memory safety is set at risk by null-pointer dereferences (NULL in C and nullptr in C++) that cause programs to crash, dangling pointers allowing access to heap allocated resources that have not lived as long as they had to, and buffer overruns allowing the program to access elements before the start or beyond the end of an array [34]. Malicious software has been taking advantage of the way C and C++ programs handle memory and exploiting bugs in the code. Hence, OSS discovered in the wild may propagate unwanted effects to derivative projects.

2.3 Rust: A Young Contender in OSS

Rust was created in order to address the challenges presented in Sect. 2.2. It follows the C++ philosophy of zero-cost abstractions and takes a step further, by incorporating memory-safety and data-race free concurrency without the need for a GC [35]. This is accomplished by statically tracking ownership and lifetimes of all variables and their references. The ownership system enables Rust to automatically deallocate and run destructors on all values immediately, when they go out of scope and prevents values from being accessed after they are destroyed. Rust applies some established techniques from academia, e.g. enums as algebraic data types, common in the ML family of languages, and traits, which enable polymorphism similar to Haskell's type classes. Similarly to JS, both procedural and functional paradigms are used, as examined by Poss [36].

Rust is available on GitHub, where all parts of the compiler and tooling are accessible for contributions [37]. The integrated command line application `cargo` serves as a complete project management tool. It is capable of instantiating new projects, building for various architectures, managing dependencies, testing, producing documentation, and more. Furthermore, `cargo` is responsible for enforcing the practices that enable OSS to be discoverable and maintainable. Interaction with C APIs is free of overheads, and the binaries produced can be called from C with no setup. As Rust utilizes LLVM for machine code emission, we were triggered to examine the possibility of utilizing this system for bridging the gap between C/C++ codebases and modern OSS development practices.

2.4 Compilation to JavaScript and WebAssembly

A strict subset of the JS programming language was designed as a compilation target, in order to allow for translation of programs written in other languages. It became known as asm.js, and the Emscripten compiler was created by Alon Zakai in 2011. This language is statically compiled and has shown near native performance [38]. One of the key benefits to its adoption was that even if a Web browser had not implemented optimizations for the subset, it could still run on every JS interpreter. That is one reason it is still in use as a fallback from the newer WebAssembly specification [39]. WebAssembly is a portable size and load-time efficient format, suitable for compilation to the Web, implemented in all major Web browsers, but still under the process of standardization via the W3C WebAssembly Working Group. It features language and platform independence, safe execution, and has shown promising performance gains of up to 5.89 times when replacing JS components with Rust code in real-use parsing scenarios [40]. Currently not all features have been finalized and garbage collection, threads, SIMD, etc. are in progress. It is relevant to both JS and C/C++/Rust OSS, because the combination of those technologies may solve the portability issue in the dissemination of multi-language OSS.

3 Exposing C/C++ OSS via Rust and Node.js

In this section the independent processes that realize our proposed methodology are presented and discussed. Each process is incremental and not mandatory, but adds to a project's exposure. The high-level architecture of our proposal is presented in Fig. 1, followed by a proof-of-concept example.

3.1 Using Rust to Package and Publish on crates.io

The processes of taking the source files of a C/C++ project and producing a package for publishing are depicted in the upper-half part of Fig. 1. By issuing the `cargo new` command, followed by the name of the package to be published, a local git repository is initiated, and the Cargo.toml file holding the project's metadata and dependencies is produced. By adding the `cc`, and `bindgen` packages to the dependencies, the project is now capable of generating bindings statically via header files, compiling the source

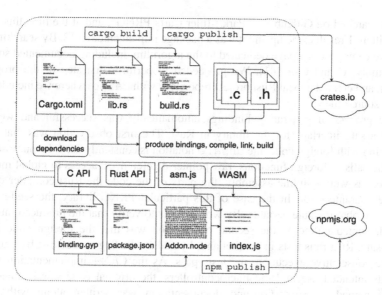

Fig. 1. The proposed high-level architecture

files and linking them automatically. By creating a build.rs file, where the build parameters are specified, the process is complete. The produced bindings can be included in lib.rs, where a new Rust API may be written. By issuing the `cargo publish` command, the package is uploaded to crates.io, the main Rust packages repository, and can be discovered by querying it. As C/C++ and Rust can all emit asm. js and WebAssembly files, portable executables may be built for reuse by JS environments.

3.2 Using Node.js to Package and Publish on npm

The second part of the process is depicted in the lower-half part of Fig. 1. Node.js uses a package.json file, to hold the project's dependencies and metadata. It can be generated by issuing the `npm init` command. The library can be used directly by utilizing the ffi module, but in order to create the more efficient Addon, the `nan` module or the official N-API dependencies can be used. A C/C++ bridge must be created to convert from C types to V8 types and provide a JS API. By instructing GYP via the binding.gyp file to use the bridge and link to the libraries produced by Rust, the Addon is created. Finally, by creating an index.js file which exports the Addon, the asm.js and WebAssembly, the process is complete. The package can be published on the npmjs. org repository by using the `npm publish` command.

3.3 The Hypothetical Park-Miller-Carta PRNG Case

For our proof of concept scenario, we hypothesize that a researcher is seeking an efficient Pseudo-Random Number Generator (PRNG) for a system's prototype. They are instructed by their colleague to use the Park-Miller-Carta PRNG.

We searched on GitHub for "Park Miller Carta PRNG", and at the time this paper was written, 1 result came up and it was a package implemented in JS. By searching the Web, we came across a page dedicated to the algorithm, including documented sources in assembly, C and C++ [41]. We proceeded to perform first step of the proposed process, and created a local Rust project repository with `cargo`, where we included the C/C++ source files.

The process of generating bindings automatically was successful and we then created a safe interface for the library in Rust. The first observation was that when interfacing with foreign code, the `unsafe` notation is constantly used. Its purpose is to mark the calls to foreign functions, raw pointer dereferences, access to global mutable variables, as well as inline assembly, the parts of the code the Rust compiler cannot provide guarantees for. In the case of this particular PRNG library, the seed-state is held in a global mutable variable. By writing tests to verify that the produced interface is implemented correctly, the second observation was that the foreign code is not thread-safe. Rust runs tests in parallel and, by adding the flag `--test-threads=1`, to force consecutive execution, the tests pass. As the C/C++ implementation would serve its intended use in 16bit microcontrollers, the original code was retained in a module named `ffi_unsafe`, and documentation was written along with inline tests-as-examples, to be part of the project's documentation. In this particular case, the library's focus is rather narrow; hence, it was trivial to replace the unsafe blocks by altering the way the state is stored and accessed. The product was an idiomatic Rust API, including a C compatible API, that have been documented and tested. The package was then pushed on GitHub and published on crates.io.

By utilizing the new C API, we compiled the library via emscripten to asm.js and WebAssembly exposed from a high-level idiomatic API in the index.js file, in order to be accessible to systems compatible with Node.js modules. The `ffi` module was used to dynamically link directly to the shared object produced by Rust. At this point, we setup a stress test to examine the potential performance degradation in each approach.

All versions were initialized with the seed 1. A for-loop cycled through each next random integer invocation for 10 million times, in order to warm-up Node.js and enable all the potential of Just-In-Time-Compilation. Then the `benchmark` library performed the evaluation of each version. For Rust, the included library Bencher was instructed to measure the execution time for 10 million integer generations, and was averaged over 10 repetitions. Table 1 contains the results in mean number of executions per second, along with the mean divergences recorded. The software and hardware specifications were the following: macOS 10.13, MacbookPro 2.3 GHz Intel Core i5, 4 GB 1333 MHz DDR3, node v8.9.1, rustc 1.25.0-nightly, clang 4.0.0, emcc 1.37.29.

Table 1. Mean executions per second and mean divergence

	Rust	ffi	WebAssembly	asm.js
Executions/second	219,159,372	180,622	25,214,517	7,969,921
Divergence	±4.89%	±1.8%	±1.78%	±1.05%

Thereafter, the ffi, WebAssembly and asm.js version, may be made available on npm for direct distribution and use in all JS environments by creating a package.json file and filling in the module's metadata.

4 Results and Discussion

By following the proposed methodology on the hypothetical, albeit pragmatic scenario, the following observations were made. The code and information related to this study are available on [42].

4.1 Discoverability Improvement

According to the popular Web metrics provider Alexa, the website hosting the examined Park-Miller-Carta PRNG implementation receives 1 page-view per day on average, with an unknown amount of those views resulting in downloads. After publishing the investigated asm.js/WebAssembly implementations derived from the type-checked code, as well as the Node.js ffi version, as a package on npm they received 161 downloads in a period of about two and a half months, which translates to about 2.15 downloads per day. Furthermore, the proof of concept package that was published on crates.io averaged 0.7 additional downloads per day, during the same period. The reported metrics suggest that re-packaged OSS according to our proposed methodology can improve the state of C/C++ codebase distribution and discovery, by multiplying the exposure to multiple repositories and providing a high-level API for easier engagement. In addition, larger codebases can be modularized into more manageable and maintainable components, and by publishing each one focused component, exposure improvements can be realized collectively.

4.2 Code Quality Control

By interfacing the foreign C/C++ code with Rust, an undocumented thread-safety weakness was discovered. An experienced programmer may have been able to realize this fragility by going through the code, but in more complex scenarios, and especially in the plane of OSS collaborations, code reviews alone cannot warrant the code's correctness. Wrapping error-prone code in Rust's unsafe blocks and documenting them, is a reasonable method to minimize the debugging surface. In addition, the process of improving the quality of the code can be performed incrementally and largely unfocused codebases can benefit from the concept of smaller components in the form of modules.

4.3 Performance Degradation

The scenario was deliberately chosen, in order to stress the performance of function invocation during context-switching interoperability and determine the overhead. Rust is able to call into C/C++ libraries without the associated overhead interpreted languages impose. Hence, calling the original PRNG library via the safe interface and auto-generated bindings, exhibited the same performance as the corrected Rust version.

Node.js-C shared object interoperability was examined via the ffi module. This choice was made in order to serve as a fair comparison against the asm.js and WebAssembly versions, as the cost is about equal in terms of programming time. Our measurements indicate that both asm.js and WebAssembly have superior performance, by a factor of 44 and 140 times respectively. Due to the fact that the time the program spends performing actual calculations, is much shorter than the time it spends switching contexts, the modules were operating at their weakest possible scenario. The V8 engine does not implement full optimizations for the asm.js subset, as it would have performed similarly to the WebAssembly otherwise. Still the minimum observed overhead by WebAssembly, while operating in a biased scenario against it, was found to impose about 8.7 times slower execution, compared to the standalone native library. The trade-off in performance vs productivity ratio appears to be improved by WebAssembly vs the more common ffi approach, as a single codebase can produce, at least, good-enough solutions for use in the most wide-spread platform, the Web.

4.4   Code Portability

The aspect of portability can be greatly improved by the proposed methodology. Asm.js is capable of executing in all JS interpreters, and with practically every system incorporating a Web browser, the coverage gains are immeasurable. WebAssembly, while still in its infancy, exhibits the same trait for current Web browsers and Node.js, but shows more future potential, with the on-progress features and its standardization. Either technology was found to be capable of realizing portable libraries from C/C++/ Rust codebases. Finally, the Emscripten compiler is capable of bridging the gap of code targeting the machine and the Web standards, and is expected be even more prominent in the future.

5   Conclusions and Future Work

In this paper, we proposed a methodology for converting existing C/C++ OSS to packages via Rust and Node.js, and publicizing them on the crates.io and npm repositories. This procedure takes into account the state of Node.js and C/C++ complexities, as well as the novel compilation to WebAssembly. Our evidence based on a realistic scenario suggests that discoverability, code quality and portability are improved, as well as the performance when compared to same cost time-wise existing alternative, all beneficial aspects to OSS. We plan to conduct a larger-scale study, and produce tooling to automate the process further. WebAssembly is still in a minimum-viable-product state, once it matures and the JS engines are optimized further, we plan to conduct research on the planned features, such as threading, which will enable more intensive C/C++ libraries to be converted through our proposed methodology.

References

1. Node.js. https://nodejs.org. Accessed 18 Jan 2018
2. V8 Repository. https://chromium.googlesource.com/v8/v8.git. Accessed 18 Jan 2018
3. Stack Overflow Survey 2017. https://insights.stackoverflow.com/survey/2017. Accessed 18 Jan 2018
4. npm. https://www.npmjs.com/. Accessed 18 Jan 2018
5. Modulecounts. http://www.modulecounts.com/. Accessed 18 Jan 2018
6. Sojer, M., Henkel, J.: Code reuse in open source software development: quantitative evidence, drivers, and impediments (2010)
7. Node.js 8: Big improvements for the debugging and native module ecosystem. https://medium.com/the-node-js-collection/node-js-8-big-improvements-for-the-debugging-and-native-module-ecosystem. Accessed 18 Jan 2018
8. Letz, S., Denoux, S., Orlarey, Y., Fober, D.: Faust audio DSP language in the Web. In: Proceedings of the Linux Audio Conference (LAC-15), Mainz, Germany, April 2015
9. Zbyszyński, M., Grierson, M., Fedden, L., Yee-King, M.: Write once run anywhere revisited: machine learning and audio tools in the browser with C++ and emscripten (2017)
10. Leclerc, G., Auerbach, J.E., Iacca, G., Floreano, D.: The seamless peer and cloud evolution framework. In: Proceedings of the Genetic and Evolutionary Computation Conference 2016, pp. 821–828. ACM, July 2016
11. Lin, Y., Blackburn, S.M., Hosking, A.L., Norrish, M.: Rust as a language for high performance GC implementation. In: Proceedings of the 2016 ACM SIGPLAN International Symposium on Memory Management, pp. 89–98. ACM, June 2016
12. Blanco-Cuaresma, S., Bolmont, E.: What can the programming language Rust do for astrophysics? Proc. Int. Astron. Union **12**(S325), 341–344 (2016)
13. List of Languages that compile to JS. https://github.com/jashkenas/coffeescript/wiki/list-of-languages-that-compile-to-js. Accessed 18 Jan 2018
14. Chaniotis, I.K., Kyriakou, K.-I.D., Tselikas, N.D.: Proximity: a real-time, location aware social web application built with Node.js and AngularJS. In: Daniel, F., Papadopoulos, G.A., Thiran, P. (eds.) MobiWIS 2013. LNCS, vol. 8093, pp. 292–295. Springer, Heidelberg (2013). https://doi.org/10.1007/978-3-642-40276-0_23
15. Chaniotis, I.K., Kyriakou, K.I.D., Tselikas, N.D.: Is Node.js a viable option for building modern web applications? A performance evaluation study. Computing **97**(10), 1023–1044 (2015)
16. Kyriakou, K.I.D., Chaniotis, I.K., Tselikas, N.D.: The GPM meta-transcompiler: harmonizing JavaScript-oriented Web development with the upcoming ECMAScript 6 "Harmony" specification. In: 12th Annual IEEE Consumer Communications and Networking Conference (CCNC), Las Vegas, NV, USA, pp. 176–181 (2015)
17. Bissyandé, T.F., Thung, F., Lo, D., Jiang, L., Réveillere, L.: Popularity, interoperability, and impact of programming languages in 100,000 open source projects. In: 2013 IEEE 37th Annual Computer Software and Applications Conference (COMPSAC), pp. 303–312. IEEE, July 2013
18. Crockford, D.: JavaScript: The Good Parts: The Good Parts. O'Reilly Media, Inc., Sebastopol (2008)
19. Daloze, B., Marr, S., Bonetta, D., Mössenböck, H.: Efficient and thread-safe objects for dynamically-typed languages. In: Proceedings of the 2016 ACM SIGPLAN International Conference on Object-Oriented Programming, Systems, Languages, and Applications, pp. 642–659 (2016)
20. libuv. http://libuv.org/. Accessed 18 Jan 2018

21. Addons Node.js. https://nodejs.org/api/addons.html. Accessed 18 Jan 2018
22. μWebSockets. https://github.com/uNetworking/uWebSockets. Accessed 18 Jan 2018
23. libxml. https://github.com/libxmljs/libxmljs. Accessed 18 Jan 2018
24. CMake. https://cmake.org/. Accessed 18 Jan 2018
25. Qmake. http://doc.qt.io/qt-5/qmake-manual.html. Accessed 18 Jan 2018
26. SCons. http://scons.org/. Accessed 18 Jan 2018
27. GYP. https://gyp.gsrc.io/. Accessed 18 Jan 2018
28. Dayani-Fard, H., Yu, Y., Mylopoulos, J., Andritsos, P.: Improving the build architecture of legacy C/C++ software systems. In: Cerioli, M. (ed.) FASE 2005. LNCS, vol. 3442, pp. 96–110. Springer, Heidelberg (2005). https://doi.org/10.1007/978-3-540-31984-9_8
29. Maven. https://maven.apache.org/. Accessed 18 Jan 2018
30. Ruby Gems. https://rubygems.org/. Accessed 18 Jan 2018
31. Pip Python. https://pypi.python.org/pypi/pip. Accessed 18 Jan 2018
32. bug#8755: "ls -l" leaks memory. https://lists.gnu.org/archive/html/bug-coreutils/2011-05/msg00062.html. Accessed 18 Jan 2018
33. Dietz, W., Li, P., Regehr, J., Adve, V.: Understanding integer overflow in C/C++. ACM Trans. Softw. Eng. Methodol. (TOSEM), 25(1), article 2 (2015)
34. Tselikis, G.S., Tselikas, N.D.: C: From Theory to Practice, 2nd edn. CRC Press, Boca Raton (2017)
35. Stroustrup, B.: Abstraction and the C++ machine model. In: Wu, Z., Chen, C., Guo, M., Bu, J. (eds.) ICESS 2004. LNCS, vol. 3605, pp. 1–13. Springer, Heidelberg (2005). https://doi.org/10.1007/11535409_1
36. Poss, R.: Rust for functional programmers. arXiv preprint arXiv:1407.5670 (2014)
37. The Rust Programming Language. https://github.com/rust-lang. Accessed 18 Jan 2018
38. Zakai, A.: Emscripten: an LLVM-to-JavaScript compiler. In: Proceedings of the ACM International Conference Companion on Object Oriented Programming Systems Languages and Applications Companion, pp. 301–312. ACM, October 2011
39. Rossberg, A.: WebAssembly: high speed at low cost for everyone. In: ML16: Proceedings of the 2016 ACM SIGPLAN Workshop on ML (2016)
40. Oxidizing Source Maps with Rust and WebAssembly. https://hacks.mozilla.org/2018/01/oxidizing-source-maps-with-rust-and-webassembly/. Accessed 26 Jan 2018
41. Park-Miller-Carta Pseudo-Random Number Generator. http://www.firstpr.com.au/dsp/rand31/. Accessed 18 Jan 2018
42. rust_node_wasm. https://github.com/kenOfYugen/rust_node_wasm.git. Accessed 26 Jan 2018

Author Index

Printed in the United States
By Bookmasters